Research Methods
for
Organizational Studies

Research Methods
for
Organizational Studies

Donald P. Schwab

Graduate School of Business and
Industrial Relations Research Institute
University of Wisconsin–Madison

LAWRENCE ERLBAUM ASSOCIATES, PUBLISHERS
1999   Mahwah, New Jersey   London

Lawrence Erlbaum Associates, Inc., Publishers
10 Industrial Avenue
Mahwah, NJ 07430

Cover design by Kathryn Houghtaling Lacey

Library of Congress Cataloging-in-Publication Data

Schwab, Donald P.
Research methods for organizational studies / Donald P. Schwab.
    p. cm.
Includes bibliographical references and indexes.
ISBN 0-8058-2972-5 (pbk. : alk. paper.)
1. Organization—Research—Methodology. I. Title.
HD30.4.S38 1999   98-24202
302.3'5'072—dc21   CIP

Books published by Lawrence Erlbaum Associates are printed on acid-free paper, and their bindings are chosen for strength and durability.

Printed in the United States of America
10 9 8 7 6 5 4 3 2 1

Contents in Brief

Contents

About the Author

Donald P. Schwab, PhD University of Minnesota, is the Rennebohm Professor of Business Research in the Graduate School of Business, University of Wisconsin–Madison. He also holds an appointment in the Industrial Relations Research Institute. Professor Schwab has also been the Donald Slichter Professor of Business Research and is a Romnes Faculty Fellow. He has also been the Chair of the Business School's Management and Human Resources Department. Professor Schwab has also been a Visiting Professor at the University of Kentucky, University of Minnesota and Purdue University.

Professor Schwab is a Fellow of the Academy of Management and of the American Psychological Association. He is a Past Chair of the Human Resources Division of the Academy of Management. In 1994, he received the Career Achievement Award from the Human Resources Division of the Academy, only the second individual to be so honored.

Professor Schwab's research has appeared in publications, including the *Academy of Management Journal, Academy of Management Review, Journal of Applied Psychology, Industrial and Labor Relations Review, Industrial Relations, Organizational Behavior and Human Decision Processes, Personnel Psychology*, and *Psychological Bulletin*. He is a co-author of nine other books. He has also served on the Editorial Board of the *Academy of Management Journal* and currently serves on the Boards of *Organizational Behavior and Human Decision Processes* and *Human Resources Management Review*. He currently teaches graduate courses in human resource management and research methods.

Preface

This book introduces students to social science methods as applied broadly to the study of issues that arise as part of organizational life. These include issues involving organizational participants such as managers, teachers, customers, patients, and clients, and transactions within and between organizations. The material in the book is an outgrowth of nearly 30 years in teaching research classes to masters and beginning doctoral students at the Universities of Wisconsin, Minnesota, and Purdue. Although these classes have been offered in management and/or industrial relations departments, students participating have come from many other programs including industrial/organizational and social psychology, educational administration, sociology, marketing, communication arts, operations management, nursing, health care administration, and industrial engineering.

Naturally, my views about research and about what constitutes good research practice have strongly influenced the content of this book. However, experiences while teaching have had the most significant impact on the organization, emphases, and tone of the book. Many students experience anxiety when they begin a course in research methods; not all students begin such a course enthusiastically. This book aims to reduce anxiety by presenting research methods in a straightforward and understandable fashion. It aims to enhance student motivation by providing practical skills needed to carry out research activities.

WHY ANOTHER BOOK ON RESEARCH METHODS?

There is no shortage of research methods books; I've taught using many of them. However, students' reactions to these books have often been unfavorable. Some methods books, although encyclopedic in terminology and techniques described, provide students with little practical guidance to actually formulate research questions or conduct research investigations. It is often difficult to believe that authors of these types of volumes actually conduct research on their own.

There are also numerous methods books written by practicing researchers. Some of these are technically elegant and useful in their treatment of specific topics. For examples, they may have an excellent chapter on experimental design, questionnaire construction, or some other topic of special interest and expertise. Frequently, however, these books are not strong throughout; furthermore, they are often written at a level that assumes students addressing research methods for the first time have more knowledge than they actually do.

A generic problem for both types of methods books just described is the lack of a compelling organizing schema. To be really helpful, a book on methods should show students how the major research activities fit together. It should help students understand that sound (valid) inferences drawn from research results depend jointly on persuasive conceptualization combined with strong design, measurement, and analysis.

HOW THIS BOOK DIFFERS FROM TRADITIONAL METHODS BOOKS

This book attempts to meet the concerns just expressed. Importantly, an integrative model is explicated in Part I of the book; this model is used throughout to explain and integrate major research activities. I have found that the model, shown on the next page, is a powerful way to communicate key research concepts, challenges, and outcomes. The model distinguishes between empirical activities carried out at an operational level and the interpretations we make of those operations at a conceptual level. The model thus illustrates the critical need for valid measurement and underscores the challenges faced by researchers in obtaining useful measures. The model also distinguishes between independent and dependent variables. Although not always explicitly stated in research reports, most organizational research is designed to draw casual inferences; the distinction between cause and consequence is essential for conducting research and, especially, for interpreting research findings.

By combining these two dimensions of research the model clearly illustrates contributions and limitations of empirical research outcomes to conceptual understanding. The model shows that the only outcome directly

EXHIBIT P.1. Empirical research model

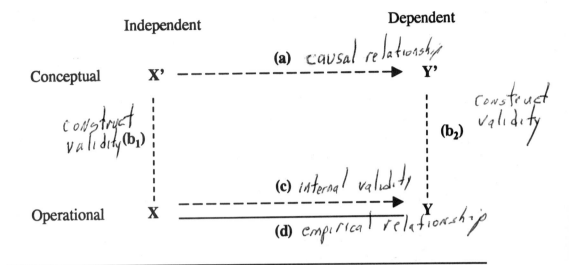

observable from empirical research is the relationship between scores (line d). All other relationships involve inferences as implied by the broken lines. Inferences are required to conclude that relationships between scores are casually or internally valid (line c). Inferences are also required to conclude that the scores obtained from measures represent their respective constructs, that they have a high degree of construct validity (lines b_1 and b_2). Finally, inferences about casual conceptual relationships (line a) require supportive evidence from all the other relationships and inferences. The model is extremely useful for showing the roles and limitations of each of the major research activities.

The model also serves as a foundation for drawing generalizations from research results. For example, it is used to show how statistical inference can be used to draw generalizations about the relationship observed by line d. Students often enter research methods classes assuming that statistical inference contributes far more to research understanding than it does. The model also serves as a foundation for the discussion of external validity where generalizations that transcend statistical inferences are at issue.

OBJECTIVES AND ORGANIZATION

My major objective in a research methods course is to see that students develop skills needed to conduct empirical research and to critically evaluate research conducted by others. This, in turn, requires that students spend a substantial portion of their time engaged in research activities. This book is designed to facilitate that objective in several ways.

First, the book has an applied orientation. Although it explicitly acknowledges the centrality of conceptualization to research understanding, it focuses primarily on empirical research activities. There are major parts devoted to measurement, design, analysis, and the inferences to be drawn from research results. Typically each part begins with a chapter on foundation issues. These include a discussion of how the activity fits into the framework provided by the model and identifies objectives for challenges in the activity. A chapter or chapters on applications then elaborates on procedures used to address the objectives and challenges of each activity.

Second, the book is designed and organized to address a serious challenge for research methods instructors. Specifically, research understanding is interactive in the sense that the more a student knows about design, for example, the easier it becomes to understand analysis or measurement, and vice versa. Yet classes must be organized in a sequential fashion. This book addresses this problem by first providing an overview of all research activities in Part I of the book. The model is used to show the roles for measurement, design, analysis, and inference. The book then proceeds sequentially through each of these topics. The discussion of measurement in Part II, for example, does not require knowledge from Part III on design or Part IV on data analysis beyond what has been discussed in Part I. The discussion of design does not require additional knowledge about analysis or inference.

The last portion of the book covers topics that draw on knowledge presented in two or more of the previous parts. In particular, measurement and design issues that require knowledge of data analysis methods are discussed at the end of the book. For example, Chapter 17 on reliability draws on information from parts on measurement and analysis. Chapter 19 on modeling serves as a capstone of sorts; it draws on information from parts on design, data analysis, and inference.

The extension chapters at the end of the book serve an additional purpose. These chapters can be used selectively as suggested by specific course objectives and student interests and capabilities. From semester to semester, even when teaching the same class, I discuss these special topics selectively depending on the unique characteristics of each class.

Finally, the book is short for two major reasons. First, it is easy for students to get information overload when reading encyclopedic methods volumes. Because my objective is to help students learn how to conduct research, I prefer to give them only information that is essential to initiating quality research projects. Much of our class discussion and student study time is spent carrying out research.

Second, I find that from semester to semester that there are substantial student differences in sophistication and substantive interests. I use outside readings along with this book, some substantive to serve as fodder for research critiques, some readings discuss research methods issues. The content and level of these papers vary depending on class composition. Consequently, this book is tightly focused, I use it as an organizing schema for the other class activities and readings.

SPECIAL FEATURES

The book has a number of additional features; although these are not unique, they are all designed to make information about research methods more accessible to students and to help teachers in the instruction process. Although this is a first edition, all of the material in it has been classroom tested at least once. In most instances, text materials have been used several times. In all cases, chapters have been revised based on student and colleague feedback.

Key terms are defined and highlighted when introduced in the text. These terms are also included in the chapter ending review section and are organized alphabetically in a glossary at the end of the volume. Chapter endings also contain review questions and, where appropriate, exercises to reinforce learning of chapter material.

Chapters usually have one or more "Research Highlights." These typically elaborate briefly on points related to a central theme in a chapter. They may serve as a basis for further class discussion. Briefly annotated bibliographies are also provided at the end of each part of the book. These are highly selective; only readings that I believe will be accessible to beginning students are included.

Several of the chapters included are novel but are consistent with the applied objectives of the book. A separate chapter is devoted to research report writing. This chapter is as useful to me as to students because it helps to improve papers that students submit as their major class project. There are also separate chapters on how to address nonresponse and missing data and on how to cope with multicollinearity.

The treatment of design is comprehensive and I believe a special strength of the book. Chapter 5 sets out the major causal challenges for design and shows how three major design decisions address these challenges. A separate chapter then describes experiments and quasi-experiments and another describes surveys and field studies. These latter chapters explain how threats to internal validity popularized by Cook and Campbell (1979) differ substantially by the type of design at issue.

Finally, I've also developed an instructor's manual that is available to teachers who use this book. This manual has sections containing lecture notes and suggestions, transparency masters, test items and recommendations for test construction and grading, and also has a number of cases. Some of these are designed to be used as exercises for learning on just one or two topics; others can serve for semester projects to be performed by individuals or teams. Data for these cases are also provided on a computer disk. Data sets are also provided that can be used for class demonstrations.

ACKNOWLEDGMENTS

I was surprised to find how much help I needed to complete this book and pleased to discover so many people who were willing to provide it. Colleagues at other universities who provided valuable help, often by reading major portions of the manuscript and in some instances class testing one or more chapters include: Alison Barber, Michigan State University, Mike Campion, Purdue University, Bob Eder, Portland State University, Barry Gerhart, Vanderbilt University, Dave Harrison, University of Texas–Arlington, Rob Heneman, Ohio State University, John Hollenbeck, Michigan State University, Pat Joynt, Henley Management College, Tom Lee, University of Washington, Tom Mahoney, Vanderbilt University, Jon Pierce, University of Minnesota–Duluth, Craig Pinder, University of British Columbia, Barb Rau, University of Wisconsin–Oshkosh, Sara Rynes, University of Iowa, and Paul Sackett, University of Minnesota.

Students and colleagues here at Madison who provided valuable assistance include Melissa Arronte, Paula Bassoff, Linda Brothers, Gil Churchill, Bob Giambatista, Herb Heneman, Bob Miller, Anne Miner, Andreas Schwab, Frank Siciliano, and Mary Zellmer. Craig Olson and Paul Peter deserve special thanks; they read, heard, talked, and argued more research methods during the course of this project than they probably wanted. Also deserving special thanks is Janet Christopher for her help in preparing and managing the manuscript.

—Donald P. Schwab

I

OVERVIEW

1

Introduction

Chapter Outline

- *Research Activities*
- *A Point of View*
- *Objectives and Organization*
- *Summary*
- *For Review*

Consider these courses of action:

- An elementary school principal establishes a set of difficult teacher goals to improve students' academic performance.
- A medical director has staff members make suggestions anonymously to encourage participation.
- A company president joins an alliance with other firms in the industry to improve returns from research and development expenditures.
- Parents take their children to a concert to stimulate an interest in music.
- A union leader calls for a strike vote to increase members' solidarity.
- A basketball coach has team members take dancing lessons to improve agility.
- A director of marketing recommends that a product be renamed, repackaged, and increased in price to attract more affluent customers.
- A captain in the Salvation Army posts names of the bell-ringers who obtain the greatest contributions each day to encourage bell-ringer solicitations.

- A human resource manager proposes a flexible benefit plan to reduce employee turnover.

These decisions have several things in common. They all take place in an organizational context, as does most human activity. These may be educational organizations such as elementary schools, health-related organizations such as clinics, business organizations such as manufacturing firms, volunteer organizations such as charitable agencies, or biological organizations such as families.

The example above all also illustrate courses of action that are undertaken as a result of expected relationships between two or more factors. The school principal believes that setting goals will influence teachers, who, in turn, are expected to influence students. The human resource manager believes that a flexible benefit plan will make the organization more attractive to employees and hence increase their motivation to retain their membership in it.

Each of the expected relationships is causal. In *causal relationships* one factor influences another. The school principal expects that the introduction of teacher goals will cause student achievement. The human resource manager expects that flexible benefits will cause employee retention. These and other expected causal relationships for the examples mentioned are summarized in Exhibit 1.1.

Emphasis is placed on the word *expected*. All these illustrative actions are based on expected relationships between factors; these expectations may or may not hold. Student achievements may increase after the principal establishes goals for the teachers, but they may not. Flexible benefits may increase employee retention, but they may not.

Empirical research can help obtain evidence on the veracity of expected causal relationships of the type described here. *Empirical research* addresses expected relationships through the systematic study of relationships between scores obtained from cases on measures.

This book describes methods for conducting empirical research on issues of the type illustrated above. Topics covered explain how the three key elements in the definition of empirical research, as shown in Exhibit 1.2, are addressed in research. *Cases* are the entities investigated in research. Cases may be individuals interacting in organizations, such as customers, patients, or students, who agree to be studied. Cases may also be organizations such as political parties, business firms, hospitals, libraries, government agencies, or religious groups. They may be formal or informal groups within organizations, such as executive policy teams in business firms, sports groups in

EXHIBIT 1.1. Causal representation of illustrative actions

School Principal

        Teacher goals ⟶ Student achievement

Medical Director

        Anonymous suggestions ⟶ Increased suggestions

Company President

        Join alliance ⟶ Improve returns

Parents

        Concert attendance ⟶ Music appreciation

Union Leader

        Strike vote ⟶ Member solidarity

Basketball Coach

        Dancing lessons ⟶ Member agility

Market Director

        Selling changes ⟶ Customer changes

Salvation Army Captain

        Bell-ringer recognition ⟶ Bell-ringer performance

Human Resources Manager

        Flexible benefit plan ⟶ Employee retention

schools, SWAT teams in police departments, or production quality improvement teams in manufacturing firms. Cases may also be events or transactions made within organizations, or linking organizations, such as sales invoices, bank checking account balances, contractual provisions, stock prices, grocery receipts, records of hospital patient prescriptions, or golf scores.

   Measures are instruments used to obtain scores on the cases studied. For example, measures may be items or questionnaires that individuals complete, or they may be items on forms that researchers fill out after they review sets of transactions or events. Finally, *scores* (or *data*) represent

EXHIBIT 1.2. Empirical research components

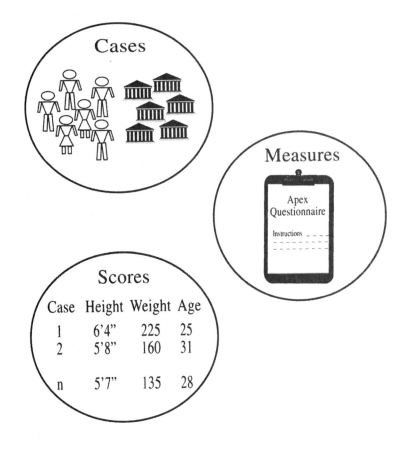

information obtained from cases on the measures employed. Typically, scores are recorded in numerical form. Researchers use these scores to identify whether relationships exist as expected.

   To illustrate, a researcher believes that increases in education lead to increases in financial success; this represents an expected causal relationship. The researcher investigates this expectation by soliciting the cooperation of a group of adult workers (cases). A questionnaire (measure) is developed that asks participants to record their highest year of education and gross income earned in the previous year. Participants' responses constitute scores that the researcher studies to see if a relationship exists as expected.

RESEARCH ACTIVITIES

The scenario described indicates that empirical research involves three activities: measurement, design, and analysis. *Measurement* involves activities associated with measuring the factors that form the expected relationship. In the example, the researcher develops questions about education and income specifically for the study conducted. In other situations, a researcher may begin with measures already developed and assess their suitability for a study at hand.

Research design establishes procedures to obtain cases for study and to determine how scores will be obtained from those cases. In the example, the choice of adult workers to study and the choice of measures and procedures to obtain scores on those measures are illustrative of the research design.

Empirical research also involves analyses of scores. *Analyses* are performed to describe scores on single measures and, especially, to identify relationships that may exist between scores across different measures. In the example, the researcher is particularly interested in the relationship between scores on the measures of education and income. Analysis methods typically involve the use of statistics.

Measurement, design, and analysis are the three major activities of empirical research as shown in Exhibit 1.3. This book describes methods to develop and evaluate measures, design research, and analyze relationships between scores.

The lines linking the three research activities signal two things. First, they signal that these research activities are related in practice. For example, decisions about design influence both measurement and analysis decisions. Second, they signal that knowledge of any one research activity is helpful in learning about the other activities. For example, the more you know about analysis, the deeper can be your understanding of measurement and design.

A POINT OF VIEW

Research is sometimes described as a major tool of "the scientific method," and that method is described in such abstract terms as to be nearly incomprehensible. Research methods may then be seen as a mysterious set of practices that only a chosen few can accomplish, probably in cloistered laboratories.

Not All Research is Empirical

Empirical research involves observation; it requires cases, measures, and scores. Not all types of research is empirical. For example, computer simulations generate scores from random number routines. Cases and measures are not involved. Analytical researchers use mathematical operations to work from initial assumptions to conclusions. There are no cases, measures, or scores.

This book is about empirical research methods only. Hereafter, *research* and *empirical research* are used interchangeably.

EXHIBIT 1.3. Empirical research activities

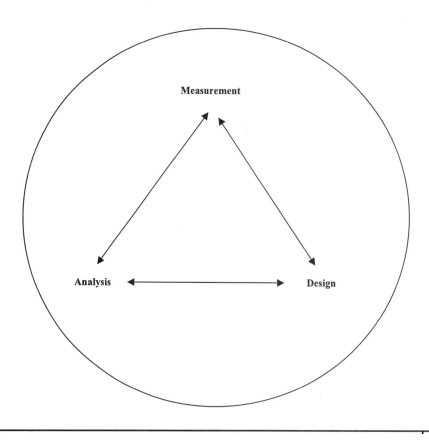

This book is written with a less deferential view of research methods. Research methods are imminently accessible. These methods do not differ qualitatively from our everyday practices of observing events and making sense of them.

This book takes the view that research methods have two advantages for obtaining knowledge, and that these are only advantages when research is appropriately conducted and reported. First, research methods properly conducted address questions systematically. Researchers carefully collect scores from cases using measures that are suitable for the question asked. Analysis of these scores is thoughtfully performed, and results obtained are carefully interpreted; probable limitations are acknowledged.

Second, research properly performed is a public process. The methods employed are reported along with the results and interpretations. This second characteristic is desirable so that others may evaluate research results and, if desired, repeat the research under similar or different conditions.

These are modest claims. Single research studies do not answer questions definitively. At best, research investigations are limited by researchers' assumptions and expectations, by the cases studied, by the measures employed, and by the methods of analysis used. Furthermore, studies involving human interactions are always bounded by context, such as the organizational setting in which they are conducted. To paraphrase Winston Churchill's view of democracy, research is the worst way to acquire knowledge except for the alternatives.

OBJECTIVES AND ORGANIZATION

Although this perspective for research is admittedly modest, it reflects a view adopted by many practicing organizational researchers. Furthermore, this perspective will hopefully suggest that you can acquire the skills needed to be a successful researcher. The book is written to help you acquire skills to conduct research with this view of research methods and outcomes in mind. Emphasis is put on the systematic nature of the research enterprise. This applies to all three major research activities: measurement, design, and analysis. Part VII of the book is devoted to reporting research studies, the public portion of the research process.

Acquiring skills to conduct research will help you be a more thoughtful and critical consumer of research performed by others, a second objective of the book. Most knowledge, even knowledge obtained by professional researchers, comes from research conducted by others. Thus, skills to critically evaluate research are often more useful than skills to conduct it.

The book is organized into eight parts consistent with its viewpoint and objectives. Part I includes this and the next chapter. Chapter 2 presents a model of the entire research enterprise. This model introduces research objectives and shows how measurement, design, and analysis contribute to knowledge generation.

Part II contains two chapters on measurement. These chapters describe measurement objectives and introduce criteria used to evaluate measures against these objectives. These chapters also describe measurement procedures commonly used in organizational studies.

Part III addresses research design. Chapter 5 identifies challenges for research design and identifies major decisions that researchers make when designing empirical research studies. The chapter also shows how these decisions affect conclusions that can appropriately be drawn from research studies. It concludes by introducing major types of designs that researchers employ. Chapters 6 and 7 elaborate on these major design types.

Chapters in Part IV focus on data analysis. Chapter 8 provides an overview of data analysis and introductory material on important characteristics of scores for analysis purposes. Chapter 9 describes methods for summarizing information about scores obtained from a single measure. These include statistics of central tendency, variability, and shape. Chapters 10 and 11 describe simple and multiple correlation and regression, respectively. These statistics provide useful ways to summarize relationships between scores from two or more measures.

Part V has two chapters on the use of statistics and probability theory for drawing inferences that transcend the relations observed on scores. These statistical inferences are made to address causal relationships and to address whether a statistic observed on the group of cases studied likely applies in the broader population from which the sample group was drawn. Chapter 12 introduces the statistical inference process. Chapter 13 describes two methods for performing generalizations: Hypothesis testing and confidence intervals.

Part VI has a chapter on other types of inferences researchers seek to make from their research. It discusses the important role of repeating research studies to obtain information on the likely generalizability of research findings. It also describes two methods that researchers employ to make these sorts of generalizations: Narrative reviews and meta-analysis.

Part VII contains a chapter on research report writing. Research reports have a special obligation to satisfy the second advantage of research mentioned earlier, namely, to provide a public record of the research for evaluation. Chapter 15 identifies the elements of research that should be included in a report to meet this obligation.

Part VIII contains four chapters that extend topics covered earlier in the book. Topics covered include: incomplete data sets, reliability, multicollinearity, and modeling.

SUMMARY

Organizational research questions usually involve *causal relationships* in which it is anticipated that one factor influences another. *Empirical research* activities contribute to causal understanding by investigating relationships between *scores* obtained from *cases* on *measures* of concepts. Three activities are needed to conduct empirical research: measurement, research design, and analysis. *Measurement* activities are aimed at obtaining scores on measures that correspond to the concepts studied. *Research design* establishes procedures to obtain participants and to determine how scores are obtained on measures. *Analyses* are performed to describe scores on single measures and to identify relationships between scores across measures.

This book takes the perspective that research methods are not greatly different from other methods for drawing conclusions about events that are observed. Research is generally superior to alternative methods because of its systematic and public nature.

Given this perspective, the book is designed to help you achieve two objectives: to learn how to conduct research and to learn how to evaluate other people's research. It does so by explaining how to perform and to record activities associated with measurement, research design, and analysis.

FOR REVIEW

Terms to Know

Causal relationship. When variation in one factor is responsible for variation in another.

Empirical research. Systematic study of relationships between scores obtained from cases on measures.

Cases. Entities (e.g., individuals, groups, organizations, transactions) investigated in research.

Measures. Instruments used to obtain scores from participants.

Scores (also, *data*). Numerical information about cases obtained on measures.

Measurement. Activities associated with measuring cases.

Research design. Overall plan of a study. Establishes procedures to obtain cases for study and to determine how scores are obtained on measures of cases.

Analyses. Used to describe scores on single measures and to identify relationships that may exist between scores across different measures; typically involve the use of statistics.

2

A Model of Empirical Research

Chapter 1 points out that decision making in organizations is typically based on expected causal relationships. For example, a decision is made to establish goals for teachers with the expectation that these goals influence teachers' behaviors and subsequently influence students' academic achievement.

Chapter 2 develops a model that explicates such causal relationships and shows how empirical research contributes to causal understanding. Master the model in this chapter, and you will see research questions just as practicing researchers see them. The model will also help you understand researchers' frames of reference when you read research reports. Most important, the model provides a good way to think about issues as you conduct and evaluate your own research.

The chapter begins with a discussion of variables; relationships between variables represent the core of research and the core of the model. The model links variables in two ways that correspond to research as typically performed. One way links variables understood at a conceptual level with variables measured and observed at an empirical or operational level. The second way links variables in a causal chain. Combined, these two methods for linking variables form a powerful way to think about empirical research methods and outcomes. The chapter also discusses issues associated with the generalization of research outcomes beyond the cases investigated in a specific study.

Topics covered in this chapter are important for the organization of this book. The model described serves as the organizing theme for Parts II through IV. The description of generalization serves as the basis for Parts V and VI.

RESEARCH VARIABLES

Variables are characteristics of objects or events that can take on two or more values. Age, height, and weight are variables that can be used to describe people. Alternatively, number of employees, number of accounts outstanding, gross receipts, and total assets are variables that can be used to describe organizations. All these characteristics are variables, because they can take on different values.

Variables are central to research. Most research is concerned with relationships between variables. For example, is there a relationship between education (one variable) and financial success (another variable)? A relationship in this case means that persons with different levels of education experience different levels of financial success.

Conceptual and Operational Variables

Empirical research activities and our understanding of research outcomes exist at two different levels of abstraction. We understand at a conceptual level. To say, "I know that education leads to financial success," expresses a belief about a causal relationship at a conceptual level.

At this level of abstraction variables are called *conceptional variables* or *constructs.* Constructs are mental definitions of characteristics of objects or events that can vary. Definitions of characteristics such as education and financial success are examples. To illustrate, the construct *education* may be defined as the knowledge and problem-solving abilities one acquires from formal learning environments. The term *construct* is used to denote conceptually defined variables from this point forward.

Empirical research activities are carried out at an operational level of abstraction. Empirical research obtains scores from cases on measures. These measures represent *operational variables.* Variables are made operational by the measures used to obtain scores from the cases studied. For example, a question that asks respondents to report the number of years they have attended school is an operational measure of education.

Dependent and Independent Variables

Another way to distinguish variables involves their location in a causal sequence. *Dependent variables* are outcomes or consequences; they are variables that researchers seek to understand, explain, and/or predict. *Independent variables* are those thought to influence or at least predict dependent variables. For example, a researcher may seek to understand why some athletic teams succeed more than others. Athletic program success is the dependent variable. Coaching quality may be an independent variable. Variation in coaching quality is expected to influence variation in athletic team success.

Dependent variables are typically influenced by many independent variables. For example, athletic success depends on the athletic ability of team members and the quality of opponents, as well as on coaching quality. Exhibit 2.1 provides a representation at the conceptual level.

Variables can be dependent in one context and independent in another. Athletic success, the dependent variable just mentioned, may serve as an independent variable in a study of athletic department revenue. Research interests determine the dependent variable in any study.

Organizational research usually includes a concern with causation. In such research, the independent variable represents a cause; the dependent variable represents the consequence. However, independent and dependent variables are not necessarily causally linked. Independent variables may simply predict dependent variables without causal linkages. For example, birds often begin

EXHIBIT 2.1. Relationship between independent and dependent variables

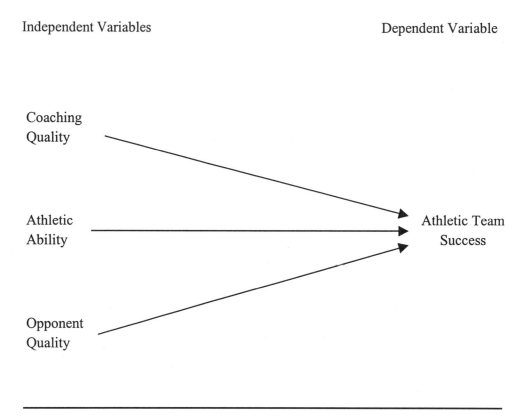

Independent Variables   Dependent Variable

Coaching Quality

Athletic Ability

Opponent Quality

Athletic Team Success

to sing shortly before sunrise; their singing predicts the sunrise but does not cause it.

THE MODEL

A model of empirical research that accounts for the two distinctions just made is shown in Exhibit 2.2. The distinction between conceptual and operational variables is represented vertically; the distinction between independent and dependent variables is represented horizontally. Only two constructs are included in the model although it can easily be extended to more than two.

Exhibit 2.2 employs three conventions used throughout the remainder of this book:

EXHIBIT 2.2. Empirical research model

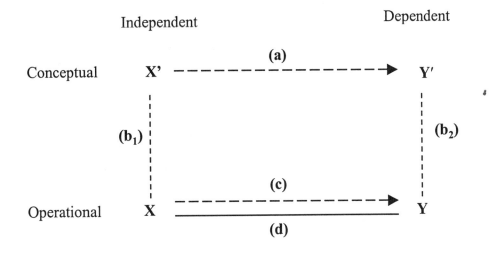

---

1. Independent and dependent variables are identified by X and Y, respectively.
2. The symbol *prime,* ', is used to designate that a variable is specified at the conceptual level.
3. Arrows represent the direction of influence or cause.

The set of variables in Exhibit 2.2 shows three types of relationships; all are important in research.

Conceptual Relationships

The top horizontal line (*a*) represents a causal conceptual relationship. A *causal conceptual relationship* describes a situation in which an independent construct is thought to influence a dependent construct. The school principal believes that teacher goals enhance student achievement. This illustrates a belief about a causal conceptual relationship.

Researchers usually have an expectation about this relationship before conducting a study. In research, such expectations are called *hypotheses,* tentative beliefs about relationships between variables. Research is done to obtain information about whether the hypothesized relationship is valid.

Validity refers to the truth of some research conclusion. In this case, validity refers to the truth of the causal conceptual relationship between X' and Y'. Because this relationship is conceptual, its validity is necessarily tentative. Line (a) in Exhibit 2.2 is broken to signal this tentative nature of the validity of the relationship.

There is always a degree of uncertainty when a conclusion or inference is held to be valid. *Verisimilitude,* meaning something having the appearance of truth, is a good way to think about validity and truth in research.

Operational Relationships

Exhibit 2.2 shows two lines connecting scores on X and Y at the operational level of measurement.

Empirical Relationships. An *empirical relationship,* represented by line (d), refers to the correspondence between scores on measures of X and Y. Line (d) is solid to signal that this relationship can actually be observed, typically using some statistical procedure (see Part IV).

Causal Relationships. When causality is an issue, research must do more than establish an empirical relationship; it must also provide evidence of causation. Line (c) signals a causal relationship between X and Y. Scores on the two measures are related, and it is because variation in X scores leads to variation in Y scores. *Internal validity* is present when variation in scores on a measure of an independent variable is responsible for variation in scores on a measure of a dependent variable.

Line (c), as (a), is broken, because internal validity cannot be established with certainty. *Internal validation* procedures (see Part III) are used to infer internal validity indirectly. Internal validity is assessed using the three criteria shown in Exhibit 2.3. The first criterion states that a relationship must be observed between scores on measures of X and Y. Although not sufficient, an empirical relationship is necessary for causation.

Furthermore, this relationship must be meaningful; it must be greater than what might be expected to occur by chance or coincidence. An empiri-

---

EXHIBIT 2.3. Internal causal criteria

1. Independent and dependent variables are meaningfuly related.

2. Variation in the independent variable is contemporaneus with, or precedes, variation in the dependable variable.

3. There is a reasonable causal explanation for the observed relationship and ther are no plausible alternative explanaitons for it.

---

cal relationship has *internal statistical validity* when it is not due to chance. *Statistical validation* (see Part V) uses probability theory to assess internal statistical validity.

The second criterion follows from a linear time perspective. It is based on an assumption that things occurring later in time are not responsible for those occurring earlier. A causal (independent) variable occurs before a consequence (dependent) variable.

The third criterion has two parts. First, it requires that there is a reasonable conceptual explanation for why X causes Y. For example, education may cause financial success because it provides people with knowledge, skills, and abilities that are valued in the market place. Second, there must be no plausible rival conceptual explanations that account for the relationship observed. This part of the third criterion is typically evaluated by entertaining alternative explanations involving some third variable(s) that may account for the relationship observed between X and Y. For example, education and financial success may be related among a group of participants only because both are related to the financial success of the parents of those being studied.

The two parts of the third criterion are closely related. A compelling explanation places a greater burden on what may be considered a plausible alternative, and vice versa.

Conceptual to Operational Relationships

Conceptual validity requires that activities conducted at the operational level be linked to the conceptual level. This link depends on relationships be-

RESEARCH HIGHLIGHT 2.1

A Research Example Using the Model

A researcher hypothesizes that work experience (X') has a positive impact on work attitudes (Y'). This expectation is studied on a group of managerial employees in a public sector organization. Work experience is measured by the number of years participants have worked for this organization (X), and work attitudes (Y) are measured with a questionnaire that managers complete.

Support for the researcher's hypothesis is obtained if three conditions are met:

1. An empirical relationship is found. Participants who have worked for the organization longer provide more favorable work attitude scores, on average, than those who have worked less time.

2. Evidence is obtained to suggest that the relationship is internally valid. It must be reasonable to suppose the relationship observed results because experience scores cause work attitude scores among the participants.

3. There is evidence that the measures, X and Y, validly represent their respective constructs, X' and Y'.

tween measures and their respective constructs; these are represented by lines (b_1) and (b_2) in Exhibit 2.2.

The construct X' is measured by the set of operations X; the construct Y' is measured by the set of operations Y. **Construct validity** is present when there is a high correspondence between the scores obtained on a measure and the mental definition of the construct it is designed to represent. Lines (b_1) and (b_2) are also broken to show that construct validity is also tentative.

Construct validation (see Part II) involves procedures researchers use to develop measures and to make inferences about a measure's construct validity. Three steps are involved in the construct validation process as shown in Exhibit 2.4. Step 1, define the construct, is central. The definition guides the choice or development of the measure (Step 2); it also provides criteria for any investigations performed on the measure (Step 3).

EXHIBIT 2.4. Construct validation steps

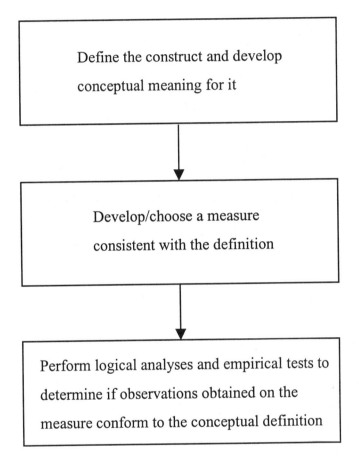

Define the construct and develop conceptual meaning for it

Develop/choose a measure consistent with the definition

Perform logical analyses and empirical tests to determine if observations obtained on the measure conform to the conceptual definition

GENERALIZING FROM THE MODEL

Empirical research provides information about relationships among scores obtained on a group of cases at one point in time. Researchers and research consumers usually are not particularly interested in this relationship, per se. They are usually more interested in knowing how the relationship generalizes beyond the specific situation studied. For example, does the relationship generalize to other groups of cases, to other times, and to other ways of assessing the relationship?

Statistical Generalization

Researchers have two methods to obtain validity evidence about research generalization. One, *statistical validation* (see Part V), uses probability theory to generalize a relationship observed on a sample of cases to the relationship that applies to the broader population from which the sample was drawn. *Statistical generalization validity* is obtained when the empirical relationship observed on a sample of cases validly estimates the relationship in the population of cases from which the sample was drawn. (Statistical validation relies on probability theory for both internal and external statistical validity.)

Exhibit 2.5 illustrates statistical generalization. An inference is made from an empirical relationship observed on a sample (d) to the corresponding, but unknown, empirical relationship (D) in the population. Public opinion polls illustrate a well-known use of statistical generalization procedures.

External Generalization

External validation (see Part VI) refers to procedures researchers use to investigate all other types of research generalization. *External validity* is present when generalizations of findings obtained in a research study, other than statistical generalization, are made appropriately. Exhibit 2.6 provides examples of external generalization.

Substantial progress has been made in methods to address external generalization during the last two decades. This external validation technology usually goes by the name *meta-analysis.* Meta-analysis is a research procedure designed to provide quantitative estimates of the generalizability of relationships across studies.

EXHIBIT 2.5. Statistical generalizations

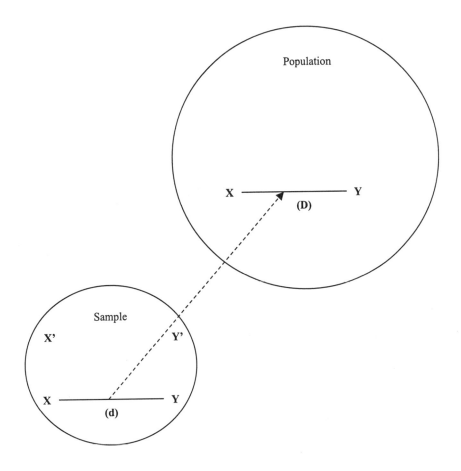

SUMMARY

Research is concerned with relationships between variables. *Variables* are characteristics of things that can take on two or more values.

A main objective of research is to assess causal relationships among conceptual variables called *constructs.* Research does so by addressing three issues: First, is there an *empirical relationship,* a relationship observed between scores on a measured *independent variable* (cause) and a *dependent variable* (effect)? Second, is it reasonable to think that the relationship is

EXHIBIT 2.6. External generalizations

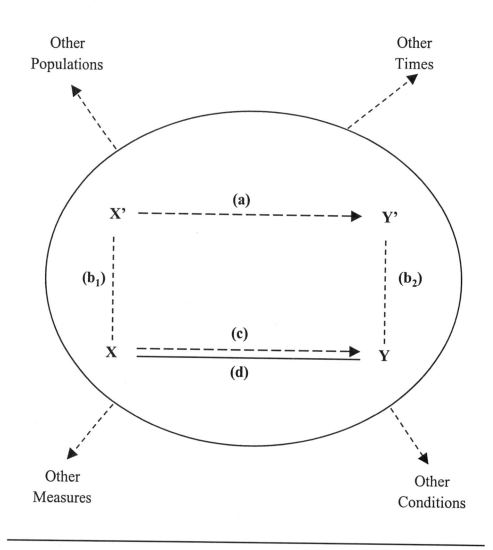

causal? *Internal validation* procedures are used to address this question. *Internal validity* is supported when the answer is affirmative. Finally, is it reasonable to suppose that scores on measures represent their respective constructs? *Construct validation* procedures are used to address this question. *Construct validity* is supported when it is reasonable to think that scores on the measures represent their respective constructs.

Once a research study has been performed, it is often of interest to know whether the results obtained generalize beyond the cases and scores at hand.

Statistical validation procedures are used to generalize from an empirical relationship observed on a sample of cases, to the population of cases from which the sample was drawn. When the generalization is warranted, there is *statistical generalization validity.*

All other sorts of generalization are called external. *External validation* procedures are used to generalize to other populations, other times, and other research methods. When such generalizations are warranted, there is *external validity.*

A final caveat to the discussion in this chapter is appropriate. Many types of validity have been described. Validity refers to truth. However, research validity and truth are always tentative; they are at best provisional, subject to change as new evidence is obtained. Researchers must settle for *verisimilitude,* the appearance of truth.

FOR REVIEW

Terms to Know

Variables. Characteristics of objects that can take on two or more values.

Conceptual variable; also a *construct.* A mental definition of a characteristic of some object that can vary.

Operational variable. Variable with a measure to obtain scores from cases.

Dependent variable. Research outcome; the consequence in a causal relationship.

Independent variable. Helps explain or predict a dependent variable; cause in a causal relationship.

Causal conceptual relationship. A relationship where variation in the independent construct is responsible for variation in the dependent construct.

Hypothesis. An expected relationship between an independent and dependent variable.

Validity. In research, when a conclusion or inference is true.

Verisimilitude. Having the appearance of truth. In research validity is best thought of as verisimilitude.

Empirical relationship. The correspondence between scores obtained from cases on measures.

Internal validity. Present when variation in scores on a measure of an independent variable is responsible for variation in scores on a measure of a dependent variable.

Internal validation. Methods used to determine whether internal validity is likely.

Internal statistical validity. Present when an empirical relationship is not due to chance.

Statistical validation. The use of probability theory to investigate internal statistical validity or statistical generalization validity.

Construct validity. Present when there is a high correspondence between cases' scores on a measure and the mental definition of the construct it is designed to represent.

Construct validation. Methods used to estimate a measure's construct validity.

Statistical generalization validity. Present when an empirical relationship observed on a sample of cases provides a correct estimate of the relationship in the population of cases from which the sample was drawn.

External validity. Present when findings obtained in a research study, other than statistical generalization, are correctly generalized.

External validation. Methods used to estimate external validity.

Meta-analysis. Procedures to review and evaluate prior research studies that depend on quantitative research methods.

Things to Know

1. Understand the model (Exhibit 2.2) and its extensions. Be able to define terms in the model. Also, be able to discuss how the constructs in the model are related. For example, how are empirical relationships and internal validity related?
    (An answer could point out that an empirical relationship is one of several requirements for internal validity. An empirical relationship is necessary, scores on the measure of the independent variable must be associated with scores on the dependent variable for internal validity. However, because internal validity also requires evidence of a

causal relationship, an empirical relationship is not sufficient. Note that this answer defines both constructs, a good idea when you are asked to compare, contrast, or otherwise connect two constructs.)

2. How do construct validation procedures address construct validity? How do internal validation procedures address internal validity?

3. What role does measurement play in the contribution of empirical research to causal conceptual validity?

Issues to Discuss

1. Territoriality is a presumed characteristic of some animals; the animal or group claims a certain territory as its own and seeks to protect it from invasion or threat by other animals, especially from members of its own species. Different animals engage in territorial behavior in different ways. Some birds sing vigorously. Some animals mark their territory with a scent, often urine.

   Sociology researchers at Pennsylvania State University did a study of territoriality among humans (reported in the *Wisconsin State Journal,* 5/13/1997). They observed people leaving shopping mall parking places in their automobiles. They found that individuals drove out of their parking spots more quickly when no one was waiting in an automobile to take their parking spot (32.2 seconds from the time they opened the door). They left more slowly (almost 7 seconds longer) when someone was waiting and more slowly still (10 seconds longer) if the waiting person honked his or her horn. The researchers concluded that humans, as many other animals, are territorial.

   a. What are the independent and dependent variable *constructs* in this illustration?

   b. What are the *operational* independent and dependent variables in this illustration?

   c. Is this study convincing regarding the expectation that humans are territorial? Why or why not?

2. Describe the following about a causal relationship of your choice involving one independent and one dependent variable.

   a. In one sentence, state the causal relationship at a conceptual level. Be sure the independent and dependent constructs are clear and be sure the direction of the relationship is clear.

    b.   Define the independent and dependent constructs in a sentence or two.

    c.   Describe a measure for each of your two constructs in a sentence or two.

II

MEASUREMENT: UNDERSTANDING CONSTRUCT VALIDITY

3

Measurement Foundations: Validity and Validation

Chapter Outline

- *Construct Definitions*
  - *Construct Domain*
  - *Nomological Networks*
- *Construct Definition Illustration*
- *Construct Validity Challenges*
  - *Random Errors*
  - *Systematic Errors*
  - *Scores Are Critical*
- *Construct Validation*
  - *Content Validity*
  - *Reliability*
  - *Convergent Validity*
  - *Discriminant Validity*
  - *Investigating Nomological Networks*
- *Summary*
- *For Review*

Part I describes how empirical research contributes to knowledge by investigating relationships between scores on measures. The value of such research depends largely on whether scores obtained on the measures used are construct valid. That is, it depends on whether there is a close correspondence between the scores and researchers' mental representations of the variables investigated.

However, construct valid measurement is confronted by an inescapable difficulty. There is no direct way to measure constructs, because they are conceptual phenomena. As a consequence, there is no direct way to assess construct validity; it must be inferred from a variety of criteria. These inferences are made by examining scores on measures and comparing them with theoretical propositions about how the scores should perform.

This chapter introduces the foundations of measurement and construct validation. It begins with a discussion of conceptual definitions and then introduces research procedures useful in construct validation.

CONSTRUCT DEFINITIONS

Measurement produces numerical values that are designed to summarize characteristics of cases under study. A measure is an instrument to record such scores. Construct valid measures yield numerical values that accurately represent the characteristic. For example, if a score of 5 represents "Very Satisfied," then a measure of satisfaction should obtain scores of 5 for all participants who are very satisfied; participants who experience other levels of satisfaction should receive other numerical values. In short, construct valid measurement results in a close correspondence between the construct of interest and the scores provided by the measure.

Defining constructs at a conceptual level is an essential first step in the development of construct valid measures. Good construct definitions are also needed to identify appropriate empirical procedures for evaluating the validity of results obtained from measures. The most useful conceptual definitions have two elements.

Construct Domain

First, useful conceptual definitions identify the nature of the construct by specifying its meaning. This element explains what a researcher has in mind for the construct; it contains a dictionary-like statement that describes the construct domain. It speaks to what is included in the construct. If there is potential confusion about what is not included, this too should be addressed in the definition.

Nomological Networks

A second element of a good construct definition specifies how values of the construct should differ across cases and conditions. For example, should the construct remain about the same over time, or is it expected to vary? Some constructs, such as human intelligence, are expected to be relatively stable over time. A measure of intelligence administered at different times should provide the same estimate of an individual's intelligence. Other constructs, such as opinions about current events, are expected to be more volatile. Scores on measures of such constructs are not necessarily expected to be similar from one administration of a measure to another.

This second element should also specify how the construct of interest relates to other constructs in a broader web of relationships called a **nomological network.** A nomological network is identical to a conceptual model in form; it differs only in purpose. In contrast to conceptual models, nomological networks are used to draw inferences about constructs and construct validity.

CONSTRUCT DEFINITION ILLUSTRATION

The following example may help solidify the ideas just developed and illustrate construct validation methods described in the following section. Suppose a researcher seeks to measure satisfaction that owners experience with personal laptop or desktop computers. The researcher may be interested in characteristics that influence satisfaction and thus view it as a dependent variable. Or, the researcher may be interested in consequences of satisfaction with computer ownership and thus view satisfaction as an independent variable. In either event, the researcher defines the construct as:

> Personal computer satisfaction is an emotional response resulting from an evaluation of the speed, durability, and initial price, but not the appearance of a personal computer. This evaluation is expected to depend on variation in the actual characteristics of the computer (e.g., speed) and on the expectations a participant has about those characteristics. When characteristics meet or exceed expectations, the evaluation is expected to be positive (satisfaction). When characteristics do not come up to expectations, the evaluation is expected to be negative (dissatisfaction). People with more education will have higher expectations and hence lower computer satisfaction than those with less education.

This example is explicit about the domain of the construct. Computer satisfaction as defined refers to speed, durability, and price. It is also explicit that satisfaction with appearance is not a part of the definition.

The definition goes on to state that the evaluation leading to satisfaction or dissatisfaction depends on a comparison of peoples' expectations for computers with their actual experience. The researcher anticipates that satisfaction will differ between participants because their computers differ in power, durability, and price, and because expectations for these three computer characteristics differ. A measure of satisfaction might ask for the evaluation directly, or it might be constructed from responses about computer expectations and computer experiences.

Finally, the definition includes a primitive form of a nomological network by relating expectations to education level. The definition states that those with higher education levels will have higher expectations and hence lower satisfaction, other things equal.

Suppose that after defining the construct the researcher finds a measure of computer satisfaction that is already developed, as shown in Exhibit 3.1. The researcher decides to perform construct validation on this measure. This measure represents an operational definition of the construct. It has six items, each anchored by a 5-point rating scale ranging from 1 (Very Dissatisfied) to 5 (Very Satisfied).

CONSTRUCT VALIDITY CHALLENGES

Construct validity is confronted by two major challenges. One involves *random errors,* completely unsystematic variation in scores. A second more difficult challenge involves *systematic errors,* consistent differences between scores obtained from a measure and meaning as defined by the construct.

Random Errors

Random or unsystematic errors are nearly always present in measurement. Fortunately, there are methods for identifying them and procedures to ameliorate their adverse consequences. Since these procedures involve the use of statistics, their formal discussion is postponed to Chapter 17. However, one such procedure is illustrated by the measure shown in Exhibit 3.1. The questionnaire has more than one item related to each characteristic of computer ownership. Items 1 and 2 relate to satisfaction with price, items 3 and 4 relate to satisfaction with speed, and so forth.

EXHIBIT 3.1. Hypothetical computer satisfaction questionnaire

---

Decide how satisfied or dissatisfied you are with each characteristic of your personal computer using the scale below. Circle the number that best describes your feelings for each statement.

Very Dissatisfied	Dissatisfied	Neither Satisfied nor Dissatisfied	Satisfied	Very Satisfied
1	2	3	4	5

My satisfaction with:

1.	Initial price of the computer	1	2	3	4	5
2.	What I paid for the computer	1	2	3	4	5
3.	How quickly the computer performs calculations	1	2	3	4	5
4.	How fast the computer runs programs	1	2	3	4	5
5.	Helpfulness of the salesperson	1	2	3	4	5
6.	How I was treated when I bought the computer	1	2	3	4	5

The use of more than one item to measure a construct is common, and it acknowledges that random errors are a common problem. Taking an average of several items designed to measure the same thing is one way to address random errors. Random errors tend to be "averaged-out" across multiple items; errors that inflate scores on one item tend to be offset by errors that understate other items. The more items, the more successfully this type of random error is controlled.

Systematic Errors

Items from the measure shown in Exhibit 3.1 also suggest two types of systematic errors that reduce construct validity. Items 5 and 6 ask about satisfaction with the purchasing experience; these are not part of the researcher's conceptual definition of the construct. A measure is *contaminated* if it captures characteristics not specifically included in the definition of the construct.

A measure can also have systematic errors because it is *deficient,* that is, when it does not capture the entire construct domain. The measure in Exhibit 3.1 is deficient, because there are no items capturing satisfaction with computer durability.

Scores Are Critical

The discussion so far actually understates the challenges faced in developing construct valid measurement. The computer satisfaction illustration identifies differences between a construct definition and a measure. Yet, construct validity (or invalidity) is not established by measures alone, it is ultimately determined by scores. Construct validity refers to the correspondence between the construct and the scores generated from a measure, not the measure per se.

Consequently, anything that influences scores can influence validity, often adversely. To illustrate, contamination may result from sources other than the measure. In the computer satisfaction example, participants may be motivated to systematically under- or overestimate their satisfaction. They may systematically report greater satisfaction than they truly feel if a representative of the computer manufacturer is present while they complete the questionnaire. The administrative environment (location, noise levels, temperature, etc.) may also influence errors regardless of the specific items in a particular measure.

Challenges for construct validity are summarized in Exhibit 3.2. The solid circle represents variability associated with the construct. In the example, this is the variability expected in satisfaction as defined conceptually. It includes the characteristics of computer speed, durability and initial price.

The circle starting on the far right represents variability in scores obtained on the measure from a group of participants. Variability in these scores is due to differences in participant responses to the items on the measure at the time

RESEARCH HIGHLIGHT 3.1

Multidimensional Constructs

Throughout this chapter, assume that researchers are interested in unidimensional constructs. Whatever the construct, it is assumed to represent a single domain.

However, there are circumstances when multidimensional constructs are of interest. Unidimensional and multidimensional constructs differ in level of abstraction; multidimensional constructs are disaggregated unidimensional constructs. In the example, computer satisfaction is considered unidimensional. A researcher could disaggregate computer satisfaction into three subdimensions: satisfaction with computer speed, computer durability, and computer price. Researchers are free to choose levels of abstraction consistent with their research interests.

completed and in the environment where the measure was administered. These scores contain both systematic and random elements.

Finally, the middle circle represents variability that reflects the consistent (systematic) variance in the observed scores. Construct valid variance must be systematic by definition. However, systematic variance may not be construct valid, because it may be contaminated or deficient. Systematic variance is sometimes called *true score* variance; this is a misnomer, since *true* implies construct valid.

Scores on a measure are construct valid (area represented by crossed lines) to the extent that systematic observed score variance overlaps with the construct valid variance. The objective of construct validation is to investigate measures and scores and ultimately to maximize this overlapping area.

Exhibit 3.2 also shows three sources of construct invalidity:

1. Scores on a measure may be less than construct valid because of deficiency. In the example, observed scores are deficient because the measure does not capture satisfaction with computer durability.
2. Scores may be less than construct valid because of systematic contamination. In the example, observed scores are contaminated because the measure includes satisfaction with the purchasing experience.

EXHIBIT 3.2. Construct validity challenges

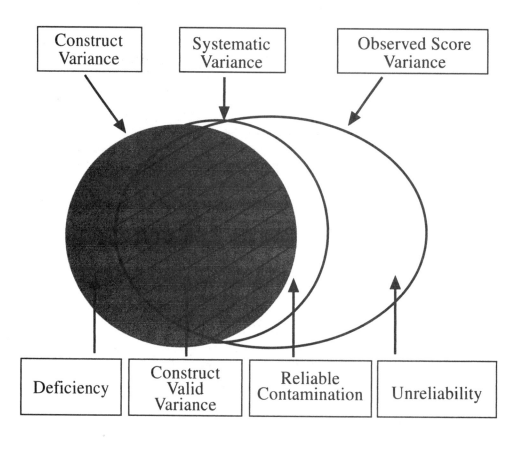

3. Finally, scores on a measure are less than construct valid to the extent that they include random errors.

CONSTRUCT VALIDATION

Because construct validity cannot be assessed directly, it cannot be directly established. However, there are procedures available to help researchers develop construct valid measures and to help evaluate those measures once they are developed. Five such procedures are described here.

RESEARCH HIGHLIGHT 3.2

Measurement by Manipulation

Measurement issues, language, and technologies have developed largely around measures that call on research participants to complete some sort of questionnaire. Examples include measures of ability, attitudes, or opinions.

However, construct validity issues are equally relevant when researchers actively manipulate values of independent variables. For example, a researcher wants to know whether "decision complexity" influences the quality of decision making. Two hypothetical decision scenarios are created to represent two levels of decision complexity. Groups of research participants are assigned to one or the other of the two scenarios; decision quality of the two groups is then compared.

All of the measurement questions and issues raised regarding questionnaires are appropriate in this case. Is decision complexity adequately defined at the conceptual level? Is the manipulation subject to random errors? Is it deficient or contaminated? For example, the scenarios may manipulate more than just decision complexity and hence be contaminated. Good research using manipulations takes steps to obtain information about the quality of the manipulations employed.

Content Validity

A measure is *content valid* when its items are judged to accurately reflect the domain of the construct as defined conceptually. *Content validation* ordinarily has experts in the subject matter of interest provide estimates of content validity.

For example, an organizational researcher develops a measure to predict performance among computer programmers. The organization wants to use this measure to help identify job applicants most likely to perform effectively if hired. As a part of development, the researcher has a panel of persons who are experts in computer programming review the measure for its

RESEARCH HIGHLIGHT 3.3

> *The Appearance of Validity*
>
> A measure is *face valid* when its items appear to reflect the construct as defined conceptually. In contrast to content validation, estimates of face validity are usually obtained from persons similar to those who serve as research participants. A measure should appear valid to participants to help motivate accurate responses.
>
> Either content or face validation would likely identify that the computer satisfaction questionnaire (Exhibit 3.1) is both deficient (no computer durability items) and contaminated (purchasing experience items).

content. Content validation of this sort provides information about potential systematic errors in measures. Expert judges can be especially helpful in identifying items that may potentially contaminate a measure.

Content validation can help improve the items that form a measure. It nevertheless is not sufficient for construct validity. In particular, content validation procedures may not provide information about potential deficiency, nor can subject matter experts provide much information about random errors that may be present in the scores that are obtained.

Reliability

Reliability refers to the systematic or consistent variance of a measure; it thus indicates the degree to which measurement scores are free of random errors. *Reliability statistics* provide estimates of the proportion of the total variability in a set of scores that is true or systematic. Reliability is shown in Exhibit 3.1 as the proportion of observed score variability (circle on the far right) that is overlapped by the middle circle representing true (systematic) score variability.

Types of Reliability. There are three common contexts in which researchers seek to assess the reliability of measurement. Chapter 17 describes a statistical procedure for estimating these types of reliability.

1. *Internal consistency reliability* refers to the similarity of item scores obtained on a measure that has multiple items. It can be assessed when items are intended to measure a single construct. In the computer example (Exhibit 3.1), satisfaction is measured with six items. The internal consistency of that questionnaire can be estimated if scores are available from a group of participants.

2. *Interrater reliability* indicates the degree to which a group of observers or raters provide consistent evaluations. For example, the observers may be a group of international judges who are asked to evaluate ice skaters performing in a competition. In this case, the judges serve as measurement repetitions just as the items serve as repetitions in the computer satisfaction questionnaire. High reliability is obtained when the judges agree on the evaluation of each skater.

3. *Stability reliability* refers to the consistency of measurement results across time. Here measurement repetitions refer to time periods (a measure is administered more than once).

Reliability and Construct Validity.   Reliability speaks only to a measure's freedom from random errors. It does not address systematic errors involving contamination or deficiency. Reliability is thus necessary for construct validity but not sufficient. It is necessary because unreliable variance must be construct invalid. It is not sufficient because systematic variance may be contaminated and because reliability simply does not account for deficiency. In short, reliability addresses only whether scores are consistent; it does not address whether scores capture a particular construct as defined conceptually.

Convergent Validity

Convergent validity is present when there is a high correspondence between scores from two or more different measures of the same construct. Convergent validity is important because it must be present if scores from both measures are construct valid. But convergent validity is not sufficient for construct validity any more than is reliability. Exhibit 3.3 shows why. The solid circle on the left represents construct variance; this variance is necessarily unknown to a researcher. The two open circles on the right of Exhibit 3.3 represent variance in scores on two measures designed to assess the construct.

EXHIBIT 3.3. Convergent validity

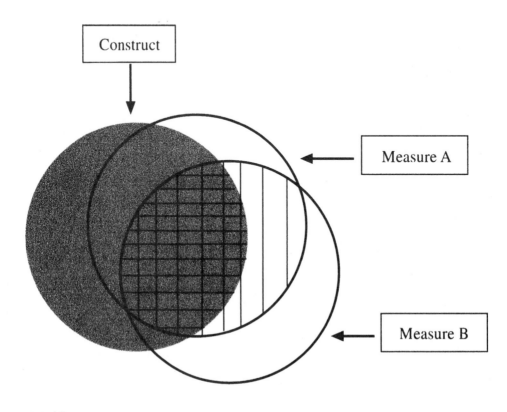

The area crossed with vertical lines shows the proportion of variance in scores from the two measures that is convergent. However, only the area also crossed with horizontal lines shows common construct valid variance. The area covered only by vertical lines shows where the two measures share variance that represents contamination from a construct validity perspective.

Convergent validity also does not address whether measures are deficient. Nor does it provide construct validity information about the proportion of variance in the two measures that do not converge. Exhibit 3.3 shows that more of the variance unique to Measure A overlaps with construct variance than variance from Measure B.

Despite these limitations, evidence of convergent validity is desirable. If two measures that are designed to measure the same construct do not converge, at least one of them is not construct valid. Alternatively, if they do converge, some evidence is obtained that they may both be construct valid. Evidence of convergent validity adds to a researcher's confidence in the construct validity of measures.

Discriminant Validity

Discriminant validity is inferred when scores from measures of different constructs do not converge. It thus provides information about whether scores from a measure of a construct are unique rather than contaminated by other constructs.

The researcher defined computer satisfaction to exclude an evaluation of the appearance of the computer. Evidence supportive of this definition would be provided by a discriminant validity investigation. If scores on the researcher's measure of computer satisfaction show little or no relationship with scores from a measure of satisfaction with computer appearance, then discriminant validity evidence is obtained.

An investigation of discriminant validity is particularly important when an investigator develops a measure of a new construct that may be redundant with other more thoroughly researched constructs. Proposed constructs should provide contributions beyond constructs already in the research domain. Consequently, measures of proposed constructs should show evidence of discriminant validity with measures of existing constructs.

Investigating Nomological Networks

Nomological networks have been described as relationships between a construct under measurement consideration and other constructs. In the chapter example, the researcher's expectation that education is related to computer satisfaction illustrates a simple nomological network, as shown in Exhibit 3.4. This nomological network is indistinguishable from a conceptual model used by researchers concerned with the relationship between education level and computer satisfaction constructs. The difference is in underlying motivations and assumptions.

Researchers with a conceptual orientation are interested in the conceptual relationship between the independent and dependent variable constructs

**EXHIBIT 3.4. Nomological network: Computer satisfaction and
education level**

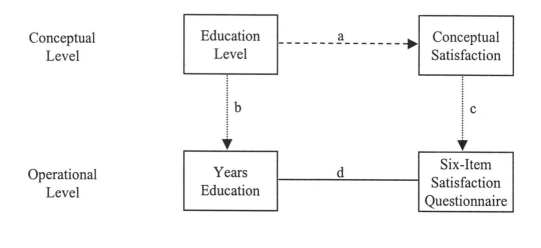

(line a in Exhibit 3.4). Such researchers use a relationship observed between scores from participants on measures of education and satisfaction (line d) to infer to the conceptual relationship (line a). To make this inference, they must assume construct validity for both satisfaction and education level (lines b and c). Given the assumptions, a negative relationship between years of education and the 6-item satisfaction questionnaire is consistent with the conceptual validity of the relationship between the two constructs.

A researcher interested in the construct validity of the 6-item measure of computer satisfaction may use the same model to draw different inferences. Specifically, the measurement researcher assumes the conceptual relationship is true (line a). Further, in the example, the measure of education level is assumed to be construct valid (line b). Given these alternative assumptions, results from an investigation of the relationship between scores on years of education and the 6-item satisfaction questionnaire (line d) provide evidence about the construct validity of the questionnaire (line c). A nega-

RESEARCH HIGHLIGHT 3.4

A Common Misconception

Sometimes research reports include a claim that a measure(s) used in the study has been construct validated; such claims are unwarranted.

The criterion in construct validation research, the construct, cannot be observed directly. Inferences made about construct validity are, therefore, necessarily tentative. They may be modified as more evidence is obtained on the measure used to represent the construct.

tive relationship between years of education and the 6-item satisfaction questionnaire is consistent with construct validity for the satisfaction questionnaire.

A relationship observed between one measured construct and a measure of another provides only limited evidence for construct validity. Thus, researchers usually seek to create more elaborate nomological networks. These may include several variables that are expected to vary with a measure of the construct. It may also include variables that are expected not to vary with it to show evidence of discriminant validity.

Evidence for construct validity mounts as empirical research supports relationships expected from a nomological network. The richer the network, and the more support, the greater the researcher's confidence that the measure is capturing variance that is construct valid.

Information obtained in the construct validation process may also lead to modification of the construct. For example, in contrast to the initial definition, the researcher may consistently find that computer appearance is related to a measure of computer satisfaction. If so, the definition of the construct may be changed to include appearance given this empirical information.

SUMMARY

Measurement represents the main link between constructs that motivate research and the empirical procedures used to address relationships between them. Definitions of constructs serve a key role in construct validation because they serve as the principle criteria for evaluating measures. A good construct definition contains a dictionary-like statement of the construct domain and a statement of how scores on a measure of the construct should behave, including how they should relate to other constructs in a *nomological network.*

Construct validity is challenged by random and systematic errors. *Random errors* produce unsystematic variation that can inflate scores in some instances, deflate them in other instances. *Systematic errors* may result from *contamination,* when scores from a measure get at characteristics that are not included in the construct. They may also result from *deficiency,* when scores from a measure do not capture a portion of variance that is in a construct. Both random and systematic errors are present in scores of all measures.

Researchers engage in construct validation to learn about and improve construct validity. Random errors in measurement are assessed by estimating *reliability* that refers to the systematic or consistent portion of observed scores obtained on a measure. Common types of reliability include *internal consistency* (consistency of measurement across items), *interrater reliability* (consistency of measurement across observers or raters), and *stability reliability* (consistency of measurement across time periods).

Evidence for construct validity is also obtained by assessing other types of validity. These include *content validity,* expert judgments about the validity of a measure; *convergent validity,* the correspondence of scores from two or more measures of the same construct; and *discriminant validity,* present when scores from measures of different constructs that should not be related are not related. Finally, evidence for construct validity is obtained when research provides support for the nomological network established for a construct.

FOR REVIEW

Terms to Know

Nomological network. Relationships between a construct under measurement consideration and other constructs. It is the measurement analog to a conceptual model of interest to causal research.

Random errors. In measurement, also called *unreliability,* errors in scores on a measure that are unsystematic. Random errors are uncorrelated with *true* (*systematic*) scores.

True scores. Also called *systematic,* the consistent (repeatable) portion of scores obtained from participants on a measure.

Systematic errors. In measurement, when scores from a measure consistently vary from construct validity because of contamination and/or deficiency.

> *Contamination.* In measurement, the portion of scores that measure something other than the defined construct.

> *Deficiency.* In measurement, the portion of the defined construct that is not captured by scores on a measure of the construct.

Content validity. When a measure is judged to be construct valid, usually by individuals who are thought to be subject matter experts.

Content validation. Procedures employed to obtain content validity.

Face validity. When a measure appears to be construct valid by individuals who use it, including participants.

Reliability. Refers to the consistency of measurement.

> *Internal consistency.* A form of reliability that addresses the consistency of scores from a set of items in a measure.

> *Interrater reliability.* A form of reliability that addresses the consistency of scores from a set of observers.

> *Stability reliability.* A form of reliability that addresses the consistency of scores across time periods.

Convergent validity. Is present when there is a high correspondence between scores from two different measures of the same construct.

Discriminant validity. Is present when measures of constructs that are supposed to be independent are found to have a low correspondence.

Things to Know

1. What construct validation purposes are served by the definition of the construct?

2. Be able to discuss how true scores are similar to constructs. How do they differ?

3. Unreliable variance in the scores from a measure are not construct valid by definition. How can reliable variance in scores not be construct valid?

4. Compare and contrast content and face validity.

5. Procedures to estimate reliability require that there be repetitions of scores. What are the repetitions in estimates of internal consistency, interrater reliability, and stability?

6. Two measures of a construct show convergent validity. Why is this not sufficient for construct validity? In what sense can you argue it is necessary? If two measures do not show evidence of convergent validity, does this mean that neither has construct validity?

7. How are conceptual models similar to nomological networks? How do they differ?

4

Measurement Applications: Research Questionnaires

Chapter Outline

- *Questionnaire Decisions*
  - *Alternatives to Questionnaire Construction*
  - *Questionnaire Type*
- *Questionnaire Construction*
  - *Content Domain*
  - *Items*
  - *Scaling*
- *Questionnaire Response Styles*
  - *Self-Reports*
  - *Observations*
  - *Implications for Questionnaire Construction and Use*
- *Pilot Testing*
- *Summary*
- *For Review*
- *Part II: Suggested Reading*

A remarkable variety of measures are used in organizational research. Some of these are designed to capture characteristics of organizations, such as information about size, longevity, organizational success, quality of products or services, and policies and practices. Some are designed to identify characteristics of individuals who interact with organizations, such as clients or customers, investors, suppliers, and employees or volunteers. Measures of the latter sort, in turn, may be designed to obtain information about a variety of individual characteristics, such as their knowledge, abilities, motivations, opinions, and behaviors.

There are also many measurement methods to obtain scores for organizational research. The present chapter discusses issues involved with one general and widely used form of measurement, namely *questionnaires.* Questionnaires are measuring instruments that ask individuals to respond to a set of questions. If the questions ask for information about the individual respondents, they are called *self-report questionnaires.* Examples of information obtained in self-report questionnaires include biographical information, attitudes and opinions, and knowledge. As examples, self-report questionnaires are used to obtain information about employee reactions to managerial work policies, consumer satisfaction and buying intentions, student evaluations of their instruction, and investor evaluations of investment opportunities.

Individuals may complete self-report questionnaires by responding to written questions or questions shown on a computer terminal. Self-reports may also be obtained through an *interview* in which another individual (the *interviewer*) asks the questions verbally and is responsible for recording responses.

Questionnaires are also used to obtain information from individuals who serve as *observers.* Observers use questionnaires to record descriptions and evaluations of organizational and individual variables. For example, questionnaires of this sort may ask supervisors to describe and/or evaluate performance behaviors of individual employees. As another example, observers may complete questionnaires to describe interaction patterns between sales personnel and customers.

These examples indicate that questionnaires have wide applicability in organizational research. This chapter discusses issues related to questionnaire construction and use. It describes decisions that researchers must make when they seek information that may be obtained from questionnaires. A major portion of the chapter is devoted to questionnaire construction. Response styles of people who complete questionnaires are also discussed, because good measurement does not depend solely on good questionnaires. Finally, the important role of pilot testing is discussed, because questionnaire construction is invariably an imperfect research activity.

QUESTIONNAIRE DECISIONS

Constructing a questionnaire is a time-consuming and demanding part of the research process. It is particularly challenging when abstract constructs must be measured. As a consequence, researchers should first consider alternatives to questionnaire construction. Two additional decisions are needed when questionnaires are used to carry out a research project. First, a decision must be made about whether the information should be obtained using a written questionnaire or through an interview. Second, if the questionnaire is designed to obtain information about individuals, a decision must be made about the source of information. Should it be obtained from outside observers or from individuals reporting on themselves?

Alternatives to Questionnaire Construction

Choosing a measurement instrument(s) depends foremost on the topic a researcher seeks to investigate. Some sorts of organizational research and some portions of specific research studies may not require that a questionnaire be constructed or may not use a questionnaire at all.

Secondary Data. Much organizational research is conducted using *secondary data,* data collected for some other purpose. When secondary data are available, a researcher does not need to be concerned with questionnaire construction or data collection. However, the researcher must still be concerned with the quality of the measures used to obtain the data. Construct validity issues identified in the previous chapter are as relevant to secondary data as to the development of new measures.

Secondary data are available from many sources. They are collected by organizations for other internal purposes, such as maintaining records to monitor and improve the quality of services or products. Secondary data are also collected by organizations to meet external requirements such as safety, affirmative action, and tax regulation. Secondary data relevant to organizational research are also collected by outside organizations, such as industry trade associations and organizations that collect and sell information about other organizations (e.g., Standard & Poor's financial reports) and individuals who interact with organizations (e.g., ACNielsen's ratings of television viewing). In addition, governments at all levels collect information that is of interest to organizational researchers. At the federal level alone, agencies such as the Census Bureau and Departments of Health and Human Services, Education, Commerce, Transportation, and Labor all collect a large amount of data that may be used in organizational research.

Secondary data is advantageous from both a cost and a time perspective when they are available and applicable. Secondary data sources should be used if research objectives can be accomplished using them. However, relevant secondary data are often not available. Even if available, secondary data may be of unacceptable or questionable quality.

Questionnaires Developed by Others.   There is another alternative to questionnaire construction. Another researcher may have already developed a questionnaire that will address your research purposes. Although data may not be available or usable, a questionnaire may be available that you can use to collect your own data. Questionnaires measuring constructs relating to many individual characteristics such as ability, personality, and interests have already been constructed. Questionnaires are also available for characteristics of individuals interacting with organizations, such as employee satisfaction. Locating these latter measures can be problematic. A good method for finding whether such measures are available is to examine research reports on topics related to your research interests.

If suitable for your research interests, questionnaires that have already been constructed are obviously advantageous in the time and effort they can save. They are especially attractive if the developer or others have additionally performed some of the construct validation procedures identified in the previous chapter.

Questionnaire Type

Secondary data or questionnaires developed by others are simply not viable options for many research projects. This is necessarily true when a researcher chooses to investigate a construct that has not been previously defined and measured. It is also true in many applied situations in which the research is aimed at investigating a topical issue, often one that applies to a specific organizational characteristic, such as a product or service. Such situations call for the construction of questionnaires as a part of a research investigation.

Self-Reports Versus Observations.   Researchers are often curious about relationships that include characteristics of individuals interacting with organizations. For example, a researcher may want to know whether academic achievement of students is related to teaching styles. Both variables in this example represent individual characteristics. As another example, a researcher may want to know whether employee performance levels are influenced by an organization's system for providing financial rewards. An individual characteristic, employee performance, represents one variable of interest.

In situations such as these, researchers must decide whether they should obtain the information from the participants studied. Some constructs require that the information be measured with responses provided by research participants. In particular, constructs that address internal mental states of individuals can only be measured by asking research participants to provide them. Attitudes and opinions, intentions, interests and preferences are all examples of such constructs.

However, there are other constructs that can be measured either internally through self-reports or externally by observation. These constructs typically involve overt behaviors, characteristics of individuals that can be observed directly. For example, the researcher interested in employee performance could ask employees to complete a questionnaire reporting on their own performance. Or, the researcher could obtain the information by having an observer complete a questionnaire that reports on employee performance.[1]

Observations are typically preferred when constructs can be assessed directly. External observers are more likely to provide consistent assessments across research participants. Furthermore, external observers may be less likely to bias responses in a way that characterizes the behavior in a favorable light.

However, the choice of using self-reports or external observers has no necessary implications for the form of the questionnaire, per se. The same questionnaire can be used for self-reports or by external observers if the information sought is the same.

Interviews Versus Written Questionnaires. A distinction is sometimes drawn between the development of interviews and the development of questionnaires. This distinction is largely unwarranted. The difference between the two procedures resides primarily in the way information is obtained from

---

[1]There may also be ways to measure performance that do not involve the use of questionnaires. For example, quantity of performance may be recorded mechanically or electronically for employees in some types of jobs that produce a physical output.

research participants. Interviews elicit information verbally; questionnaires elicit information in written form. The same care must be taken in developing interview questions and response formats as is taken in developing questionnaires.

A case can be made that interviews allow greater flexibility. Interviewers can follow up on answers with questions that probe respondents' thinking in greater depth. Interviewers can record responses and interviewee behaviors that are not available as formal questionnaire responses.

These are differences that make interviews attractive in the early stages of instrument development. Interviews can help researchers refine the questions to be asked and the response formats to be used. However, when finalized, when a researcher is ready to collect data that will be used to investigate the main research expectations, a typical interview schedule will look much like a typical questionnaire.

The decision about whether to use an interview or questionnaire as the final measurement instrument depends on other criteria. Assuming the same care in construction, questionnaires are usually less expensive to administer. The decision to use an interview or a questionnaire must also take account of respondents' abilities and motivations. Reading abilities among some members of heterogeneous populations may make the use of questionnaires problematic. Interviews may also be advantageous from a motivational perspective. The interaction that takes place between the interviewer and interviewee may be used advantageously to motivate participation and complete responses.

Interaction between interviewers and interviewees also poses dangers for interviews. There is a greater risk that the administration of questions differs from interview to interview. Furthermore, because there is interaction, interviewee responses may be influenced by the particular individual conducting the interview.

It is generally desirable to use questionnaires when possible. The importance of uniformity in questions and response coding favors questionnaires. When interviews are used, it is important that they be conducted as systematically as possible.

QUESTIONNAIRE CONSTRUCTION

Questionnaires, whether administered in written form or through interviews, have two essential characteristics. First, they have items designed to elicit the information of research interest. Second, they have a protocol for

EXHIBIT 4.1. **Two questionnaires designed to measure satisfaction with pay**

Question	Response Format				
Minnesota Satisfaction Questionnaire	VD	D	N	S	VS
1. The amount of pay for the work I do.	☐	☐	☐	☐	☐
2. The chance to make as much money as my friends.	☐	☐	☐	☐	☐
3. How my pay compares with that for similar jobs in other companies.	☐	☐	☐	☐	☐
4. My pay and the amount of work I do.	☐	☐	☐	☐	☐
5. How my pay compares with that of other workers.	☐	☐	☐	☐	☐

Cornell Job Descriptive Index			
1. Income adequate for normal expenses (+).	Yes	?	No
2. Satisfactory profit sharing (+).	Yes	?	No
3. Barely live on income (−).	Yes	?	No
4. Bad (−).	Yes	?	No
5. Income provides luxuries (+).	Yes	?	No
6. Insecure (−).	Yes	?	No
7. Less than I deserve (−).	Yes	?	No
8. Highly paid (+).	Yes	?	No
9. Underpaid (−).	Yes	?	No

Note: Minnesota Satisfaction Questionnaire from Weiss, Davis, England and Lofquist (1967). Items are scaled from Very Dissatisfied (VD) = 1; Dissatisfied (D) = 2; Neither Dissatisfied or Satisfied (N) = 3; Satisfied (S) = 4; to Very Satisfied (VS) = 5. Cornell Job Descriptive Index from Smith, Kendall and Hulin (1969). Positive (+) items are scaled Yes = 3 and No = 0. Negative (-) items are scaled Yes = 0 and No = 3. For both positive and negative items ? = 1. Both scales shown are with permission from the authors.

recording responses. For example, Exhibit 4.1 shows sets of items and response scales from the pay portions of two well-known job satisfaction questionnaires. The Minnesota Satisfaction Questionnaire (MSQ) has five items designed to measure satisfaction with pay. Each has a 5-point response scale ranging from Very Dissatisfied to Very Satisfied. The Cornell Job Descriptive Index (JDI) has nine items to measure satisfaction with pay. Participants respond by indicating only whether each item applies (Yes), does not apply (No), or they cannot decide whether the item applies in describing their pay (?).

Content Domain

A properly designed study will already have identified the variables to be measured by the time questionnaire development becomes an issue. If one or more constructs are included, these should be carefully defined as described in Chapter 3. Item construction for constructs should follow closely from the definitions.

Typically, researchers will also want to obtain additional information from their questionnaires. At the very least, information will usually be sought regarding personal descriptive characteristics of the questionnaire respondents, such as their organizational role (e.g., manager, student, customer), education, age, and gender. Respondents in the role of describing characteristics of organizations will typically be asked to provide descriptive information such as size, location, and type of products or services provided.

Interesting side issues are likely to occur while the questionnaire is being developed. As a consequence, it is often tempting to add items that are not central to the research investigation. Resist this temptation. Attend to developing a set of items that focus directly and unequivocally on your research topic. Diverting attention to related items and issues will likely reduce the quality of items that are essential. Furthermore, response rates inevitably decline as questionnaire length increases.

Items

Item wording and the arrangement of items obviously impact the responses that are obtained on a questionnaire. Indeed, the content of the questionnaire influences whether research participants will provide responses at all. There is a great deal of research showing the importance of item wording and item arrangement on questionnaire responses.

Item Wording. Despite this research, recommendations for item wording are difficult to make, because each questionnaire is potentially unique in important ways. Four recommendations that serve as general guidelines follow.

1. *Keep the respondent in mind.* This is perhaps the most important recommendation. It is very easy to overestimate participants' knowledge and interest in a topic because of your knowledge and interest. Who will be responding to the questionnaire? What knowledge will they have? What knowledge will they be willing to share? Do not ask for information that participants cannot or will not provide.

2. *Make it simple.* Make sure that the words in each item are understandable to respondents. It is nearly always reasonable to suppose that verbal understanding levels of at least some respondents are low. Thus, regardless of whether you use a written questionnaire or an interview, keep the words and questions simple. Construct items so that demands on respondents' knowledge, attention, and memory are reasonable. Use technical words and jargon reluctantly even if respondents are technical specialists.

3. *Be specific.* It is dangerous to assume that respondents will share your frame of reference; at least some of them probably will not. As a consequence, it is important to be explicit about relevant contextual features such as who, what, when, where, and how.

4. *Be honest.* It is easy to manipulate results in one direction or another, because questionnaire responses are so sensitive to item wording. Thus, guard against leading respondents to the answers you believe or hope will occur. An examination of your own assumptions and values can help you evaluate question wording for potential implicit biases.

Item Sequence. The way items are ordered in a questionnaire is constrained by the type of items included. For example, order is of little consequence if items are all similar. However, order can influence responses and response rates when items vary in content.

Research respondents are often hesitant to begin a questionnaire. They may be anxious about whether they can answer the questions. Or they may be reluctant to provide information. As a consequence, it is helpful to start a questionnaire with items that participants find interesting and are easy to complete.

Ask for demographic information last. People are often reluctant to provide personal information. Asking for it last increases the likelihood that it will be provided, because respondents have already made a commitment by completing the earlier part of the questionnaire. Furthermore, you will have obtained useful information even if the respondents do not provide the personal information.

Scaling

There are many ways that questionnaire item responses can be recorded. An *open-ended response format* permits respondents to answer questions in their own words. They are sometimes used on small groups of participants early in the questionnaire development process to make sure that the full range of potential responses is captured. They are also sometimes used in interviews, particularly when the questions are designed to elicit complex responses.

However, most questionnaire items are provided with *closed-ended response formats* in which respondents are asked to choose the one category that most closely applies. Closed-ended responses are easy to complete; they are also easy to code reliably. The MSQ and JDI pay scales shown in Exhibit 4.1 illustrate closed-ended response formats.

Constructs measured by items calling for self-reports or observer ratings are often scaled using closed-ended categories. When these categories are arranged in order, such as positive to negative or satisfied to dissatisfied, response categories are usually designed to yield equal-appearing intervals between categories. Researchers typically assign numerical values to these categories although these values may or may not be shown on the questionnaire. Exhibit 4.2 shows three equal-appearing scales for measuring satisfaction with some object.

Categories with equal intervals are attractive for conducting statistical analyses on scores, as discussed in Part 4. As a consequence, there is a large body of research on methods for constructing scales that have equal intervals between response categories; these methods are often complex and laborious to carry out. Fortunately, there is evidence to suggest that rating scales with equal-appearing categories, such as those shown in Exhibit 4.2, perform about the same as more elegantly derived scale formats.

RESEARCH HIGHLIGHT 4.1

Words to Avoid in Questionnaires

Absolutes. Words expressing absolutes such as *always, never, everyone,* or *all* create logical problems because statements including them are almost always false.

And. The word *and* usually signals that the item is getting at two ideas not one—a double-barreled question. Double-barreled questions are problematic because responses may differ depending on which "barrel" is considered.

You. You is problematic if there can be any question about whether it refers to the respondent or to a group the respondent represents (e.g., an organization).

Adjectives to describe frequency. Words such as *occasionally, sometimes, frequently,* or *often* mean different things to different people. One person's occasionally may be equivalent, numerically, to another persons frequently. Use numerical values when you want to obtain numerical information.

QUESTIONNAIRE RESPONSE STYLES

In Chapter 3, it was noted that scores are critical for establishing the construct validity of measures. This is a reminder that the value of information obtained from questionnaires is determined by the quality of scores obtained. Items and scaling formats alone, no matter how good, do not guarantee successful questionnaire outcomes.

Research has established that characteristics of the individuals completing questionnaires and the environments in which they complete them often impact the results obtained. Some of these characteristics have been studied in situations involving self-reports; others have been studied on observational ratings.

EXHIBIT 4.2. Equal-appearing response for scaling satisfaction

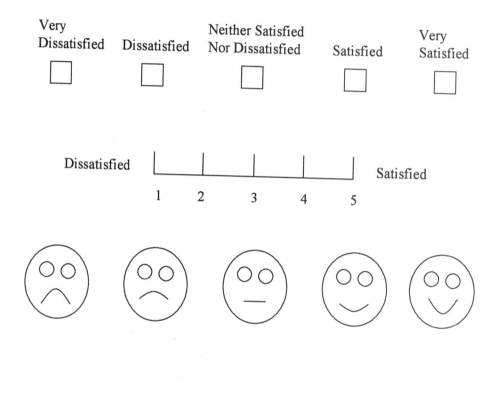

Self-Reports

Two tendencies that influence self-report responses have received substantial attention. *Social desirability* refers to the tendency to present oneself in a publicly favorable light. For example, a socially desirable response expresses approval for a public policy (e.g., the Supreme Court's decision on abortion) because the respondent believes others approve. *Response acquiescence* or *yea-saying* is a tendency to agree with a statement regardless of its content. Of the two, social desirability appears to be a more general problem for questionnaire responses.

Named Scaling Formats

Researchers have developed a wide variety of formats to scale questionnaire items. You may see reference to the following in organizational studies:

Thurstone Scale. This is an attitude scale that is designed to generate items with equal intervals between them. The procedure uses judges to identify the degree to which items represent the favorability or unfavorability toward some object (e.g., birth control). Twenty items are retained that cover the entire range of favorability or unfavorability from the subset of items that judges agree have the same favorability or unfavorability value. Respondents check whether they agree or disagree with each of the retained items. Their scores are based on the average numerical values assigned to each item by the judges.

Behaviorally Anchored Observation or Rating Scales. A procedure similar to the Thurstone method, this format is used to develop scales to measure behavior rather than attitudes. The scales have been used frequently in organizational research in which observers (e.g., supervisors) are asked to rate the performance behavior of employees.

Likert Scale. This scale is designed to measure attitudes with equal intervals between categories, like the Thurstone scale. Participants in the development stage are asked to indicate their own agreement or disagreement with a large number of items about an attitude on a 5-point scale. Item analysis is then used to compare scores on each item with the total score made up from the sum of all items. Items are retained for the questionnaire if scores correspond closely with the total scores. Scales are often referred to as Likert scales even if the developer does not evaluate the items using the item analysis procedure recommended.

Semantic Differential Scale. This scale is designed to measure the meaning that participants attribute to some object using 7-point bipolar adjectives such as good–bad, strong–weak, and active–passive. Most of the adjective pairs measure participants' evaluation of the object; the sum of these evaluations is often taken to represent an individual's attitude toward the object.

Observations

A number of response styles have also been identified when individuals are asked to make observations about some object. These include *leniency error*, a tendency to systematically provide a more favorable response than is warranted. *Severity error*, a tendency to systematically provide less favorable responses than warranted, is less frequent. Alternatively, *central tendency error* is present if an observer clusters responses in the middle of a scale when more variable responses should be recorded. *Halo error* is present when an observer evaluates an object in an undifferentiated manner. For example, a student may provide favorable evaluations to an instructor on all dimensions of teaching effectiveness because the instructor is very effective on one dimension of teaching.

Implications for Questionnaire Construction and Use

Self-report and observer errors are difficult to identify in practice. For example, leniency error cannot necessarily be inferred because an observer provides high evaluations of all cases rated. It may be that all cases deserve to obtain high evaluations; in this case, high evaluations are valid, not evidence of leniency error.

Furthermore, attempts to control for either self-report response styles or observational errors through questionnaire construction have had only limited success. For example, researchers have attempted to reduce social desirability and leniency errors through the choice of response categories. *Forced-choice scales* are designed to provide respondents with choices that appear to be equal in social desirability or equal in favorability. Behaviorally anchored observation or rating scales (see Research Highlight 4.2) are designed to yield more accurate ratings by providing respondents with meaningful scale anchors to help generate scores that are less susceptible to rating errors. Unfortunately, research investigations comparing questionnaire formats on common self-report and observational problems have not found one format to be systematically better than others.

Errors introduced by response styles can be reduced by insuring that respondents have the ability and are motivated to complete the questionnaire task. For example, errors such as central tendency or leniency are more likely when observers do not have sufficient information to complete a questionnaire accurately. Improperly motivated respondents are also problematic.

PILOT TESTING

No matter how much care is used, questionnaire construction remains an imprecise research procedure. Before using a questionnaire for substantive research, it is essential to obtain information by pilot testing the questionnaire on persons similar to those who will be asked to complete it as a part of the substantive research. Two types of pilot tests are desirable.

One type asks individuals, preferably like those who will complete the final questionnaire, to provide their interpretation and understanding of each item. This assessment will help identify errors in assumptions about participants' frames of reference. It also helps identify items that are difficult to understand. Pilot tests of this sort will almost always lead to at least some changes in the design of a research questionnaire. As a result, it can be useful in increasing response rates, reducing missing data, and obtaining more valid responses to the final questionnaire.

A second type of pilot test is more like a regular research study; a large number of participants is desirable. Data from this type of pilot test are used to see if scores behave as expected. Are average scores reasonable? Do scores on items vary as expected? Analyses assessing relationships between items are also useful in this type of pilot test. For example, internal consistency reliability of multi-item measures can be assessed using a procedure described in Chapter 17. Indeed, this second type of pilot test can be viewed as a first step in construct validation as described in the last chapter. However, its preliminary nature must be emphasized. Changes in items will almost always be suggested the first time that scores from a new questionnaire are analyzed.

SUMMARY

Questionnaires, measuring instruments that ask research participants to respond to questions, are often used in organizational research. Questionnaires may ask for *self-reports,* in which respondents provide information about themselves. They are also used to ask observers to describe or evaluate some externally visible characteristic (e.g., a behavior) of individuals or organizations. Getting information through observers often leads to more systematic measurement when there is a choice of methods.

Researchers should check to see whether the research question of interest could be addressed in some other way before developing a questionnaire. *Secondary data,* information collected for some other purpose, is often available for research use or another researcher may have already developed a questionnaire that is satisfactory for your purposes.

Questionnaires may be administered in written form or they may be administered as *interviews* where an *interviewer* asks questions verbally. Interviews are useful early in the research process to help refine questions and possible responses. Alternatively, written questionnaires are typically more efficient to administer when the final research study is conducted. The choice between interviews and written questionnaires also depends on the accessibility of research participants and their language proficiency.

Questionnaire construction begins by defining the domain of information to be obtained. In developing questions, researchers need to attend to the ability and motivation of the individuals who will be asked to respond. Words and questions should be simple and specific, and researchers need to be honest in their efforts to obtain accurate information.

When possible, questionnaires should be designed so that participants are drawn in with interesting questions. Questions asking for personal information are best saved until the end of the questionnaire.

Questionnaires sometimes use *open-ended response formats* in which respondents provide their own answers. Alternatively, respondents are asked to choose a fixed category when questions have *closed-ended response formats.* Questions with closed-ended response formats are attractive because they are easy to complete and because they are easy to code. When response categories are arranged in order (e.g., from more to less), equal-appearing closed-ended response formats are typically constructed.

The quality of results provided by questionnaires depends largely on the care and attention participants give them. Self-reporting errors that can be problematic include *social desirability,* in which respondents attempt to present themselves in a favorable light and *acquiescence* (or *yea-saying*), in which respondents tend to agree with a questionnaire item regardless of its content. Errors made by observers include *leniency* (*severity*), in which scores are systematically inflated (deflated), *central tendency,* in which scores have insufficient variability, and *halo,* in which evaluations of an object are made in an undifferentiated fashion.

Questionnaires need to be pilot tested before they are used for research purposes no matter how carefully constructed. It is useful to have individuals evaluate each question for interpretation and understanding. It is also useful to obtain information from a large number of individuals so that statistical properties of the scores can be examined. Results from pilot testing invariably suggest questionnaire modifications.

FOR REVIEW

Terms to Know

Questionnaires. Measuring instruments that ask individuals to respond to a set of questions in verbal or written form.

Self-report questionnaires. Questionnaires that ask respondents to provide information about themselves.

Interviews. Measuring instruments in which another individual (the interviewer) asks the questions verbally and is responsible for recording responses.

Secondary data. Information collected for other purposes that is used for research .

Open-ended response format. Questionnaire scaling that has participants respond in their own words.

Close-ended response formats. Questionnaire scaling in which the researcher provides participants with fixed response categories.

Social desirability. A self-report response style designed to present the respondent in a publicly favorable light.

Response acquiescence (also *yea-saying*). A self-report response style in which the respondent tends to agree with a questionnaire item regardless of its content.

Leniency error. Present when an observer systematically inflates ratings of a group of objects.

Severity error. Present when an observer systematically deflates ratings of a group of objects.

Central tendency error. Present when an observer clusters responses in the middle of a scale when more variable responses should be recorded.

Halo error. Present when an observer evaluates an object in an undifferentiated manner.

Forced choice scales. Scales in which response categories are equated on favorability or other characteristics to control for response styles.

Things to Know

1. Under what circumstances would you consider self-reports over observations? Observations over self-reports?
2. Under what circumstances would you consider using written questionnaires rather than interviews? Interviews rather than written questionnaires?
3. Are there any advantages to using an open-ended response format over a closed-ended response format?
4. What are characteristics of good questionnaire items?
5. How should questionnaire items be sequenced?
6. How do social desirability and response acquiescence differ?
7. Compare and contrast social desirability and leniency.
8. What types of pilot testing should be performed on new questionnaires?

PART II: SUGGESTED READING

There are many books available on measurement methods for the social sciences; many of these are quite demanding in terms of the statistical knowledge required for understanding. I recommend any edition of Nunnally (1967; 1978; Nunnally & Bernstein 1994). All are excellent yet understandable treatments of many measurement issues. Ghiselli, Campbell, and Zedeck's (1981) book is also good, and it too is accessible.

There are also more specific treatments of construct validity and related topics. Although a challenge to understand, Cronbach and Meehl (1955) wrote a seminal paper on construct validity. Barrett (1992), Blalock (1968) and Schwab (1980) provide useful elaborations on the topic. Schwab uses the general model of this book to frame his discussion. Although their methodology is now challenged, Campbell and Fiske (1959) present an understandable description of the logic of convergent and discriminant validity. For readings on reliability see Chapter 17.

Sudman and Bradburn's (1982) book on questionnaire items is useful. Payne's (1951) book, *The Art of Asking Questions,* is a classic. There are also specialized volumes on particular types of questions, such as Schwarz and Sudman's (1994) book on obtaining retrospective reports from respondents. Price and Mueller (1986) provide a compilation of measures available for organizational research. White (1986) provides a bibliography of material on questionnaire construction.

III

DESIGN: ADDRESSING INTERNAL VALIDITY

5

Research Design Foundations

Chapter Outline

- *Causal Challenges*
  - *Causal Direction*
  - *Uncontrolled (Nuisance) Variables*
- *Using Design to Address Causal Challenges*
  - *Sampling: Selecting Cases to Study*
  - *Measurement Decisions*
  - *Administering Measures to Cases*
- *Design Types*
  - *Experiments*
  - *Quasi-Experiments*
  - *Field Studies and Surveys*
- *Summary*
- *For Review*

Movie and commercial television portrayals of violence by humans to humans have increased in the last several decades, as has the perpetuation of violence in real life. There is a relationship between the depiction of violence and actual violence.

Does the portrayal of violence lead to violence in society? Or, does societal violence lead to its depiction? Or, are the two reciprocal? Or, are they only coincidental? These questions illustrate that the greatest challenge for research is not whether relationships can be found between variables, but why? What are the reasons for relationships between variables?

Researchers use two sources to help draw causal inferences from relationships observed among variables. They draw on conceptual models formulated to explain relationships in causal terms. And, they employ research designs to help address challenges to causal understanding.

This chapter is concerned with contributions research design makes to causal understanding. It begins with a discussion of challenges to causal understanding. It then explores decisions researchers make to confront these challenges through research design. Finally, the chapter describes how these decisions combine to identify four common research design types. These designs are developed more fully in the following two chapters.

CAUSAL CHALLENGES

Internal validity is present when variation in an independent variable is responsible for variation in a dependent variable. Exhibit 5.1 summarizes the three criteria introduced in Chapter 2 that help establish internal validity.

EXHIBIT 5.1. Internal causal criteria

1. Independent and dependent variables are meaningfully related.
2. Variation in the independent variable is contemporaneous with, or precedes, variation in the dependent variable.
3. There is a reasonable causal explanation for the observed relationship and there are no plausible alternative explanations for it.

The first criterion refers to an empirical relationship, the association between the independent (*X*) and dependent variables (*Y*). Such relationships are typically investigated using statistical procedures described in Parts IV and V of this book. In this chapter, assume that an empirical relationship is established between X and Y.

Thus, this chapter focuses on the latter two criteria. Does variation in the independent variable occur with, or before, variation in the dependent variable? And, particularly, are there other plausible explanations for the observed relationship?

These criteria suggest two general problems for concluding that an observed relationship means that an independent variable causes a dependent variable ($X \rightarrow Y$). One involves the direction of causation. The other involves possible consequences of uncontrolled variables that may be responsible for the relationship observed between the independent and dependent variable. Different research designs offer different degrees of protection against these challenges to internal validity.

Causal Direction

A conceptual model states that there is a causal conceptual relationship between an independent and dependent variable ($X' \rightarrow Y'$). Suppose also that a relationship between X and Y is observed on a set of scores. Exhibit 5.2 shows two alternative explanations that involve causal direction. The top panel illustrates a possibility that $Y \rightarrow X$, not $X \rightarrow Y$.

For example, it is often assumed that a supervisor's leadership style (X') influences subordinate work behavior (Y'). However, one study obtained evidence suggesting that cause goes from Y' to X' (Lowin & Craig, 1968). In the study, a ***research confederate*** (given the pseudonym Charlie) was used to act as a subordinate for participants who role-played as supervisors. (A research confederate is, unknown to the research participants, a member of the research team.) Charlie engaged in systematically different work behaviors for different supervisor participants. He worked efficiently for some of the participants and inefficiently for others.

Research participants who supervised an efficient Charlie used different leadership styles than participants who supervised an inefficient Charlie. Subordinate behavior thus influenced supervisory behavior. This causal direction is illustrated in the top panel of Exhibit 5.2.

This study is causally persuasive for two reasons. First, Charlie's behavior occurred before the supervisors' behavior was recorded; the second criterion for causality was satisfied. More important, Charlie's behavior was controlled by the researchers. It was carefully scripted so that causal influence could only go from Charlie to the participant supervisors, not the reverse.

The lower panel in Exhibit 5.2 illustrates another difficulty in reaching causal conclusions; it shows causation going both ways. Economists often use the term *simultaneity* to describe a situation in which causation is reciprocal. The relationship between leadership style and subordinate behavior may be simultaneous. That is, supervisors' leadership styles may influence subordinate behavior and subordinates' behavior may also influence supervisory style.[1]

Uncontrolled (Nuisance) Variables

Typically, causal models are more complex than the models researchers actually study. The underlying causal models include variables and relationships that are not of interest and may not be accounted for in a study. For example, a researcher may measure and study a relationship between education level and subsequent employment income. Other variables that also influence income, such as years of work experience and type of occupation, may not be of interest.

However, the nature of any causal relationship between education and income is misrepresented if these other causal variables are not considered. The effect of education on income may be overstated or understated depending on how each is related to other variables in the more complete causal model. Thus, other variables that play a role in a causal model present a serious challenge to understanding if uncontrolled. When uncontrolled, such variables are called *nuisance variables.* They provide potential alternative explanations for the relationship(s) of interest.

Consequences for causal understanding resulting from nuisance variables depend on how they are related to the independent and dependent variables studied. Six types of nuisance variables are described here using the consumer computer satisfaction example introduced in Chapter 3. As in Chapter 3, relationships described are offered to illustrate research issues and not to explain consumer satisfaction.

---

[1]Lowin and Craig did not rule out the possibility that leaders generally influence subordinates. They simply ruled out that possibility in their study; they could thus concentrate on subordinates' role in the influence process.

EXHIBIT 5.2. Causal direction problems

Reverse causal direction

Independent (X)   Dependent (Y)

Leader   ◄─────────────────────────────   Subordinate
Behavior   Behavior

Joint causation: Simultaneity

Independent (X)   Dependent (Y)

Leader   ◄─────────────────────────────►   Subordinate
Behavior   Behavior

Bias. One serious result of nuisance variables is *bias,* when the causal relationship between an independent variable is systematically under- or overstated. A *biased relationship* occurs when a nuisance variable is causally related to the dependent variable and is related to the independent variable(s), causally or otherwise. To illustrate, suppose a researcher believes that consumer satisfaction depends on computer speed. Greater speed is expected to lead to higher satisfaction. However, the researcher does not account for computer memory, which also influences satisfaction. The larger the memory, the greater the satisfaction. Furthermore, computer speed and memory are related. Manufacturers make computers faster as they increase computer memory. These relationships are shown in the top panel of Exhibit 5.3.

EXHIBIT 5.3. Computer speed and memory as determinants of satisfaction

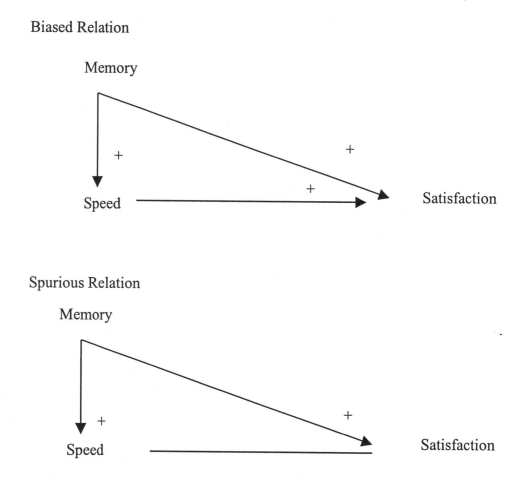

The relationship between computer speed and satisfaction that is observed will overstate the causal relationship if computer memory is not controlled. Part of the speed–satisfaction relationship that is observed results because computer memory is related to both satisfaction and speed. Memory thus biases the relationship between speed and satisfaction; it must be controlled to remove the bias.

Spurious Relationships.   A ***spurious relationship*** is a special case of bias. It occurs when a nuisance variable accounts for all of the observed relationship between a dependent and independent variable(s). Assume, as stated previously, memory influences satisfaction and is related to speed. However, now assume the improbable, that there is no causal relation between speed and satisfaction. A study that investigates only speed and satisfaction will nevertheless find the two related. They are related spuriously because of their joint relationships with memory. These relationships are shown in the bottom panel of Exhibit 5.3.

Biased relationships are typically inflated. An observed relationship overstates the true causal relationship between an independent and dependent variable because a nuisance variable(s) is not taken into account.

Suppressor Variables.   However, nuisance variables may also ***suppress*** causal relationships; they may lead to an understatement of the true causal relationship. ***Suppressor variables*** most commonly have a positive relationship with the independent variable and no relationship or a small negative relationship with the dependent variable. For example, memory would suppress rather than inflate the relationship between speed and satisfaction in the top panel of Exhibit 5.3 if it is positively related to speed but has no relationship with satisfaction. In this case, failure to control for computer memory leads to an understatement of the relationship between speed and satisfaction.[2]

Nuisance variables that are related to the independent variable(s) under study thus seriously challenge causal interpretation. Depending on the strength and direction of their relationships, they may inflate (bias), deflate (suppress), or even make spurious the observed relationship between independent and dependent variables.

---

[2]This result may seem counter intuitive. Chapter 11 shows how suppressor variables operate using formulas for multiple correlation and regression.

Noise.   A *noisy relationship* is more benign; a noise variable is related to the dependent variable but unrelated to the independent variable(s). Consumer affability illustrates such a possibility. More affable consumers report higher satisfaction with their computers because they are more satisfied generally than are less affable consumers. However, there is no reason to suppose that affability is related to computer speed. The relationships are shown in Exhibit 5.4.

EXHIBIT 5.4. Computer speed and consumer affability as determinants of satisfaction

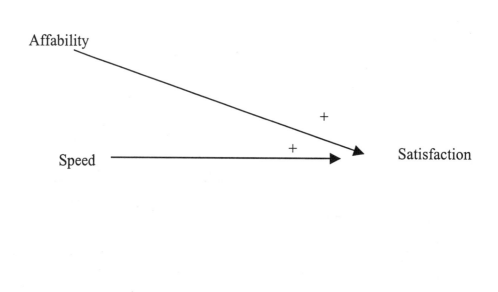

Noisy Relation

Noise variables do not misrepresent the strength of relationship between a dependent and independent variable(s); they are benign in that sense. However, they do influence the dependent variable. They introduce variability in the dependent variable that is not accounted for by the independent variable(s) of interest. As a consequence, researchers are unable to explain as much of the variability in the dependent variable as is true if the noise variables are controlled. This is especially problematical for internal statistical and statistical generalization validation (see Part V).

Mediators. Independent variables are ordinarily thought to influence dependent variables directly; variability in *X* leads immediately to variability in *Y*. *Mediator* or *intervening variables* come between an independent and a dependent variable in a causal chain. If a mediator is present, then some or all the influence of the independent variable operates indirectly on the dependent variable through the mediator.

Consider a conceptual model in which a researcher expects satisfaction with computers to be negatively influenced by computer weight. However, unknown to the researcher, weight influences price (lower weight is only achieved at a price). Price also influences satisfaction negatively.

The top panel of Exhibit 5.5 shows a case where price *fully mediates* the relationship between weight and satisfaction. A relationship is observed if only weight and satisfaction are studied. However, if price is also included in the model studied, weight is found to have no direct effect on satisfaction. Its effect is only indirect, due to its effect on price.

The bottom panel of Exhibit 5.5 shows a case where price *partially mediates* the weight–satisfaction relationship. Weight has a direct effect on satisfaction and an indirect effect (through price). If price is uncontrolled, the influence of weight will erroneously appear to be a direct effect.

Mediator variables are ubiquitous in research. Relationships between independent and dependent variables typically have variables that intervene. Indeed, mediator variables are often used to help explain why an independent variable influences a dependent variable. For example, the impact of weight on price can help explain the impact of weight on satisfaction.

Researchers choose to include or exclude mediator variables based on the type of understanding they seek. For example, a researcher likely would include price in a model explaining satisfaction, because price is important to consumers. Alternatively, computer manufacturing cost probably would not be included in a study of consumer satisfaction. Although cost mediates weight and price from a manufacturer's perspective, cost, per se, is probably not considered by consumers.

Moderators. *Moderator variables* have values that are associated with different relationships between an independent and dependent variable.[3] The strength and/or direction of relationships between independent and dependent variables depend on values of a moderator variable.

---

[3]In psychology, moderator variables are often also called *interaction variables*. In sociology moderators are sometimes called *boundary conditions*.

**EXHIBIT 5.5. Price as a mediator of the weight-satisfaction
relationship**

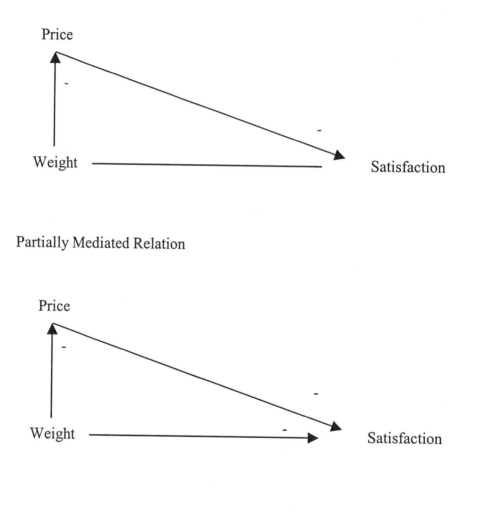

Fully Mediated Relation

Partially Mediated Relation

Consider again a model where weight is expected to have a negative influence on computer satisfaction. Such a relationship may exist only among owners of laptop computers; there may be no relationship between weight and satisfaction for desktop computer owners. If so, type of computer (laptop or desktop) moderates the relationship between computer weight and computer satisfaction.

EXHIBIT 5.6. Computer type as a mediator of the weight-satis-faction relationship

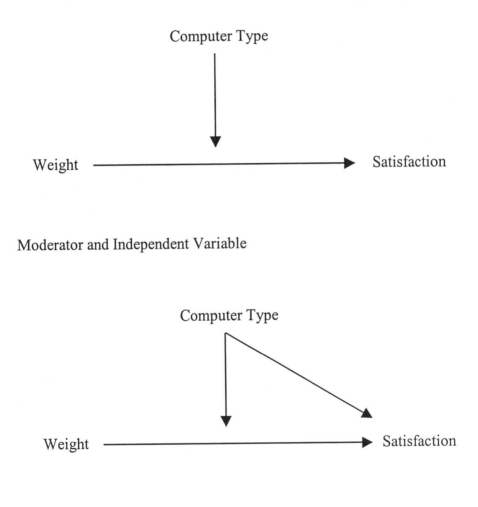

Failure to account for the moderator misrepresents the causal relationship between weight and satisfaction for both computer types. The relationship will be overstated for desktop computer owners and understated for laptop computer owners.

The top panel of Exhibit 5.6 illustrates the scenario just described. The bottom panel of Exhibit 5.6 illustrates a case where type of computer serves

RESEARCH HIGHLIGHT 5.1

Difficulties Identifying Causally Problematic Variables

Empirical relationships among the variables of central interest and potential nuisance variables tell little about causal roles the latter variables may serve. For example, there is no way to decide if a variable acts as a moderator from its relationships with the independent or dependent variables. A moderator may be related to an independent and/or dependent variable, or it may not be related to either. The only way to identify a moderator variable is to test it directly. For example, a moderator can be investigated by subgrouping, as illustrated in the discussion of Exhibit 5.6. Moderator variables can also be assessed statistically as described in Chapter 20.

As another example, relationships observed do not allow one to distinguish between a mediator variable and a nuisance variable that biases the relationship between an independent and dependent variable. The distinction between these two variables hinges on the causal direction of their relationship with the independent variable. The independent variable is a cause of the mediator, but it is a consequence of the biasing nuisance variable.

Thus, by themselves, relationships observed among a set of variables provide little causal information. Conceptual models and design decisions described in this chapter are essential for causal clarification in most instances.

as both a moderator and an independent variable. Type of computer may moderate the relationship between weight and satisfaction as described above. However, in addition, type of computer ownership may have a direct effect on satisfaction. Laptop computer owners may be more (or less) satisfied with their computers, regardless of weight.

USING DESIGN TO ADDRESS
CAUSAL CHALLENGES

All the examples described previously include an observed relationship between the independent and dependent variables. However, the examples also show that interpreting these relationships may be causally problematic. The causal relation between the variables may not be in the expected direction. Or, an additional variable(s) that operates in the causal model may obscure the relationship(s) of interest if not controlled.

The examples also suggest how important strong conceptual models are for addressing causal concerns. A good conceptual model can make a compelling case for the direction of causation. A good model can also help identify variables that require control.

Research design also may help meet causal challenges, especially when coupled with strong conceptualization. This section identifies three key characteristics of research design; these are sampling cases, measurement, and the administration of measures to cases. The section emphasizes how decisions about these design characteristics can contribute to causal clarity.

Sampling: Selecting Cases to Study

Decisions regarding samples to study often emphasize generalization of research results. Part V describes how statistical generalization procedures can be used to generalize sample findings to cases in a larger population when probability rules are used to select the samples. *Probability sampling* of this sort is contrasted with other types, typically called *convenience* or *judgment sampling.* Probability sampling permits statistical validation, convenience sampling does not.

Sampling decisions also have implications for causal inferences. These apply to both probability and convenience samples. Two sampling decisions that bear on the control of nuisance and moderator variables are discussed here.

Restriction of Range.   Cases may be selected so that variation in a nuisance or moderator variable(s) is restricted or eliminated. *Restriction of range* reduces relationships between nuisance and other variables.

To illustrate, consider the example in which computer memory is a nuisance variable affecting the relationship between speed and satisfaction (the top panel in Exhibit 5.3). One way to control the nuisance variable memory is to restrict its variability. For example, include only consumers with computers of one memory size. Eliminating the variation in computer memory through sample selection eliminates its effect on the speed-satisfaction relationship. Moderator variables can be controlled the same way. From Exhibit 5.6, only participants with laptop (or desktop) computers may be studied.

There is a down side to restricting the range of nuisance or moderator variables; generalization of research results is limited. For example, if only laptop owners are studied, then generalization of the speed-satisfaction relationship cannot be made to owners of desktop computers.

Comparison Groups. Some research designs compare dependent variable scores across *comparison groups*—two or more groups of participants. The groups are chosen to represent different levels of an independent variable. However, efforts are made to insure that the groups are similar on potential nuisance variables.

For example, a researcher is again interested in the effect of computer speed on consumer satisfaction. An organization is found that purchased computers for its office employees. Employees in some departments were provided faster computers than employees in other departments. If the researcher can assume that employees and computers are otherwise similar, computer satisfaction of the two employee groups can be compared to investigate the effect of computer speed.

Measurement Decisions

Part II described how measurement decisions influence construct validity. Decisions in this realm are designed to enhance the correspondence between scores and the underlying constructs of conceptual interest. Measurement decisions also have causal implications. Decisions about independent variables and variables to control are especially important in this latter context.

Control Over Independent Variables. The purpose of causally motivated research is to determine how independent variables influence dependent variable responses. Thus, values of the dependent variable are always a characteristic of the cases studied; the cases control or determine values of the dependent variable. Indeed, researchers must take care so that dependent variables are not influenced by the procedures used to measure them.

There is more latitude about measures of independent variables. Often independent variables represent responses from cases much as dependent variables. Consider a study of the relationship between education (X') and income (Y'). A researcher would likely have participants report both their level of educational achievement and the amount of their income.

In such cases, the measurement of the independent variable contributes little to internal validity. There is nothing about this design to rule out the possibility that $Y' \rightarrow X'$, because values of both variables are obtained from the cases investigated.[4] Further, nuisance variables (e.g., occupation level) are also likely to be problematical in this design, because they are often related to educational achievement.

Two alternative forms of measurement remove control of the independent variable from the cases investigated; levels of the independent variable are established externally. First, this control may be exercised by some exogenous event. For example, a researcher may study property insurance purchases (Y) in two communities, one having recently experienced a hurricane and the other not. In this instance, the exogenous determination of values of the independent variable (hurricane or no hurricane) rules out the possibility that $Y \rightarrow X$.

Second, a researcher may exercise direct control over levels of an independent variable. The leadership study described early in this chapter is illustrative. In that study, researchers established two levels of subordinate behavior carried out by their research confederate; these levels represent the operationalization of the independent variable. The research participants who role-played supervisors had no control over the confederate, hence no control over the levels of the independent variable they experienced. Although any relationship between subordinate behavior and leadership behavior might still be biased by other uncontrolled variables, the design does rule out the possibility that a relationship resulted because the dependent variable influenced the independent variable.

Measurement and Statistical Control. Measurement combined with data analysis procedures can also contribute to the control of nuisance, mediator, and moderator variables. Specifically, when researchers measure variables that require control, they can include them in statistical models de-

---

[4]Of course, a conceptual model may help rule out the possibility that income levels lead to educational achievement

signed to deal with more than one causal variable. For example, a researcher studies the relationship between education level and income but recognizes that, if uncontrolled, occupation level may bias the relationship. In such instances multiple correlation or regression (Chapter 11) may be used to investigate the relationship between income and education controlling for occupation level. Statistical models for addressing causal issues are discussed in Chapter 19.

Administering Measures to Cases

Powerful causal designs can be built when researchers not only control levels of an independent variable(s) but also determine what cases experience each level. Such designs address both directional challenges and nuisance variables.[5]

The objective of these designs is to assign cases in a way that equalizes values of nuisance variables across levels of the independent variable. In the leadership study, for example, suppose leader assertiveness is a potential nuisance variable. Suppose further that the researchers assign participants to the two levels of subordinate behavior so that they are on average equal in assertiveness. Subsequent differences across the two subordinate behaviors cannot be due to differences in assertiveness. Even though assertiveness may influence leader behavior, its effect will be the same in the two groups. There are two general procedures to equate values of nuisance variables across different levels of an independent variable.

Matching. One procedure involves *matching* (equating) cases that receive different levels of the independent variable on a nuisance variable(s). For example, assume a researcher is interested in the relationship between computer type (laptop or desktop) and satisfaction; computer speed and memory are recognized to be nuisance variables. The researcher sorts among a group of computer owners matching each laptop owner with a desktop owner whose computer has the same speed and memory. Subsequent satisfaction differences between laptop and desktop owners cannot be due to

---

[5]They do not, however, eliminate challenges created by moderator variables. Moderator variables must be measured and explicitly addressed with sampling or statistics

differences in these two nuisance variables, because each group has a similar mix of computer speed and computer memory.

Matching is a powerful form of control, but it is often difficult to achieve. The number of potential cases in the group to be matched may have to be large. It may be difficult, for example, to find desktop and laptop participants who have computers with the same speed and memory. Further, as the number of nuisance variables increases, so too does the difficulty of finding cases that meet the matching criteria.

Random Assignment.   **_Random assignment_** is another way researchers seek to equalize groups on nuisance variables; cases are randomly assigned to different levels of an independent variable(s). This was the actual procedure used in the leadership study. Participants who role-played leaders were randomly assigned to the two levels of subordinate behavior carried out by the research confederate.

Random assignment of supervisor participants to subordinate behavior is attractive because it should average out the effect of personal characteristics that may serve as nuisance variables. Average assertiveness of those participants who were exposed to the efficient subordinate should be about the same as for those who experienced the inefficient subordinate. Other supervisor differences should also be approximately equated across the two subordinate behavior levels.

Random assignment has two potential advantages over matching. When successful, it controls for nuisance variables whether or not researchers are aware of them. Second, because random assignment does not require knowledge of specific nuisance variables, researchers do not have to measure them.[6]

However, random assignment is not always successful in equating groups on nuisance variables. Just as 10 flips of a coin may occasionally lead to 8, 9, or even 10 heads (instead of the expected 5), random assignment of cases to levels of an independent variable may not equate the resulting groups on nuisance variables. The larger the groups formed by random assignment, the more likely that they will be equivalent on nuisance variables (see Part V).

---

[6]Nevertheless, measurement of nuisance variables is often still desirable to see whether randomization is successful.

DESIGN TYPES

The characteristics outlined call for decisions in all research designs. Researchers must make decisions about cases to study, measures, and the administration of measures to cases.

Exhibit 5.7 shows how these decisions combine to describe four common types of research. These four are introduced here and developed more fully in the next two chapters.

EXHIBIT 5.7. Typology of research designs

Design	Assignment of Cases	Sample	Independent Variable Control
Experiment	Random	Probability/ Convenience	Researcher
Quasi-experiment	Nonrandom	Probability/ Convenience	Researcher/ Exogenous event
Survey	Nonrandom	Probability	Cases
Field study	Nonrandom	Convenience	Cases

Experiments

Experiments are characterized by random assignment of participants to levels of an independent variable(s). Researchers must be able to control (manipulate) levels of the independent variable(s) in experiments. The leadership study illustrates an experiment; the researchers randomly assigned supervisor participants to the two levels of subordinate behavior. Cases in experiments may be from some intact group (e.g., all members of a department in an organization). Or, cases may be obtained using a sample from some larger population.

Quasi-Experiments

Quasi-experiments share several characteristics of experiments. They also use an independent variable(s) that is not controlled by the cases studied.

Also as in experiments, cases to study may be obtained by probability or convenience sampling.

Quasi-experiments differ from experiments regarding the assignment of cases to levels of an independent variable. In quasi-experiments, assignment is not done randomly. Thus, researchers can try to match cases on a nuisance variable(s), or they can try to obtain comparable groups of cases for each level of the independent variable.

Field Studies and Surveys

Field studies and *surveys* differ from experiments and quasi-experiments regarding the independent variable. In both, responses on the independent variable are provided by the cases studied, not the researcher.

What differentiates field studies from surveys is how cases are sampled. Field studies obtain cases through a convenience sampling procedure. Surveys employ probability sampling to obtain cases from a larger population. This is done so that statistical inferences can be made from the sample to that larger population.

Experiments and quasi-experiments are potentially strong designs when causal direction is a concern, because values of the independent variable are determined outside the cases studied in both. Experiments are also strong for ruling out alternative explanations involving nuisance variables. Quasi-experiments can also be good in this regard, although they are generally less powerful than experiments.

Surveys and field studies are not strong designs for addressing causal direction. However, researchers who use these two designs often measure variables that may serve to obscure causal relationships if uncontrolled. They then couple these designs with statistical analysis procedures to control for potential biasing variables (see Chapter 20).

SUMMARY

Research design is the main empirical research activity to attain internal validity. Internal validity involves the causal relationship between scores on measures of an independent and dependent variable.

Given an observed relationship between independent and dependent variables, internal validity is challenged in two ways. One involves the direction

RESEARCH HIGHLIGHT 5.2

> ### *Don't Confuse Research Design with Research Setting*
>
> Types of research design are to be thought of in terms of the characteristics in Exhibit 5.7. The four designs differ in sampling, in measurement of the independent variables, and in the assignment of cases to measurement. They do not necessarily differ in where they are conducted. Thus, field studies do not have to be carried out in the "field"; experiments do not have to be conducted in laboratories.

of causality. Does an observed relationship warrant the conclusion that variation in the independent variable leads to variation in the dependent variable?

A second challenge involves potential roles of variables that are not accounted for in the research model investigated. A *nuisance variable* is an uncontrolled variable operating in the causal model studied. Nuisance variables may *bias* relationships, typically by inflating the causal relationship between an independent and dependent variable. But nuisance variables may also *suppress* causal relationships, or even make them *spurious.* A nuisance variable that results in *noise* makes it more difficult to identify a relationship between an independent and dependent variable. However it does not affect the expected size of the causal relationship.

Mediator variables (also called *intervening variables*) come between independent and dependent variables. *Full mediation* occurs when an independent variable causes the mediator, not the dependent, and the mediator causes the dependent variable. *Partial mediation* occurs when an independent variable causes the mediator and the dependent variable, and the mediator causes the dependent variable.

Moderator variables (also called *interactions* and *boundary conditions*) may or may not be independent variables. However, they do influence the relationship between the dependent and some other independent variable. The relationship (direction and/or magnitude) between the dependent and an independent variable depends on values of a moderator variable.

A research design involves three sets of decisions. Each set has implications for causal direction and/or control of variables not accounted for in the research model investigated.

1. Decisions about the cases studied can help control nuisance and moderator variables. One way is to *restrict the range* of such variables through the group studied. Nuisance variables can also be controlled if they are equated among *comparison groups* that experience each value of the independent variable.

2. Decisions about how an independent variable is measured can help make the causal direction between an independent and dependent variable unambiguous. Greater understanding of causal direction is possible when values of the independent variable are not determined by the cases studied. Measuring potential problematic variables can also contribute to internal validity when combined with statistical analysis procedures.

3. Decisions about how measures are administered to cases can help control both directional and nuisance variable challenges. This can be achieved through *matching* or *random assignment.*

Characteristics of these three sets of decisions can also be used to identify four common types of research design. *Experiments* provide researchers greatest control over the research environment. Researchers control the levels of independent variables and randomly assign cases to those levels. Experiments may thus provide high internal validity. Although *quasi-experiments* do not include random assignment, researchers nevertheless maintain substantial control over the research process. Quasi-experiments can also provide strong internal validity if a researcher can successfully match participants on nuisance variables or can find comparable comparison groups. *Field studies* and *surveys* do not provide strong evidence for causal direction. However, they may be designed to control for potential nuisance, mediator, and moderator variables.

FOR REVIEW

Terms to Know

Research Confederate. A member of the research team who interacts with participants but is not known by participants to be a member of the research team.

Simultaneity. When causal influence goes from the independent to the dependent variable and vice versa.

Nuisance variable. A variable in the causal model that is not controlled in a research study.

Biased relationship. An observed relationship between an independent and dependent variable that under- or overstates the causal relationship. Occurs if a nuisance variable is causally related to the dependent variable and is related to the independent variable(s).

Spurious relationship. An observed relationship between an independent and dependent variable but no causal relationship. Occurs when a nuisance variable accounts for all of the observed relationship between a dependent and independent variable(s).

Suppressor variable. A nuisance variable that biases an observed relationship between an independent variable downward; usually occurs when a nuisance variable has a positive relationship with the independent variable and a small negative relationship with the dependent variable.

Noisy relationship. Occurs when a nuisance variable is related to the dependent variable but not to the independent variable(s).

Mediator variable. Also *intervening variable*; comes between an independent and dependent variable in a causal chain.

Full mediation. The relationship between an independent and dependent variable operates only through a mediator variable. The independent variable has no direct effect on the dependent variable.

Partial mediation. The relationship between an independent and dependent variable operates partially through a mediator variable. The independent variable has a direct effect on the dependent variable and an indirect effect through the mediator.

Moderator variable. A variable whose values are associated with different relationships between an independent and dependent variable. May or may not be an independent variable.

Interaction variable. Synonym for *moderator variable.* A relationship between an independent and dependent variable depends on the value of another independent variable.

Boundary condition. Synonym for *moderator variable.* A relationship between an independent and dependent variable depends on the value (boundary) of another independent variable.

Probability sampling. The selection of a subset of cases obtained from a larger population of cases using rules of probability.

Convenience sampling (also *judgment sampling*). The selection of cases (usually an intact group) to study using nonprobability methods.

Restriction of range. A reduction in the variance of a variable through selection of cases.

Comparison groups. Groups of research cases thought to be comparable on levels of potential nuisance variables.

Matching. Cases are selected for research so that those who experience different levels of an independent variable(s) are equated on levels of nuisance variables.

Random assignment. Allocation of cases to levels of an independent variable(s) without order; a procedure designed to match cases on levels of nuisance variables.

Experiments. A research design in which cases are randomly assigned to levels of an independent variable(s).

Quasi-experiments. A research design in which cases do not control the levels of the independent variable(s) they experience; cases are not randomly assigned to levels of the independent variable(s).

Field study. A research design in which values of the independent variable(s) are characteristics of the cases studied and where cases are not randomly selected from some larger population.

Survey study. A research design in which values of the independent variable(s) are characteristics of the cases studied and where cases are randomly selected from some larger population.

Questions for Review

1. Be able to differentiate between spurious and biased relationships brought about by nuisance variables.

2.   How are mediator and moderator variables similar? How do they differ?

3.   What key characteristics (e.g., sampling) differentiate experiments, quasi-experiments, surveys, and field studies?

4.   How can sampling be used to control for nuisance variables? What limitations does sampling have as a method of control?

5.   How are matching and comparison groups similar as forms of control? How do they differ? Which would you prefer to use as a form of control for nuisance variables? Why?

6.   What design(s) would you recommend if you were concerned about causal direction but not nuisance variables? Why?

Issues to Discuss

1.   How does random assignment of cases to levels of some independent variable operate to control for bias or spuriousness?

2.   Does random assignment of cases to levels of some independent variable control for moderator and mediator variables? Why or why not?

3.   From a design perspective, why is it attractive that cases not provide responses to the independent variable?

6

Design Applications:
Experiments and Quasi-Experiments

Chapter Outline

Quasi-experiments, and especially experiments, are attractive when researchers seek to address causal issues through research design. These designs establish values of an independent variable outside the control of the cases studied; a researcher or an exogenous event is responsible for levels of the independent variable. As a consequence, variation in the dependent variable cannot be responsible for variation in the independent variable. Causal influence, if it exists, must go from the independent to the dependent variable.

Furthermore, quasi-experiments and experiments may provide opportunities to assign cases to different levels of an independent variable. In experiments, researchers randomly assign cases to levels of an independent variable. In quasi-experiments, cases are allocated to levels of an independent variable using a method other than random assignment. In either case, opportunities to assign cases to different levels of an independent variable may help control alternative explanations due to nuisance variables.

Nevertheless, both quasi-experiments and experiments are subject to internal validity challenges. Both experience *threats to internal validity,* characteristics of research studies that make causal claims vulnerable to alternative explanations.

Chapter 6 describes several experimental and quasi-experimental designs. It also evaluates these designs for threats to internal validity.

BASIC DESIGNS

There are two broad categories of experimental and quasi-experimental designs. *Between-cases designs* involve two or more groups. These designs are typically *cross-sectional* in which the independent and dependent variables are measured only once. Causal inferences are drawn by comparing scores on a dependent variable across two or more groups of cases that experience different levels of an independent variable.

Within-case designs involve only one group of cases. They must also be *longitudinal designs* in which the dependent (and perhaps, independent) variable is measured more than once. Within-case designs address causal relationships by measuring the dependent variable both before and after a change in values on an independent variable. Evidence consistent with a causal relationship is obtained if values of the dependent variable change systematically as values of the independent variable change.

The two designs described next illustrate major differences between longitudinal within-case designs and cross-sectional between-cases designs. More complicated designs are discussed later in the chapter.

Design A1: Cross-Sectional Between-Cases Design[1]

Design A1 in Exhibit 6.1 illustrates the simplest form of between-cases design; it is cross-sectional. It has one independent variable X with two val-

---

[1] The number 1 follows A to signal that an analogous design exists for surveys and field studies (A2), discussed in Chapter 7.

ues ($X = 0$ and $X = 1$). Each value is assigned to a group of cases represented by the vertical boxes. The effect of the independent variable is determined by whether Y scores differ between the two groups, if $\mu_{Y|0}$ (read as, mean of Y given that $X = 0$) $\neq \mu_{Y|1}$.

Basic research design

EXHIBIT 6.1. Design A1: Cross-sectional between-cases experimental or quasi-experimental design

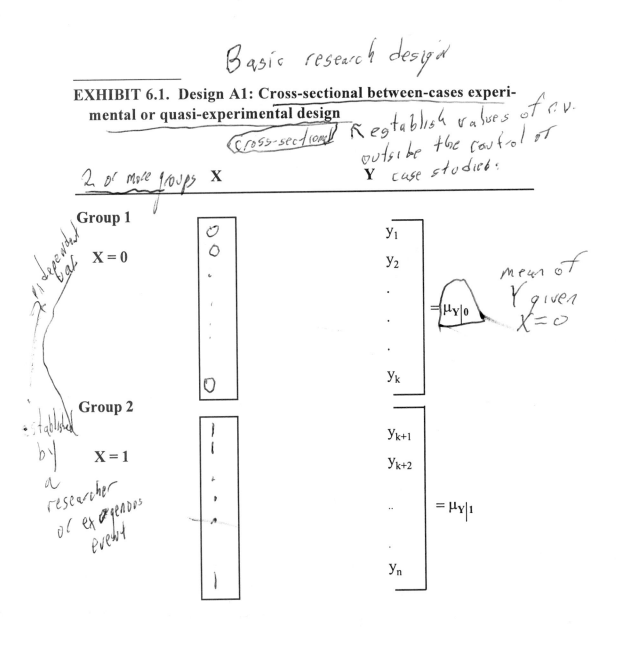

For example, an organization may be interested in evaluating a training program aimed at providing employees with skills to diagnose and repair production problems that arise in the manufacture of a product. Y is a measure of product quality.

One group of employees receives training, $X = 1$; the other serves as a control group, $X = 0$. The effect of training on product quality is observed by comparing subsequent mean scores on product quality between the two groups.

Design B1: Longitudinal Within-Cases Design

Design B1, shown in Exhibit 6.2, illustrates a simple longitudinal within-cases design. The results of a change in an independent variable are studied on a single group. The dependent variable is measured before, Y^b, and after, Y^a, the independent variable value $X = 1$ is introduced. An effect of X is concluded if $\mu_Y^a \neq \mu_Y^b$.

EXHIBIT 6.2. Design B1: Longitudinal within-cases design

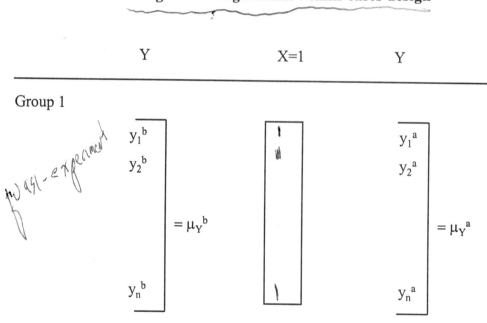

	Y	X=1	Y
Group 1	y_1^b		y_1^a
	y_2^b		y_2^a
	$= \mu_Y^b$		$= \mu_Y^a$
	y_n^b		y_n^a

A longitudinal within-cases design could also be used to assess the influence of training. The organization measures product quality among a group of employees before training is introduced. It then trains all employees ($X = 1$) followed by another measurement of product quality at a later date. The effect of training is assessed by a comparison of μ_Y^a with μ_Y^b.

Both Designs A1 and B1 study results following a contrast between one level of an independent variable with another. In Design A1, the contrast is explicit between two groups; in Design B1, it is made implicitly on a single group.

Design A1 may be either an experiment or a quasi-experiment. It is an experiment if cases are randomly assigned to the two X groups. It is a quasi-experiment if cases are assigned to the two levels of X in some other way, such as matching. Design B1 must be a quasi-experiment since only one group is studied. Cases cannot be randomly assigned to different levels of X.

THREATS TO INTERNAL VALIDITY

This section describes three classes of threats to internal validity that potentially trouble experiments and/or quasi-experiments of the type described.[2] These threats are summarized in Exhibit 6.3 and are discussed next. They include threats generated by the research environment. They also include threats associated specifically with between-cases or longitudinal experiments and/or quasi-experiments.

Threats from the Research Environment

Ironically, the very control that makes experiments and quasi-experiments attractive for addressing some threats to internal validity makes them vulnerable to others. Briefly, control over the research environment risks inadvertently influencing cases' scores on Y. The greater the control, the greater the danger that the research environment influences Y scores. This results in part because greater control means that the research study intervenes more explicitly on cases. It also results because greater control provides researchers more opportunity to influence Y scores in ways other than through X. Although these two threats work together, they are discussed separately.

---

[2]Many of these threats also trouble surveys and field studies, as is discussed in Chapter 7.

EXHIBIT 6.3. Summary: Threats to internal validity

Research Environment Threats

> Demand characteristics

> Expectancy effects

Between-Cases Threats

> Selection

> Intragroup history

> Treatment contamination

Longitudinal Threats

> History

> Maturation

> Mortality

> Testing

> Instrumentation

> Regression

Demands on Participants.   Typically, human participants know that they are involved in a research study. They have some knowledge before they participate in a study. They acquire additional knowledge based on its stated purposes, instructions, interactions with researchers, and information they are asked to provide once in the study.

These cues may serve as ***demand characteristics***; they provide participants with expectations about what is being investigated. These, coupled with motivation (e.g., to be a good or bad participant), may lead to Y scores that depend on expectations and motivation instead of, or along with, the level of X experienced. These influences threaten the internal validity of the relationship observed between the independent and dependent variables. In the language of

Chapter 5, these expectations and motivations serve as potential nuisance variables.

Researcher Expectations.   Researchers are also influenced by environmental characteristics. These shape researchers' attitudes and behaviors and may impact on the research study and research outcomes. Of particular concern are unintended effects researchers may have on the dependent variable. For example, a researcher who treats participants in a warm and friendly manner may obtain different responses than one who is cool and aloof.

An *expectancy effect* occurs when researchers treat participants in ways that increase the likelihood of obtaining a desired result. For example, participants experiencing one form of training may perform better on some task than those who receive another form of training. These differences may be the result of a researcher's belief that one form of training is better; the researcher inadvertently treats the two groups differently in ways not related to the training itself. Such differences may involve subtle psychological processes that even the researcher is unaware of, such as various forms of nonverbal communication (e.g., body language).

Differential treatment of this type illustrates a form of nuisance variable. Furthermore, nuisance variables of this type serve to bias, or potentially make spurious, an observed relationship between X and Y, because they are related to levels of the independent variable.

Threats from the research environment can never be eliminated entirely. However, they can be minimized through design activities aimed at their control. For example, researcher expectancy may be controlled if confederates, who are not aware of a researcher's expectations, administer the independent variable treatments.

Threats in Between-Cases Designs

There are several potential threats to internal validity that apply particularly to between-cases designs. First, *selection* is a threat to internal validity when there are pre-existing differences between groups experiencing different levels of X. These differences, rather than different levels of X, may account for Y differences.

In the previous employee training in production diagnostics and repair illustration: one group of employees is trained and one untrained group serves as a control. Preexisting group differences, such as in motivation or ability

RESEARCH HIGHLIGHT 6.1

Selection Threats and Omitted Variables

The concept of an omitted variable represents another way to think about the selection problem. An *omitted variable* is an independent variable that operates in the causal system studied but is not, as the name implies, included in it.

Selection is typically discussed when there is concern that cases which experience alternative levels of an independent variable systematically differ in some way that may influence the relationship observed between that independent variable and Y. Alternatively, omitted variables are usually discussed when there is a concern that a research study does not include all the variables warranted by the conceptual model being tested. The two concepts address the same issue. A potential independent variable(s) serves as a nuisance, because it is not accounted for in a research study. The omission of this variable may result in a misinterpretation of the relationship between X and Y.

It is also the case that selection threats are discussed more frequently in the literature of experiments and quasi-experiments. Omitted variables are often discussed in survey and field study literatures.

levels, are possible alternative explanations for differences in average product quality measured after the training.

Selection is a serious threat, because there are many ways that groups of cases may differ. These differences can produce the entire gauntlet of nuisance variable(s) possibilities involving bias, spuriousness, or suppression.

A second potential threat to between-cases designs, *intragroup history,* represents an exogenous event(s) that has a different impact on one group than another. For example, the trained group may work with better or poorer materials or equipment; it may have better or poorer supervision. These intragroup history effects are nuisance variables that appear to represent an effect of X if uncontrolled.

Third, between-cases designs may be subject to *treatment contamination* that occurs when a level of X assigned to one group is communicated to another. For example, an untrained control group of employees may reduce or increase product quality through greater or less effort if they learn another group is receiving training. Or, trained employees may transfer their learning to the untrained employees.

Threats in Longitudinal Designs

Longitudinal designs are also subject to internal validity threats. One is called *history,* an outside event that occurs between measurements of the dependent variable; the historical event occurs along with the change in X. For example, the quality of the material used to produce the product in the training example is illustrative of a potential history effect. Any change in material quality between measurements of the dependent variable will appear to be a result of the training.

Another threat to longitudinal designs, *maturation,* refers to changes in the participants investigated that occur between the measurements of the dependent variable. For example, suppose training is implemented among a group of new employees. Changes in product quality may then result simply because employees acquire experience with their jobs, not because of the training.

Still another potential threat is *mortality,* which occurs when some cases terminate between measurements of Y. Cases that terminate before a study is completed often differ from those that stay. If so, an alternative explanation is provided for changes in Y. For example, if low performing employees disproportionately leave the organization, average product quality may increase, because employees remaining are more effective performers.

Additional longitudinal threats involve measurement of the dependent variable. *Testing* is a threat if the initial measurement of Y influences scores when it is measured again. For example, human participants may remember how they responded to an initial questionnaire measuring Y when they are asked to complete it a second time. They may then try to "improve" (change) their scores independent of the research treatment.

Instrumentation refers to changes in the measure of Y. For example, the procedures used to measure product quality may become more sophisticated over time. Product quality may thus appear to be decreasing. The training is seen as unsuccessful when the measuring system is simply getting more discriminating at identifying quality.

One additional threat to longitudinal designs is called *regression*; it depends on two circumstances. First, it depends on unreliable measurement of the dependent variable. Unreliability results in scores that are sometimes too high, sometimes too low. Repeated measurements tend to average out these highs and lows (see Chapter 17).

Second, regression as a threat requires that cases be chosen for extreme (high or low) Y scores on the first measurement. If both circumstances are true, regression results in scores moving from the extreme toward average on a subsequent measurement.

For example, suppose the organization measures product quality on several groups of employees. It then chooses the group with the lowest average quality for training. Quality may increase on a second measurement. However, this increase may be due to regression, not training.

Although threats to internal validity are ubiquitous, different designs are more or less vulnerable to different threats. Skilled researchers capitalize on this knowledge. They choose designs that are least vulnerable to those threats that are likely given the conceptual model investigated.

ADDITIONAL DESIGNS

Designs A1 and B1 are elementary; both have only one independent variable with just two levels. The cross-sectional Design A1 has only two groups and the longitudinal Design B1 has only one.

These characteristics can all be extended to make more sophisticated designs. By doing so, researchers can often accomplish two important objectives: they can study more complicated conceptual models, and they can control some of the previously identified threats to internal validity.

Three alternatives are described to provide a flavor for ways experiments and quasi-experiments can be designed. The first shows how cross-sectional designs can be combined with longitudinal designs. The last two illustrate how additional independent variables can be added to experimental and quasi-experimental designs.

Design C1: Longitudinal Between-Cases

Exhibit 6.4 illustrates a design (C1) that is made from between-cases characteristics of Design A1 and longitudinal characteristics of Design B1. The dependent variable is measured before and after groups of cases experience either of the two levels of an independent variable.

EXHIBIT 6.4. Design C1: Longitudinal between-subjects experimental or quasi-experimental design

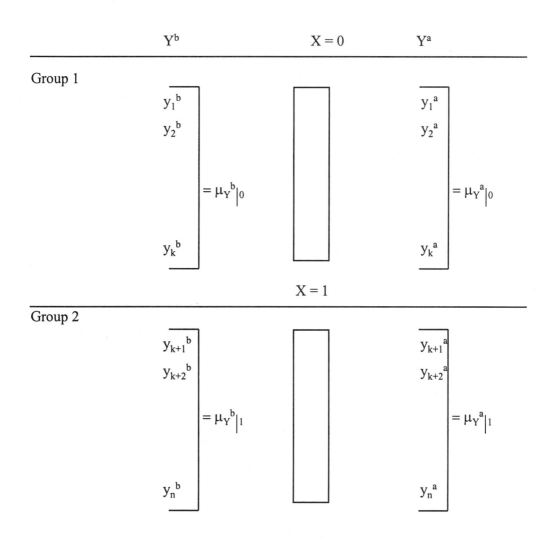

Design C1 potentially adds threats of longitudinal designs (e.g., testing) to threats of cross-sectional designs (e.g., treatment contamination). So why use it? The term *potentially,* is the key word; Design C1 is attractive when selection is a likely threat and potential threats of longitudinal designs are less likely.

The first measurement of the dependent variable serves to identify whether groups are comparable before X is introduced. This is particularly advantageous in quasi-experiments in which intact comparison groups are employed. Selection as a threat is probable if $\mu_Y{}^b|_0 \neq \mu_Y{}^b|_1$.

Exhibit 6.5 shows two possible outcomes from a longitudinal between-cases design. In each example, $X = 1$ represents a treatment condition such as training and $X = 0$ represents a control. Also, in each example, the control group experiences an increase in average Y scores of $5 - 3 = 2$. These score increases may reflect maturation or other threats associated with longitudinal designs. Also, the treatment group in each example appears to increase Y scores more than the control.

The top panel of Exhibit 6.5 reports results that suggest no selection threat, $\mu_Y{}^b|_0 \cong \mu_Y{}^b|_1$. This is an expected result if cases are randomly assigned to $X = 0$ and $X = 1$. In that case, the effect of X on Y can be assessed by looking at the difference between $\mu_Y{}^a|_1$ and $\mu_Y{}^a|_0$, $7 - 5 = 2$.[3]

The bottom panel of Exhibit 6.5 shows results where a selection threat is probable. $\mu_Y{}^b|_0 \neq \mu_Y{}^b|_1$. In this case, an effect of X can be assessed by calculating the difference of differences $[(\mu_Y{}^a|_1 - \mu_Y{}^a|_0) - (\mu_Y{}^b|_1 - \mu_Y{}^b|_0)]$. The group experiencing $X = 1$ has an average Y score of 5 before and 9 after. The control group has scores of 3 and 5. The difference of differences, $[(9 - 5) - (5 - 3)] = 2$, suggests an effect of training on Y relative to the control.

Regrettably, results as shown in the bottom panel of Exhibit 6.5 may present internal validity problems not necessarily overcome by taking the difference of differences. Whatever leads to the pretest differences in Y scores may work in combination with X to influence post-test Y scores.

For example, the trained group may be more motivated to perform well. This accounts for its higher average Y scores in the first time period. Furthermore, this group may take greater advantage of the training because of its higher motivation. The improvement in Y scores for the (motivated) trained

---

[3]If cases are randomly assigned to groups, it is doubtful whether Y should be measured before the introduction of the levels of X. Randomization should equalize the groups on Y before X levels are introduced. The benefit of knowing whether Y scores are equal is likely more than offset by the potential threats introduced by a longitudinal design.

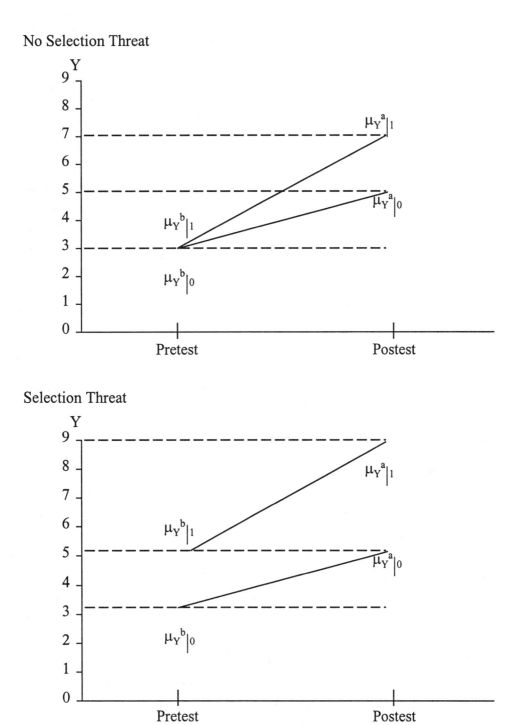

EXHIBIT 6.5. Illustrative results from a longitudinal beween-subjects design.

No Selection Threat

Selection Threat

group is thus greater than would be the case if the control group experienced the training. Motivation moderates the relationships between X and Y.

Design D: Cross-Sectional Factorial Design

The designs discussed to this point study only one independent variable; yet dependent variables are typically influenced by several independent variables. Researchers often seek to account for several independent variables in their research designs.

One form of this design occurs when researchers control the assignment of cases to levels of two or more independent variables. Designs with two or more independent variables that are manipulated by a researcher are called *factorial designs*; factor is a synonym for an independent variable that is under the control of a researcher. Exhibit 6.6 illustrates such a design. It has two independent variables (XA and XB), and each has just two levels. The dependent variable is measured once making this a cross-sectional design.

For example, an organization may want to know if employee performance (Y) is influenced by training (XA) and monetary incentives (XB). $XA = XB = 0$ represents a control condition in each case. $XA = XB = 1$ represents training and monetary incentive conditions, respectively.

Two studies using Design A1 could be used to investigate the effects of training and monetary incentives separately. However, studying the variables in a factorial design has two important advantages.

First, a study using Design D is more efficient than two studies using Design A1. To illustrate, assume a researcher wants to include 20 cases in each group. A study of training requires 40 cases (20 in a treatment condition, 20 in a control). A study of monetary incentives also requires 40 cases. Eighty cases are required to do the two studies separately.

Alternatively, a single factorial design of both training and monetary incentives requires just 40 cases as illustrated in Exhibit 6.7. Twenty cases who receive training (n_{10} plus n_{11}) can be contrasted with 20 training controls (n_{00} plus n_{01}). Analogously, 20 cases that experience monetary incentives (n_{01} plus n_{11}) can be contrasted with 20 controls (n_{00} plus n_{10}).

Second, one study using Design D provides more information than two studies using Design A. This is a beauty of factorial designs; it allows researchers to investigate moderator variables (interactions) directly.[4]

---

[4]The term *interaction* is frequently used in the language of experiments and quasi-experiments.

EXHIBIT 6.6. Design D: Factorial design with two independent variables

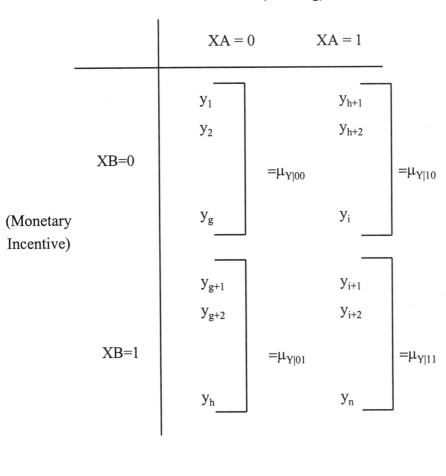

(Training)

| | XA = 0 | XA = 1 |

Exhibit 6.8 shows a graph of how training and a monetary incentive might influence performance. $\mu_{Y|11}$ ($= 70$) and $\mu_{Y|10}$ ($= 25$) are greater than $\mu_{Y|01}$ ($= 35$) and $\mu_{Y|00}$ ($= 20$). These indicate a training effect. Similarly, $\mu_{Y|01}$ and $\mu_{Y|11}$ are greater than $\mu_{Y|00}$ and $\mu_{Y|10}$ indicating an effect of monetary incentives. A moderating or interaction effect is shown because $\mu_{Y|11}$ (representing the performance of the group experiencing both training and monetary

EXHIBIT 6.7. Participants in a factorial design of training and
   monetary incentives

XA (Training)

XB (Monetary Incentive)	XA=0	XA=1
XB=0	$n_{00} = 10$	$n_{10} = 10$
XB=1	$n_{01} = 10$	$n_{11} = 10$

incentives) is greater than the effects of training and monetary incentives added together. The effect is shown by the lack of parallelism between the solid lines in Exhibit 6.8.

Both moderator variables and interactions indicate that effects of one independent variable on a dependent variable depend on the values of another independent variable. In the example, the effect of monetary incentives on performance is greater when training is present than when it is not present. It works either way. The effect of training is greater when monetary incentives are present than when they are not.

Design E: Cross-Sectional Design with Covariate

Another cross-sectional design combines independent variables that are assigned to cases with variables that represent cases' responses. These latter independent variables are called *covariates.*

Exhibit 6.9 illustrates the simplest case. It shows an independent variable (XA) that is assigned to cases at one of two levels ($XA = 0$ or $XA = 1$). It also

EXHIBIT 6.8. Effects of training (*XA*) and monetary incentives
  (*XB*) on performance (*Y*)

Performance

shows a covariate (*XB*). Covariates are often continuously scaled variables
(e.g., age, income). A unique subscript is given each case on *XB* to acknowledge that each may have a unique value.

  For example, a wholesaler may be interested in sales of designer sunglasses as a function of the way the item is displayed in retail stores. Stores
represent cases and sunglasses sales per store represents the dependent variable. The glasses are displayed one way in half the stores studied (*XA* = 0),
another way in the other half (*XA* = 1). The firm also believes that sales of de-

EXHIBIT 6.9. Design E: Cross-sectional design with a covariate

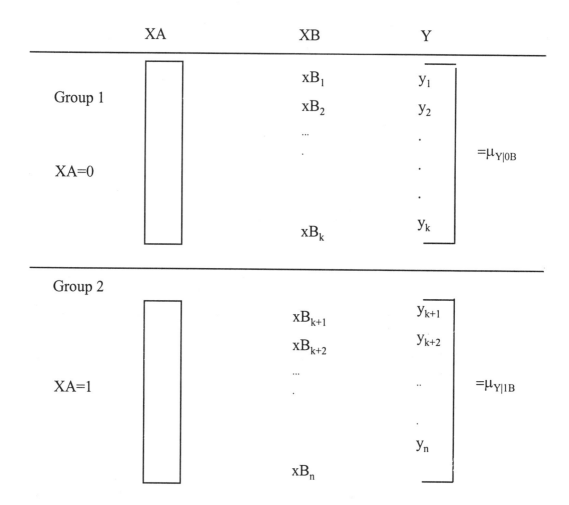

Note: Each case has a potentially unique score on XB.

signer sunglasses depend on customer income. Thus, average customer income per store is treated as a covariate (*XB*).[5]

The value of a covariate design depends on how *XB* is related to *Y* and *XA*. If *XB* is only a noise variable (related to *Y*, but not *XA*),[6] covariate analysis makes the assessment of the effect of the independent variable more precise by reducing the amount of unexplained *Y* variation.

Covariate design and analysis may also be useful if *XB* is a biasing variable (related to *Y* and *XA*). In this case, the analysis adjusts *Y* for *XB* differences in *XA*. In the example, an adjustment in *Y* is made if customer income averages differ between stores with the two different displays. This adjustment is analogous to taking the difference of differences in Design C; it holds the same dangers. Covariate analysis does control for a selection threat to internal validity insofar as *XB* is concerned. However, if groups differ on a measured covariate, they may also differ on potential covariates not measured and hence not controlled by this analysis.[7]

Design Extensions

The designs introduced here only scratch the surface. Each can be extended, usually in straightforward ways. For example, more levels of the independent variable can be added to Designs A1 through E. The dependent variable can be measured additional times, either before and/or after the introduction of *X* in the longitudinal Designs B1 and C1. More independent variables can be added to Design D. Independent variables and/or covariates can be added to Design E.

The choice of a particular design should depend on the research issue investigated, tempered by constraints placed on the study; compromises are always required. The objective for researchers is to develop a satisfactory design, not an ideal design. Satisfactory designs help rule out plausible alternative explanations, not all alternative explanations.

---

[5]Income might be estimated from a questionnaire survey of a sample of customers.

[6]This is the same as saying there is no multicollinearity. For a discussion of analysis issues related to covariate analysis, with and without multicollinearity, see Chapter 19.

[7]Further, as in the case of the difference of differences in Design C, covariate analysis does not control for the possibility that *XB* moderates the relationship between *Y* and *XA*. A more complicated analysis method described in Chapter 19 does account for a moderating effect of *XB*.

SUMMARY

Experiments and quasi-experiments are designed to investigate systematic differences in a dependent variable between groups who experience different levels of an independent variable. Design A1 provides a simple illustration of a *cross-sectional between-cases design.* It is cross-sectional because X and Y scores are obtained from cases only once. Changes in Y scores as levels of X change can also be studied in *longitudinal within-cases designs* as illustrated by Design B1. Y scores are measured before and after some change in X is introduced.

Experiments and quasi-experiments are subject to some *internal validity threats* regardless of specific design type. *Demands* placed on cases by virtue of their participation in a research study can potentially alter relationships observed among the variables investigated. *Researcher expectations* can also threaten the internal validity of any study.

Additional threats are associated with specific types of research designs. *Selection* is a threat to between-cases designs when the cases that experience different levels of X are different in some other way(s). A selection threat is similar to an *omitted variable* threat. In both cases, there is a danger that the XY relationship studied is misrepresented because some independent variable(s) has not been taken into account.

Intragroup history effects also threaten between-cases designs. They refer to exogenous events that influence groups experiencing different levels of an independent variable differently. Between-cases designs are also threatened by the possibility of communication between groups experiencing different levels of X that may lead to *treatment contamination.*

Longitudinal designs are subject to a different set of threats. *History* or *maturation effects* may occur between measurements of Y and thus appear as an effect due to the introduction of an independent variable. *Mortality* is a threat if cases drop out of the study between measurements of the dependent variable.

Measurement issues also serve as potential threats in longitudinal designs. *Testing* is a threat if cases respond differently on repeated measurements of Y. *Instrumentation* is a threat if the procedure for measuring Y changes over time. *Regression* occurs if a group is chosen for study because it has extreme high (or low) scores on Y and Y is unreliably measured. In that case, a second measurement of Y will move (regress) toward average, suggesting an effect of the change in the independent variable.

Many alternative experimental and quasi-experimental designs are available. These designs can address more complex research issues than are possible with Designs A1 and B1. These alternatives can also be useful in ruling out certain threats to internal validity.

A longitudinal between-cases design, C1, adds a longitudinal dimension to a between-cases design. Y scores are obtained before the introduction of X as well as after. Design C1 is potentially useful when selection is a threat. Selection as a threat is suggested if groups differ on the measure of Y taken before the introduction of X.

Design D illustrates how cross-sectional designs can be extended when researchers control values on more than one independent variable. *Factorial designs* are more efficient than studies of each independent variable separately. They also provide more information because they permit investigation of interactions among the X variables. Interactions, like moderators, indicate that the effect of one X on Y depends on the level of another X.

Design E also describes an experiment or quasi-experiment with a second independent variable. However, in this case, the second X variable is a *covariate,* a case response on some variable. In quasi-experiments, inclusion of a covariate may help control for a selection effect. However, inclusion of a covariate that is related to Y can help more precisely identify the effect of the manipulated X variable even if the covariate does not serve as a selection threat.

The designs described are all simple. They can be extended in many ways to address more complex research topics.

FOR REVIEW

Terms to Know

Threats to internal validity. Characteristics of research studies which make a causal claim that an independent variable leads to a dependent variable vulnerable to alternative explanations.

Between-cases design. Design that uses two or more cases or groups of cases in which each case or group experiences different levels of an independent variable. Effect of an independent variable is assessed by comparing dependent variable scores across the cases or groups of cases.

Cross-sectional design. Design in which the independent and dependent variables are measured only once. The relationship between the variables is taken as evidence of the influence of X on Y.

Within-cases design. Design that uses one case or one group of cases. Effect of an independent variable is assessed by measuring the dependent variable before and after a change in the level of the independent variable.

Longitudinal design. Design in which the dependent (and perhaps, independent) variable is measured more than once.

Demand characteristics. Characteristics of a research study that motivate participants' expectations about what is investigated; a threat to internal validity.

Expectancy effects. A nuisance variable that influences the dependent variable because a researcher treats some cases differently from others based on assumptions made about expected research results; a threat to internal validity.

Selection. A threat to internal validity when there are preexisting differences between groups experiencing different levels of an independent variable. These differences may account for differences observed on the dependent variable.

Omitted variable. An independent variable that operates in the causal system studied but is not included in the model studied. Serves as a threat to internal validity in the same way as selection is a threat.

Intragroup history. An exogenous event(s) that has impact on a group of cases that experience one level of an independent variable differently than the event influences groups experiencing other levels of the independent variable; a threat to internal validity.

Treatment contamination. Occurs when a level of an independent variable assigned to one group of participants is communicated to another; a threat to internal validity.

History. An exogenous event that occurs between measurements of the dependent variable; a threat to internal validity in longitudinal designs.

Maturation. Changes in cases between measurements of the dependent variable; a threat to internal validity in longitudinal designs.

Mortality. Occurs when some cases terminate between measurements of the dependent variable; a threat to internal validity in longitudinal designs.

Testing. A threat to internal validity in longitudinal designs when the initial measurement of a dependent variable influences participants' responses to the dependent variable on a subsequent measurement of it.

Instrumentation. A threat to internal validity in longitudinal designs when the measure of the dependent variable changes over time.

Regression. A threat to internal validity in longitudinal designs when (a) groups are chosen for levels of the independent variable based on dependent variable performance on a first measurement, and (b) there is unreliability in the dependent variable measure.

Factorial design. Studies with two or more independent variables. Factor is a synonym for independent variable, which is under the control of a researcher.

Covariate. A synonym for an independent variable that is not manipulated by a researcher in experiments and quasi-experiments.

Questions for Review

1. Be able to explain how experiments and quasi-experiments rule out the threat that a relationship between an independent and dependent variable is due to the influence of the latter on the former.
2. Compare and contrast testing and instrumentation as threats to internal validity in longitudinal designs.
3. Compare and contrast intragroup history and history as threats to internal validity.
4. Under what conditions would you consider using Design C1 instead of Design A1?
5. Explain why taking the difference of differences in Design C1 may not account for a selection threat when the pretest scores on Y differ across levels of the independent variable studied.
6. In what way(s) is a factorial design attractive relative to doing separate studies of each factor?

Issues to Discuss

1. Cross-sectional between-cases Design A1 may be experimental or quasi-experimental. What threat(s) does an experimental design reduce or rule out relative to a quasi-experimental design of this sort?

Why? What threats to this design are present regardless of whether experimentation is used?

2. A covariate, if unaccounted for, is a potential nuisance variable. What is the effect of covariate analysis if the covariate is a noise variable? What problems remain for covariate analysis if the covariate is a biasing variable?

3. A researcher believes that observing violent television programs leads to violent behavior. A quasi-experiment is chosen to address this expectation. Two levels of violent television will be investigated, and violent behavior will subsequently be measured by using official records (e.g., reports of school rule infractions, police arrest records).

   a. What group(s) of participants would you try to obtain for your study and how would you motivate this group to participate in the study? Would you try to match participants across the two levels, or would you seek comparison groups? In either case, what variables would you seek to control through matching or comparison groups?

   b. How would you make the two levels of television violence operational?

   c. What are the major threats to internal validity of your design decisions? Can you change your design decisions in any way to reduce these threats?

   d. How could you change your design so that it was an experiment rather than a quasi-experiment? Are there any threats that would be reduced or eliminated by this change? Are there remaining threats or new threats?

7

Design Applications:
Field Studies and Surveys

Chapter Outline

- *Basic Designs*
  - *Design A2: Between-Cases Design*
  - *Design B2: Within-Cases Time Series*
  - *Design C2: Longitudinal Between-Cases Panel Studies*
  - *Design Extensions*
- *Threats to Internal Validity*
  - *Concerns About Causal Direction*
  - *Biases Introduced by a Single Source and Similar Method*
- *Praise for Surveys and Field Studies*
  - *Internal Validity May Not Be a Concern*
  - *Causation May Not Be a Concern*
  - *Design Constraints*
- *Summary*
- *For Review*
- *Part III: Suggested Reading*

Unlike experiments and quasi-experiments, field and survey studies obtain scores on independent variables from the cases studied. On human participants, these may be biographical characteristics, such as age; variables representing ability, such as intelligence; or attitudes, such as satisfaction. Examples when organizations represent cases are size, such as number of employees; success, such as market value; or longevity, such as years since founding.

Surveys differ from field studies by how cases are chosen. Surveys use probability samples to obtain cases from a larger population (see Part V). Field studies obtain cases some other way; typically some intact group of cases is studied. For example, a study of student absenteeism may include all students from some elementary school. This procedure for obtaining a group of cases is called *convenience sampling*.

The two types of studies often also differ in conceptual complexity. Surveys usually focus on relatively simple research issues, such as voter or consumer opinions. Such studies usually investigate one or a few independent variables in straightforward ways. For example, a survey of political opinion may compare proportions of likely voters who prefer one candidate to others by their political affiliation, race, or sex.

Field studies are often more complex. They are frequently used to test conceptual models with a number of independent variables. These variables may be combined in complex (e.g., nonlinear) ways. For example, field studies are often used to investigate consumer, client, student, or investor motivations to behave in various ways.

This chapter introduces three basic designs used in survey and field studies. Similarities and differences between these and quasi-experimental or experimental designs are noted. Also noted are ways that these designs can be extended to address more complicated issues.

The second part of the chapter addresses threats to the internal validity of surveys and field studies. Many of these threats are also present in experiments and quasi-experiments as discussed in Chapter 6. Emphasis is placed on threats that are more specifically associated with surveys and field studies.

The discussion shows that surveys and field studies are generally more susceptible to internal validity threats than experiments or quasi-experiments. Of course, internal validity is not the sole criterion for evaluating research designs. The chapter closes with a discussion of situations in which surveys and field studies are attractive designs.

BASIC DESIGNS

Survey and field study designs can be classified as between-cases or within-case just as experiments and quasi-experiments. A between-cases field or survey study involves a group of cases. A within-case field or survey study refers literally to one case in contrast to longitudinal quasi-experiments that typically study a group of cases. Surveys and field studies focus on relationships between individual cases whereas experiments and quasi-experiments focus on differences between groups of cases.

These designs can also be classified as cross-sectional or longitudinal. Cross-sectional field or survey studies measure independent and dependent variables only once. Both independent and dependent variables are typically measured more than once in longitudinal surveys or field studies.

Design A2: Between-Cases Design

The most common form of field or survey study employs a cross-sectional between-cases design. Scores on measures of independent and dependent variables are obtained once.

The design, A2, is shown in Exhibit 7.1; it is a straightforward adaptation of the cross-sectional between-cases Design A1 shown in Chapter 6 as Exhibit 6.1. Design A2 is modified to account for the measurement of X at an individual case level. Subscripts, $1, \ldots, i, \ldots, n,$ refer to individual cases to acknowledge that each case may have a unique score on X. For example, a survey might be conducted to estimate citizen opinion on a local government bonding referendum (Y). Information on participants' age serves as an independent variable (X).

Design B2: Within-Case Time Series

Time series studies provide information about how a dependent variable, Y, changes over time. It does so by obtaining scores from a case at several regular intervals, such as each month or year. A design with one independent, X, and one dependent, Y, variable is illustrated in Exhibit 7.2. Superscripts, $1, \ldots, j, \ldots, t,$ refer to time periods. Because time series designs use only one case, they are almost always field studies, not surveys. There is little advantage to using a probability sample when the sample size is equal to one.

Time series are field study analogs to longitudinal within-case designs. Y is measured in more than one time period, often many time periods. However, time series typically differ from quasi-experimental within-case designs by also measuring an independent variable(s) each time Y is measured.

EXHIBIT 7.1. Design A2: Cross-sectional between-cases design

X	Y
x_1	y_1
x_2	y_2
$\vdots$	$\vdots$
x_i	y_i
$\vdots$	$\vdots$
x_n	y_n

Note. Subscripts refer to individual cases.

Time series can be performed on individuals as cases. However, in organizational research, time series studies commonly use an institutional case. For example, a time series might be performed on the relationship between a hospital's occupancy rate (Y) and the number of medical doctors affiliated with it (X); the hospital represents the case. Or, a time series might be conducted to determine if changes in unionization rates (X) in an industry are associated with changes in real salary levels (Y); the industry represents the case.

Time series can be constructed to look at instantaneous changes between Y and X or lagged changes. In *instantaneous models* a change is studied within each time period. *Lagged models* are motivated by an assumption that it

EXHIBIT 7.2. Design B2: Time series

Time 1		Time j		Time t	
x^1_1	y^1_1	x^j_1	y^j_1	x^t_1	y^t_1

Note. Superscripts refer to time periods; subscripts refer to the case.

takes some time for a change in X to result in a change in Y. For example, changes in the number of doctors affiliated with a hospital may take several time periods before they are translated into changes in hospital occupancy.

Time series analyses are ordinarily performed on data that have been generated in the past. For example, historical data for a study of the relationship between the United States unemployment rate (X) and average wage rates in the United States can be obtained from Department of Labor sources.

Design C2: Longitudinal Between-Cases Panel Studies

Panel studies add a cross-sectional dimension to the time series design just described. X and Y scores are obtained on a group of cases in two or more time periods. As in time series, however, interest is in how Y scores change as X scores change over time.

A simple panel design is diagrammed in Exhibit 7.3. Scores on one independent and one dependent variable are obtained from several cases at two times. Subscripts refer to cases, and superscripts refer to time periods.

EXHIBIT 7.3. Design C2: Two time period study panel

Time 1		Time 2	
x^1_1	y^1_1	x^2_1	y^2_1
x^1_2	y^1_2	x^2_2	y^2_2
.	.	.	.
x^1_i	y^1_i	x^2_i	y^2_i
:	:	:	:
x^1_n	y^1_n	x^2_n	y^2_n

Note. Subscripts refer to individual cases; superscripts refer to time periods.

To illustrate, a sample of full-time employees in a geographical area may be surveyed twice with a year's separation. Y is hourly wage and X is union membership ($X^t_i = 0$, not a member; $X^t_i = 1$, a member). Analysis that investigates the relationship between the difference in wage ($Y^2_i - Y^1_i$) and the difference in union membership status ($X^2_i - X^1_i$) provides information about how changes in union membership influence wage levels.

Panel studies are attractive because they control for between-cases differences that do not change over time. For example, research has established that men obtain higher wages than women, on average. However, gender should influence income similarly in both time periods. Thus, an analysis of difference scores accounts for gender effects by "differencing" them away.

By contrast, a cross-sectional survey or field study may provide an erroneous estimate of the effects of union membership on wages if it does not explicitly account for gender. The union membership estimate will be biased if gender and union status are related.

Design Extensions

Modifications and extensions of all three of these designs are common. These changes are typically straightforward as is also true of the experimental and quasi-experimental designs described in the previous chapter.

In particular, all three designs can account for more than one independent variable. Except in the simplest cross-sectional surveys, Design A2 is usually extended to include several independent variables. This is nearly always true in field study investigations of conceptual models. For example, a study of personal income may include measures of education and work experience as major independent variables. It may also measure biographical variables such as age, race and gender, and work environment variables such as union membership status and type of industry to serve as control variables.

Panel studies (Design C2) also often include more than two time periods. Analysis issues are somewhat complicated when more than two time periods are involved. However, data from more than two time periods generally helps reduce alternative explanations.

THREATS TO INTERNAL VALIDITY

Surveys and field studies are generally vulnerable to the same internal validity threats that distress experiments and quasi-experiments. All the major threats to the internal validity of experiments and quasi-experiments described in Chapter 6 apply; that discussion may be useful as a review.

Threats from the research environment exist. Although a field study or survey may not be as intrusive as an experiment or quasi-experiment, human participants nevertheless know that they are participating in a research study. Demands on participants thus remain. Indeed, this problem may be exacerbated in field and survey studies when participants' provide responses on measures of both independent and dependent variables.

Researcher effects also threaten surveys and field studies; they bring expectations to surveys and field studies just as they do to experiments and quasi-experiments. It is true that researchers do not intentionally manipulate levels of some X variable in surveys and field studies. However, when designs use measures involving interaction between researchers and participants, such as interviews, surveys and field studies are potentially as vulnerable to researcher effects as studies involving more active manipulation of an independent variable.

Time series and panel studies are also susceptible to the threats associated with longitudinal designs described in the previous chapter. These threats are sometimes greater in time series and panel studies when more measurements of the variables are taken. In such situations, instrumentation is a likely threat because measures often change over time. Even when instrumentation is not a threat, repeated measurement may lead to testing effects.

History and maturation also pose problems for panels and time series. For example, a study may be performed to see how changes in income (X) influence buying behavior (Y). A panel of consumers is studied several years to investigate this issue. Over that time, historical events such as the amount and type of television advertising, and possibly maturation, may vary with changes in income.

The internal validity of time series and panel studies is also threatened by systematic trends in scores obtained on the variables. These trends may represent long-term increases or decreases in scores, such as yearly changes in wage rates, or repeating variations, such as seasonal changes in retail clothing sales. Trends and repeating variations bias estimates of the effect of X variables on Y. Fortunately, these threats can often be statistically removed before a relationship between X and Y is estimated.

Mortality is also a serious threat to panel studies. (Since time series are usually constructed on historical data and only involve one case, mortality is generally not a threat.) Mortality may result because cases literally expire (e.g., people die, organizations cease operations). It may also result because cases move and can no longer be located or tire of participation and drop out of the research study. The longer a panel study obtains scores, the greater the threat of mortality.

Surveys and field studies are also vulnerable to internal validity threats not present in experiments and quasi-experiments. Two are of particular concern.

Concerns about Causal Direction

Levels of independent variables are established outside of cases in experiments and quasi-experiments. This exogenous determination of X levels is advantageous for causal statements since such designs preclude the possibility that a relationship results because Y leads to X. Sometimes the nature of the X variable in surveys or field studies is also obviously exogenous to the causal system of interest. For example, an observed relationship between chronological age (X) and political party affiliation (Y) does not plausibly result because Y leads to X.

However, the direction of a causal relationship is often uncertain in surveys and field studies. Investigation of relationships between attitudes and behaviors is illustrative. Consider a field study that measures employee satisfaction and employee performance. A relationship obtained between these two variables contributes little to causal understanding. Satisfaction may cause performance, or the reverse; or, the relationship may be biased or even spurious.

Does the temporal sequence of measurement address the causal issue? The second causal criterion, which was summarized in Exhibit 5.1, states that X should occur with or before Y. What are the causal implications if job satisfaction is measured before job performance in a field study?

It is desirable design practice to measure the presumed causal variable before or with the presumed consequence, certainly not after. However, temporal sequence typically adds little to the internal validity of surveys or field studies. A relationship may be observed regardless of measurement order when participant responses serve as both independent and dependent variables. For example, both employee satisfaction and performance are likely to be relatively stable over time. A high performer in one time period is likely to be a high performer in subsequent time periods. Satisfaction, too, tends to be stable. Thus, any relationship between the two probably does not depend on which variable is measured first.

Biases Introduced by a Single Source and Similar Method

Additional threats to internal validity are common when human cases provide scores on both X and Y variables. One is a form of demand effects introduced in the last chapter. It occurs when participants believe they see an expected relationship between the independent and dependent variables being measured and respond accordingly. For example, a participant believes that perceived product quality (X) leads to purchasing intentions (Y). The participant completes a questionnaire stating a belief that a particular product is high quality. The questionnaire then asks about purchasing intentions. To be consistent with the belief stated previously, the participant indicates an intention to buy the product, whether or not this reflects a true intention.

Another threat involves differences in predispositions that participants bring to any social situation. For example, participants likely differ in their inclination to be agreeable or disagreeable. A study where both X and Y call for degrees of agreement may obtain a relationship that reflects only differences in participants' predispositions.

Exhibit 7.4 illustrates the problem. Three participants, A, B, and C, are asked to provide evaluations of X and Y statements that call for responses on a 5-point scale ranging from 1, "Strongly Disagree," to 5, "Strongly Agree."

Assume all three participants are neutral on both variables. They "Neither Agree nor Disagree" (scale point 3) with the constructs X' and Y'. However, Participant A is inherently critical and reports scores of $X = 2$, $Y = 1$. C is inherently agreeable (scores of 5 and 4), and B is neither agreeable nor disagreeable (scores of 3 and 3). As Exhibit 7.4 shows, a relationship between X and Y is observed. Given the assumption, this relationship results from differences in participants' predispositions to agree or disagree; there is no relationship between X' and Y' at the construct level.

The threat illustrated in Exhibit 7.4 can be viewed as a measurement problem, a problem of construct invalidity. Measures that capture general predispositions rather than true construct variance are contaminated. The issue is raised here because the contamination operates on both the independent and dependent variable. Contamination operates to suggest an empirical relationship between variables when none exists; thus, it illustrates a threat to internal validity.

A related problem is also suggested by this example. The similarity of measurement procedures for X and Y variables can contribute to inflated or even spurious relationships. In the example, both X and Y are measured using

EXHIBIT 7.4. **Spurious relationship between** *X* **and** *Y* **due to pre-disposition differences**

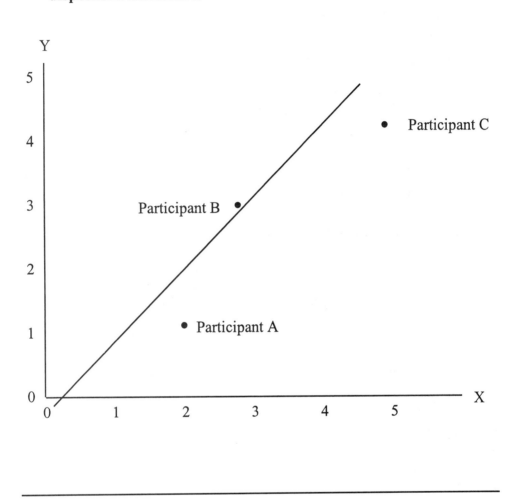

a common 5-point scale of agreement and disagreement. Similarity in thes format (e.g., wording) of items used to measure independent and dependent constructs can also contribute to inflated relationships.

PRAISE FOR SURVEYS AND FIELD STUDIES

It is clear that design characteristics of surveys and field studies make them more vulnerable to internal validity threats than experiments and quasi-experiments. Simply stated, surveys and field studies, especially when cross-sectional, are not attractive for addressing causal concerns. However, that does not mean surveys and field studies are unattractive research designs.

Internal Validity May Not Be a Concern

There are times when causation is important, but a design providing high internal validity is not. These situations occur where researchers are confident that causal relationships are not in question. This confidence is often based on a well-accepted conceptual explanation.

For example, human capital theory predicts that investments, such as education and training, influence success in subsequent life experience, such as financial attainment. Field studies and surveys are conducted to estimate the strength of relationships; questions regarding causality are answered conceptually.

Causation May Not Be a Concern

In other situations, noncausal relationships are of interest. Often these involve information about people's opinions, expectations or preferences. For example, surveys are conducted to identify voter opinions or consumer product preferences. Statistical generalization is more important in such situations than are causal issues.

As another example, a researcher develops a short inexpensive alternative to a time-consuming and expensive test of some ability. The time consuming and expensive test is known to be valuable in predicting important behaviors (e.g., educational performance). The short form may serve as a substitute for the more involved form if a strong relationship is demonstrated between the two. The researcher is interested in the strength of the relationship between the two test forms, not whether one causes the other. A field study can effectively address the issue.

Design Constraints

There are still other situations in which experimentation is desirable but impractical. For example, there is great personal and public policy interest in whether smoking causes cancer. Experimentation could clearly inform this issue. Random assignment of a large group of individuals to smoking and nonsmoking conditions would answer many criticisms of other types of research raised by the tobacco industry. Of course, such a study is illegal (people cannot be required to smoke—or not smoke) and unethical. Knowledge about the relationship between smoking and cancer must be made from nonexperimental research.

These illustrations suggest that designs cannot be arranged in a single hierarchy; one is not uniformly superior to others. The appropriate design for any situation depends on validity issues taking the conceptual state of the model investigated into account. Practically speaking, it also depends on the constraints imposed on the research environment.

SUMMARY

Surveys and field studies can use between-cases or within-case designs. They can also be cross-sectional where X and Y are measured only once. Or, they can be longitudinal involving several measurements of X and Y over time.

Variations of Design A2, between-cases design, are widely used for both surveys and field studies. X and Y scores are obtained from cases once. In practice, cross-sectional between-cases field studies and surveys usually obtain scores on a variety of independent variables.

Time series are less widely used. They obtain repeated scores from a single case, often on an organization or larger unit such as an industry. Frequently scores are obtained over a long time period. The time series described here, Design B2, included one independent and one dependent variable. The design is used to show how changes in values of X correspond to changes in values of Y.

Panel studies combine multiple cases with multiple time periods. Like time series, they are typically used to study within-case changes in Y values as X values change. Panel studies control for stable between-cases variables that can serve as selection threats in cross-sectional studies.

Surveys and field studies are subject to the same internal validity threats present in quasi-experiments and experiments. Researcher and participant effects brought about through the research environment are present in surveys and field studies as they are in experiments and quasi-experiments. Experiments and quasi-experiments may be intrusive through their manipulation of levels of the independent variable. However, the measurement procedures of surveys and field studies may also be intrusive.

Surveys and field studies that obtain multiple measurements of independent and dependent variables are also prone to the longitudinal threats identified in experiments and quasi-experiments. History, maturation, instrumentation, and testing are frequent possibilities. These threats may be more serious for longitudinal survey and field studies, because oftentimes more measurements are taken.

Additional internal validity threats are present in surveys and field studies, because independent variables are measured using participant responses. Even the causal direction of a relationship between X and Y is in doubt in these situations. Participants' responses also raise problems, because nuisance variables represented by case demand effects and predispositions can produce misleading relationships between independent and dependent variables. These difficulties are especially likely when the instruments used to measure X and Y are similar.

Surveys and field studies are often attractive designs for causal inference, despite their many difficulties. They are attractive in many situations in which causation is not a concern. They are also useful when alternative designs are impractical or cannot be employed.

FOR REVIEW

Terms to Know

Time series. Design to investigate longitudinal changes in a dependent variable; independent and dependent variables are measured more than once over time.

Instantaneous model. Time series model in which changes in the independent and dependent variables are assumed to occur without an intervening time interval.

Lagged model. Time series model in which changes in the independent variable are assumed to take some time to influence the dependent variable.

Panel studies. Independent and dependent variables are measured two or more times on a group of cases; design to measure changes in the dependent variable as a function of changes in an independent variable(s).

Questions for Review

1. Compare and contrast field studies and surveys.
2. Distinguish between lagged and instantaneous time series models.
3. Be able to describe internal validity threats to surveys and field studies not present in experiments or quasi-experiments.

Issues to Discuss

1. How are panel study designs potentially superior to cross-sectional between-cases designs? Are they less advantageous in any way(s)?
2. Identify a research topic in which a field study would be more attractive than an experiment or quasi-experiment. Why is a field study the most attractive way to address this topic? Which specific Design, A2, B2, or C2 would you recommend to carry out this field study?

PART III: SUGGESTED READING

Cook and Campbell's (1979) book on quasi-experimentation is probably the most influential work on design in the social sciences. In particular, their discussions of causal evidence and threats to internal validity are broadly accepted. The volume also contains chapters on quasi-experimental designs and analysis methods. An article by Cook and Shadish (1994) provides an update on many of the issues in the original volume. An earlier volume by Campbell and Stanley (1963) offers a less technical discussion of threats to internal validity.

Many books that purport to be on research design actually focus more on statistical analysis, given a design, than they do on design itself. Fortunately, there are several excellent exceptions. I like Keppel's (1982) book on experiments; it offers a readable treatment of experimental design and analysis. Design issues are not slighted; Keppel also gives more attention to within-cases designs than some other books of this type.

Cochran (1982) and Kish (1987) are two excellent treatments of research design generally. Emphasis is placed on quasi-experiments and field studies, although both use experiments as a point of departure. Kish also had things to say about the design of survey research. Both Cochran and Kish emphasize design issues over analysis, although at least an intermediate level of statistical knowledge makes these books more understandable.

IV

ANALYSIS: INVESTIGATING EMPIRICAL RELATIONSHIPS

8

Data Analysis Foundations

Chapter Outline

- At most colleges and universities, students' first (or only) exposure to research method activities is a course in statistics.
- Statistics courses are typically taught by statisticians.

These unremarkable observations may nevertheless be important for your mindset about research. If your introduction to research methods was as described, you probably started this book believing that statistics represent the main empirical research activity.

Hopefully that idea was dispelled in Part I, where it was argued that empirical research is aimed at enhancing conceptual understanding. It does so by providing information about probable relationships between scores that validly represent the constructs at issue. Statistics are helpful in this process;

but statistics are far from sufficient. Causal relationships and relationships that correspond to conceptual meanings also require sound design and measurement.

But why the observation—statisticians teach statistics? It's a matter of perspective. Statisticians are understandably most interested in advancing knowledge about the field of statistics. Alternatively, empirical researchers are interested in statistics as a tool for advancing knowledge about conceptual relationships. These differences lead to different concerns and emphases.

An important difference has to do with the way scores are viewed. To statisticians, scores illustrate how statistical procedures operate. Hypothetical scores are as good as scores from real cases for their purposes.

Not so for empirical researchers; information provided by scores from real cases are central empirical ingredients. Moreover, these scores typically do not satisfy statistical assumptions; they frequently are in error, or even missing. Empirical researchers must seek to make appropriate inferences to the conceptual level from an operational environment of fallible scores. (Appendix 8A discusses errors in data sets and methods to minimize them. Chapter 16 describes statistical procedures that are available to address missing data.)

DATA ANALYSIS AND STATISTICS

Data is another term for scores. Data often refer to a set of scores on two or more variables. (*Datum* is singular and refers to one score.) For researchers, the data are as challenging as the statistical procedures used to analyze them. This book adopts a research orientation to analysis; it emphasizes data analysis, not statistical analysis, per se.

The chapter begins with a definition of statistics and describes how statistics contribute to research. It then describes characteristics of scores for research purposes. These characteristics have implications for decisions regarding use of statistical procedures. It concludes with a description of conventions for statistical operations on scores used in the remainder of this book.

The term *statistic* is used in several ways. Sometimes it refers to a field of study. Sometimes it describes procedures developed by statisticians or procedures that researchers use to analyze data. Sometimes the term is used to characterize outcomes of statistical procedures.

In this book, the term *statistic* is used to designate a summary characteristic of scores. For example, a mean is a statistic whose values describe the central tendency of a set of scores on some measure. A simple correlation coefficient is a statistic whose values describe the degree of relationship between scores on two variables.

Statistical Information

There are many statistics, many ways to summarize data. Means and correlation coefficients are just examples. However, statistics almost always provide information about just two issues. First, some statistics provide summary information on scores obtained on a single variable. The mean, which identifies the weighted middle of a set of cases' scores, is one example. Chapter 9 discusses statistics that decribe scores on a single variable.

Second, statistics provide information about how values on two or more variables vary together. In this role, statistics are used to address the central issue in research, namely relations between variables. Chapters 10 and 11 discuss statistics that describe relationships.

Statistical Purposes

Statistics also serve two purposes. First, they are used to summarize scores and empirical relationships among the cases studied. The present section describes statistics for this purpose.

Second, statistical procedures are used to address two types of validity introduced in Chapter 2. One of these involves the contribution of statistics to causal analysis—internal statistical validity and validation. The other applies when statistics are used in generalization—statistical generalization validity and validation. Both of these procedures rely heavily on probability, and their discussion is postponed to Part V.

PROPERTIES OF SCORES

An operational variable has a measure that is used to obtain scores on the cases studied. These scores are numerical, and there are several ways to classify them. Two such ways have implications for data analyses and interpretation.

Levels of Measurement

Numerical values assigned in measurement refer to characteristics of cases on some variable of interest. However, the amount of information conveyed by the numerical values can vary. Four *levels of measurement* representing different amounts of information are commonly identified. Examples of each level are shown in Exhibit 8.1.

EXHIBIT 8.1. Examples of levels of measurement

Nominal		
	Branches of Govenment	Legislative, Executive, Judicial
Ordinal		
	Job Level	Professor, Associate Professor, Assistant Professor
	Theatre Popcorn Sizes	Small, Large, Jumbo
Interval		
	Temperature (Celsius or Fahrenheit)	
	Calendar Time	
Ratio		
	Salary	
	Age	

Nominal (or *categorical*) *variables* signify that different numbers mean only that values represent different things. No order is implied by the numerical values assigned. For example, numbers can be assigned to a nominal variable that identifies members of the three branches of government; it has the values legislative, judicial, and executive. Legislative members can be assigned 1s, judicial 2s and executive 3s. All members with values of 1 are different than members with values of 2, and so forth.

But the assignment of numbers is arbitrary. Members of the legislature can be assigned a value of 3, executive branch members, a value of 1. In fact, any number can be assigned to members of any branch of government as long as it is not the same number assigned to another branch. The numbers convey only similarities (same number) or differences (different number).

Three additional measurement levels connote increasingly sophisticated degrees of order. Numerical values of *ordinal variables* imply only order—"most" to "least," or vice versa. For example, job titles often represent ordinal variables. A professor has a higher job level than an associate professor who has a higher level than an assistant professor. However, only order is implied, not magnitude of difference between the titles; any numbers that preserve the order are thus permissible. Professors can be assigned 1, associates, 2, and assistants, 3. Assigning professors 3, associates 7, and assistants 10 also suffices since the same order is implied (though it is reversed).

Interval variables have ordinal characteristics, and the distance between them is meaningful. However, interval variables do not provide information about the absolute level of a variable.

Temperature measured by Celsius or Fahrenheit illustrates an interval variable. Temperature differences of 10 degrees Celsius are the same anywhere on the variable. The difference between 10 and 20 degrees is the same as the difference between 35 and 45 degrees. However, neither Celsius nor Fahrenheit variables provide information about the absolute temperature level; zero temperature is arbitrary in both cases. Consequently, one cannot say that a Fahrenheit temperature of 50 degrees is twice as warm as a temperature of 25 degrees.

Finally, *ratio variables* have interval characteristics and a true zero point. Salary is an example. The difference between a yearly salary of $25,000 and $35,000 is the same as a difference betwen $90,000 and $100,000. Furthermore, a yearly salary of $100,000 is twice as large as a salary of $50,000.

Recognizing differences between these levels of measurement is important for the choice of statistics in some instances; it is also important for the interpretation of statistical output. Statistics that provide information about relationships between variables, in particular, are sometimes sensitive to levels of measurement.

Discrete and Continuous Variables

Another measurement distinction is between discrete and continuous variables. *Discrete variables* have a countable number of values. For example, gender is a discrete variable that can assume two values, male and female. Nominal and ordinal variables are always discrete.

RESEARCH HIGHLIGHT 8.1

Nearly Interval Measurement

Researchers disagree about whether certain widely used types of measures such as attitude questionnaires meet interval measurement requirements. For example, are the intervals on a response scale that ask people to indicate 1 "Strongly Disagree," 2 "Disagree," 3 "Neither Disagree or Agree," 4 "Agree," or 5 "Strongly Agree" really equal? Or, do they satisfy only ordinal requirements? Further, there is disagreement about whether statistics that rely on meaningful intervals can be used for these types of measures.

This book takes the view that such measures, if not strictly interval, are nearly interval. Furthermore, statistics that require meaningful intervals can be used without serious difficulty as long as measures are nearly interval.

Alternatively, ***continuous variables*** are infinitely divisible between any two values. For example, age can be scaled in years, but it can be divided into months, weeks, days, hours, and so forth. Interval and ratio variables are continuous.

The distinction between discrete and continuous variables is important for some types of statistical validation procedures (see Part V) and for reporting scores in research reports (see Chapter 9). For simplicity, researchers report continuous variables as discrete. For example, they may round continuous age values to the nearest whole year.

CONVENTIONS

Mathematical formulae and operations in Part IV are modest; symbols used are shown in Exhibit 8.2. Letters are used to designate what meaning should be attached to variables. These conventions are shown in Exhibit 8.3.

When shown, scores are placed in a ***data matrix.*** A data matrix is a rectangular array of scores with cases in the rows and variables in the columns as represented in Exhibit 8.4. This representation can help you understand for-

---

EXHIBIT 8.2. Math symbol conventions

Symbol	Interpretation
+	add
-	subtract
$\pm$	add and subtract, or plus and minus
*	multiply
—	divide
=	equal
$\approx$	approximately equal
$\neq$	not equal
>	greater than
$\geq$	greater than or equal
<	less than
$\leq$	less than or equal
$\sum_{i=1}^{N}(y_i)$	$= y_1 + y_2 + \ldots + y_i + \ldots + y_N$, where i designates the ith case, $i = 1$, indicates that summing begins with the first case and N designates that the summing continues through the Nth case. The complete representation is shortened to, $\Sigma(y_i)$, since in this book the summing always begins with the first case and continues through all cases.
x^2	$x * x$
$\sqrt{}$	take the square root

mulae and other statistical operations. Create a mental picture of rows (cases) and columns (variables).

SUMMARY

Data analysis contributes to conceptual understanding along with design and measurement. Statistics are often calculated as a part of this activity. A *statistic* is a characteristic of scores. It describes scores on single measures or relationships between scores among two or more measures.

Scores representing variables differ in ways that have consequences for types of statistics calculated on them and their interpretation. Numbers only

EXHIBIT 8.3. Letter conventions

Letter	Interpretation

1) **One variable**. If only one variable is considered, it is designated X. An independent variable is also designated X and a dependent variable is designated Y.

X	variable or independent variable
x_i	value of the ith case on X where i goes from 1 to N cases
N	total number of cases
Y	dependent variable
y_i	value of the ith case on Y where i goes from 1 to N cases

2) **Two or more variables.** When two or more independent variables are considered (or when independent/dependent variable status is not an issue) variables are designated X with a subscript:

Xj	j^{th} variable where j goes from 1 to k variables
k	total number of X variables
Xj_i	value of the ith case on the jth variable

EXHIBIT 8.4. A data matrix

				Variables			
Cases	Y	X1	X2	. . .	Xj	. . .	Xk
1	y_1	$x1_1$	$x2_1$		xj_1		xk_1
2	y_2	$x1_2$	$x2_2$		xj_2		xk_2
3	y_3	$x1_3$	$x2_3$		xj_3		xk_3
.							
.							
.							
I	y_i	$x1_i$	$x2_i$		xj_i		xk_i
.							
.							
N	y_N	$x1_N$	$x2_N$		xj_N		xk_N

identify similarity and dissimilarity among *nominal variables.* Numbers additionally imply order (more than, less than) among *ordinal variables. Interval variables* have the added property that the differences between values are meaningful. Finally, *ratio variables* have the characteristics of an interval variable plus a true zero point.

Discrete variables have a countable number of values. *Continuous variables* are infinitely divisible between values.

FOR REVIEW

Terms to Know

Data. Scores characterizing cases obtained on measures. *Datum* refers to one score.

Statistics. Refers to a field of study, procedures to analyze data, or a term to describe outcomes of statistical procedures. It also refers to a summary characteristic of scores.

Levels of measurement. Refers to the amount of information provided by scores.

Nominal (categorical) variable. Variable in which similar values signal the same thing, different values signal different things.

Ordinal variable. Variable with nominal properties, and values signal order from highest to lowest (or lowest to highest).

Interval variable. Variable with ordinal properties, and the distance between values is meaningful.

Ratio variable. Variable with interval properties, and there is a true zero point.

Discrete variable. Variable with a countable number of values.

Continuous variable. Variable that is infinitely divisible between any two values.

Data matrix. A rectangular array of scores with cases in the rows and variables in the columns.

Questions for Review

1. You learn the values of the following variables that apply to an individual:

Gender
Age
Whether the individual owns an automobile
Years of work experience
Number of books the individual owns
Political party affiliation
Whether the individual is a union member
How many telephones the individual has at home

Specify the level of measurement for each of these variables.
Classify each variable as discrete or continuous.

2. A student takes four college classes: Economics 100, a 3-credit course that meets 3 times a week; Psychology 100, a 3-credit course that meets 3 times a week; Algebra 100, a 5-credit course that meets 4 times a week; Golf 100, a 1-credit course that meets once a week. Arrange this information in a data matrix in which classes represent the cases, and the two variables are the number of credits and the number of days classes meet.

3. Professors rank higher than associate professors who rank higher than assistant professors. Assign numbers to these three ranks that satisfy a nominal scale but violate an ordinal scale.

Rank	*Number*
Professors	
Associate Professors	
Assistant Professors	

APPENDIX 8A: ON CLEAN DATA

Computers and statistical software are a great help to research and data analysis. Many analyses now performed are virtually impossible without a computer because of the number of calculations required. Even analyses that can be done by hand, or on a calculator, are greatly speeded with a computer. Once data is entered, a computer can perform calculations with unerring accuracy.

But there is a rub; data must be correctly entered. This appendix identifies data error sources. It also makes recommendations for minimizing errors when creating data sets and for locating them in existing data files.

Errors Made on Measuring Instruments

Most serious errors occur when information is recorded on the original measuring instrument, such as a self-report questionnaire or an interview form. Participants completing self-report questionnaires may generate errors. For example, they may respond incorrectly because they do not understand a question. Errors are also likely when research observers complete measurement instruments. For example, an observer may not have access to correct information or may misinterpret information provided.

Errors by participants or observers are difficult to correct. They are best minimized before data are collected. Two precautions help. First, the measuring instrument should be constructed with a concern for missing data in mind. Keep it simple to complete; make questions unambiguous. Second, do not assume that participants or observers have your knowledge or motivation. Provide training to obtain knowledge and incentives to obtain motivation.

Data File Errors

A second source for errors occurs when data are transcribed from the original measuring instruments into a file for subsequent analysis. Such errors can be minimized at the outset. Three things can help. First, use a rectangular format for data sets. Maintain a separate row for scores on each case and a separate column for each variable. Missing responses are much easier to account for if this suggestion is followed.

Second, make the job of recording original data simple. For example, suppose you want to record gender by making male equal 1; female equal 0. However, participants are asked to circle *M* if male; *F* if female on a questionnaire. *M*s and *F*s should be entered in the computer file. The letters *M* and *F* can be transformed to the numbers 1 and 0 by the software program in the computer without errors.

Finally, if resources permit, all data should be recorded twice. The two data files can then be compared; any differences can be resolved by an examination of the original data source.

Missing Values

Research studies are almost always plagued by missing data; these present a serious problem (Chapter 16 discusses methods to address missing data at the analysis stage of a research study). Two recommendations are made here for recording information about missing data. First, record a specific value to identify all missing data rather than leaving cells in the data set blank. This helps the individuals transcribing the data maintain values in the correct rows and columns. Second, if possible, assign the same value to missing responses across all variables. This is another way to help transcribers minimize errors. In doing so, however, make sure that values to identify missing values cannot be legitimate responses for any of the variables.

Evaluating Secondary Data Sets

Research is often conducted on data that have been collected and recorded by someone else. Although you can never be certain about the accuracy of such data, you can evaluate them for values that are impossible, improbable, or inconsistent.

Suppose a variable is measured using a 5-point rating scale that ranges from 1 (low) to 5 (high). Any numerical value outside this range is impossible; it must be incorrect. Similarly, some values are possible but improbable. For example, it is improbable that an employee is 94 years old.

Impossible and improbable values can be identified one variable at a time. Inconsistent values must be examined in the context of two or more variables. For example, it is inconsistent for a student to be younger than the number of years of education.

Sometimes you can correct impossible, improbable, or inconsistent data using responses to other variables measures. Often, however, such variables must be treated as missing values.

9

Analysis Applications: Describing Scores on a Single Variable

Chapter Outline

- *A Data Matrix*
- *Tables and Graphs*
  - *Tables*
  - *Graphs*
- *Statistical Representation of Scores*
  - *Central Tendency*
  - *Variability*
  - *Shape*
- *Relationships Between Statistics*
  - *Skew and Central Tendency*
  - *Skew and Variability*
- *Summary*
- *For Review*

Statistics describe scores on a variable or describe empirical relationships between scores obtained on two or more variables. This chapter presents a selective review of statistics and other methods to describe scores on a single variable.

There are at least three reasons to investigate scores on single variables before looking at relationships between variables:

1. Investigation is needed to decide whether the scores are ready, or can be made ready, for analyses of relationships between variables. Such investigation is needed because data files usually contain errors after initial construction (see Chapter 8, Appendix 8A, and Chapter 16).
2. Statistics that summarize scores on single variables can aid in understanding the cases studied and generalizations that may follow from a study. For example, knowledge of biographical information about research participants, such as age, education, and gender, suggest how research findings may generalize to other persons.
3. Knowledge about how scores are distributed on each variable also helps researchers understand statistics of relationships among variables. Subsequent chapters show that both the variability and shape of score distributions on single variables influence relationships that may be obtained between variables.

The chapter begins by describing ways to summarize scores on a measure using tables and graphs. Statistics that describe three characteristics of score distributions, central tendency, variability, and symmetry or asymmetry are then defined. Relationships between these statistics are also discussed.

A DATA MATRIX

Exhibit 9.1 shows a data matrix of scores on four variables obtained from 19 cases. The first two, $X1$ and $X2$, are discrete and range from 1 to 7. They are ordered interval scales and may represent, for example, levels of satisfaction ranging from 1, "Very Dissatisfied," to 7, "Very Satisfied." $X3$ is age and $X4$ is weight. These are ordered continuous scales rounded to the first decimal place.

It is difficult to obtain much information from a visual inspection of Exhibit 9.1 even though there are only 19 scores on each variable. Summarizing such scores in frequency tables, in graphs, and/or statistically, can aid interpretation and understanding.

TABLES AND GRAPHS

Researchers sometimes do not appreciate how useful tables and graphs can be for summarizing scores.

EXHIBIT 9.1. Data matrix: Scores from 19 cases on four variables

	7-Point Rating Scales		Age	Weight
Case	X1	X2	X3	X4
1	3	4	38.6	126.1
2	5	7	54.5	147.1
3	6	7	63.8	163.7
4	2	3	26.2	116.5
5	1	1	28.4	110.5
6	4	6	46.0	135.6
7	4	6	45.2	138.1
8	5	6	51.3	143.3
9	6	7	62.7	155.1
10	7	7	68.9	174.8
11	3	5	39.7	128.9
12	3	4	35.5	124.6
13	5	7	56.6	150.9
14	3	3	32.1	121.2
15	2	2	25.3	112.3
16	4	5	44.9	132.4
17	4	6	48.1	137.8
18	5	6	53.4	146.5
19	4	5	42.8	129.0

Tables

A *frequency table* provides a summary of scores from a data matrix by reporting the number (and/or percentage or proportion) of cases at each level of a discrete variable, or within each interval of a continuous variable. Exhibit 9.2 shows a frequency table for $X1$, a discrete 7-value variable, and Exhibit 9.3 shows a frequency table for age, $X3$, a continuous variable. Intervals have been created in Exhibit 9.3 and cases with ages that fall within each interval are grouped together.

EXHIBIT 9.2. Frequency table for $X1$, a 7-point ordered scale

Value	Frequency	Percentage
1	1	5.3
2	2	10.5
3	4	21.1
4	5	26.3
5	4	21.0
6	2	10.5
7	1	5.3
Total	19	100.0

EXHIBIT 9.3. Frequency table for $X3$, age

Age Intervals	Frequency	Percentage
20 < 30	3	15.8
30 < 40	4	21.1
40 < 50	5	26.3
50 < 60	4	21.0
60 < 70	3	15.8
Total	19	100.0

Graphs

A graph of scores on a variable provides a picture of the data that is often more informative than a frequency table. A ***bar chart*** reports the values of a discrete variable on one axis and the frequency (number and/or proportion or percentage) of cases with scores at each value on the other. Exhibit 9.4 shows a bar chart for $X1$; the values are on the horizontal axis and the frequency on the vertical axis.

EXHIBIT 9.4. Bar chart of scores on *X1*, a 7-value ordered scale

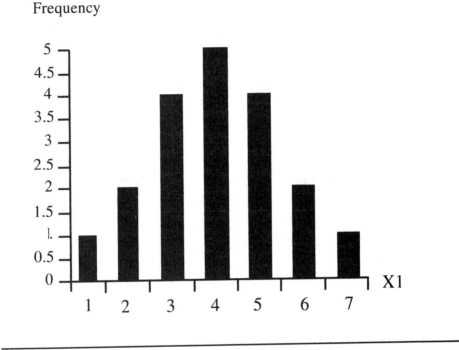

Histograms graph continuous variables. A histogram reports values of a continuous variable placed in intervals as illustrated for age, *X3*, in Exhibit 9.5.

STATISTICAL REPRESENTATION OF SCORES

Statistics are also available to describe characteristics of distributions, such as those shown in Exhibits 9.2 and 9.3.

Central Tendency

The middle of a distribution of scores, is called its ***central tendency.*** Two statistics describing central tendency are the median and the mean. The ***median*** is the middle score (or if there is an even number of scores, the sum of the two middlemost scores divided by 2).

The ***mean*** is the sum of the values of each score divided by the number of scores:

EXHIBIT 9.5. Histogram of _X3_, age

$$\mu_x = \frac{\Sigma x_i}{N} = \frac{\left(x_1 + x_2 + \dots x_i + \dots + x_N\right)}{N} \qquad (9.1)$$

where μ_X = mean of _X_

x_i = score of the ith case on _X_

N = number of cases

The **_mode_** is the most frequent score in a distribution. It is sometimes of interest in describing the central tendency of nominal variables. Further, it is of interest to know whether a distribution has one (unimodal) or more modes. For example, a bimodal distribution might have peaks at the extremes rather than one peak in the middle.

In most cases, however, the median or mean is of more interest. Hereafter, the mode is only used to distinguish distributions that have one or more peaks.

Variability

Variability refers to the spread in the distribution of scores. A useful and intuitively meaningful statistic indicating variability is the *standard deviation,* the average variability of scores around the mean:

$$\sigma_x = \sqrt{\frac{\Sigma(x_i - \mu_x)^2}{N}} \qquad (9.2)$$

where σ_X = standard deviation of X

Formula 9.2 is worth study. When calculations are completed, the square and square root leave the values of the deviations between each x_i and the mean unchanged but with a positive number. Dividing by N is analogous to dividing by N in Formula 9.1. It creates an average. However, the average now refers to the deviations around the mean of the distribution.

Exhibit 9.6 summarizes steps to calculate the standard deviation of $X1$ from Exhibit 9.1. The mean is calculated first from Formula 9.1, $\mu_{X1} = 76/19 = 4.00$. The mean is then subtracted from each value of $X1$ in the column ($x_1 - \mu_{X1}$); this column must sum to 0.0. The deviations are squared in the last column. The sum of this column is divided by N, and its square root is taken. The standard deviation, $\sigma_{X1} = \sqrt{42/19} = \sqrt{2.21} = 1.49$. The average variability of $X1$ scores about its mean is 1.49.

Although not as intuitively meaningful, variance is useful for certain mathematical operations involving statistics. *Variance* is the standard deviation squared.

$$\sigma^2 x = \frac{\Sigma(X_i - \mu_x)^2}{N} \qquad (9.3)$$

where $\sigma^2 x$ = variance of X

**EXHIBIT 9.6. Calculation of the standard deviation ($X1$ from
Exhibit 9.1)**

Case	$X1$	$(X1 - \mu_{X1})$	$(X1 - \mu_{X1})^2$
1	3	−1	1
2	5	1	1
3	6	2	4
4	2	−2	4
5	1	−3	9
6	4	0	0
7	4	0	0
8	5	1	1
9	6	2	4
10	7	3	9
11	3	−1	1
12	3	−1	1
13	5	1	1
14	3	−1	1
15	2	−2	4
16	4	0	0
17	4	0	0
18	5	1	1
19	4	0	0
Σ	76	0	42
μ	4		

Shape

The *shape of a distribution* of scores is described by its symmetry around
the central tendency and by its peakedness or flatness. The reference point
for shape is a *normal distribution.* It describes a continuously scaled

RESEARCH HIGHLIGHT 9.1

Another Standard Deviation Statistic

You may see Formula 9.2 with $n - 1$ in the denominator rather than N. The denominator, $n - 1$, is appropriate when estimating a population standard deviation from a sample (where n refers to the sample size) that has been randomly drawn from it. In this section, the cases studied are assumed to represent the population of participants, N, thus Formula 9.2 is appropriate.

EXHIBIT 9.7. A normal distribution

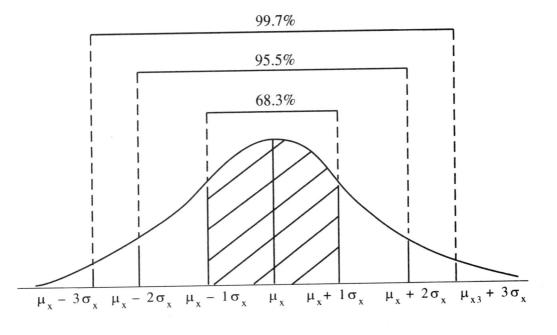

EXHIBIT 9.8. A standard normal distribution: $\mu_{ZX} = 0$, $\sigma_{ZX} = 1$

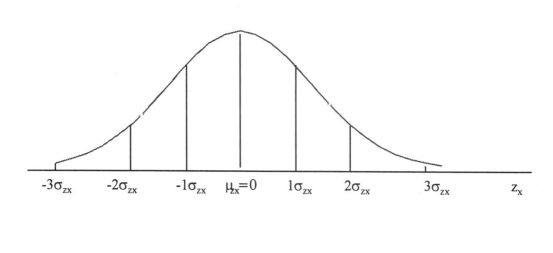

unimodal variable that has 68.3 percent of scores falling within ± (read plus or minus) one standard deviation of the mean, 95.5 percent of scores falling within ± two standard deviations of the mean, and 99.7 percent of scores falling within ± three standard deviations of the mean.

Exhibit 9.7 shows a normal distribution. The distribution is shown under a smooth curve to illustrate a continuous variable. Because a continuous variable is infinitely divisible between values, it is not appropriate to assign a frequency to any particular value. Thus, areas under the curve are identified to represent proportions or percentages of scores that are contained in the total distribution of scores. The crosshatched area between negative and positive one standard deviations in Exhibit 9.7 contain 68.3 percent of the scores.

A normal distribution can have any mean or standard deviation, hence there are many normal distributions. However, all are symmetrical as described, all have the same percentages of scores falling within the sets of standard deviations as described. A *standard normal distribution* has mean = 0.00 and standard deviation = 1.00. Exhibit 9.8 shows a standard normal distribution.

EXHIBIT 9.9. Histogram of scores on $X4$, weight

EXHIBIT 9.10. Bar chart of scores on $X2$

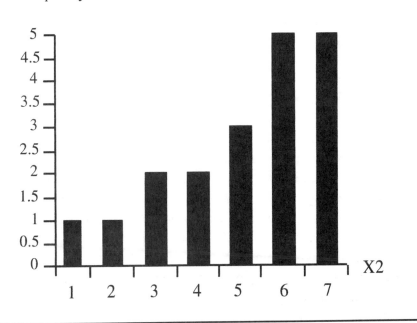

Distributions of scores on many variables approximate the normal distribution. For example, physical characteristics of human and other animal populations often approximate a normal distribution. Part V shows that a normal distribution is also often approximated in many sampling situations in which generalizations from a sample to a population are desired. Thus, normal distributions are widely used in statistical work and have become a standard for judging other types of distributions.

Skew.   *Skew* describes the symmetry or asymmetry of a distribution, relative to a normal distribution. When a distribution is symmetrical, as the normal distribution, skew = 0.0. When the distribution is asymmetrical and the tail is toward the right, skew > 0.0. Exhibit 9.9 shows a histogram of $X4$ from the data in Exhibit 9.1. It is an asymmetrical distribution with a positive skew > 0.0. Exhibit 9.10 shows a bar chart of $X2$ in Exhibit 9.1. The tail is to the left, skew < 0.0.

Kurtosis.   *Kurtosis* shows the peakedness or flatness of a distribution relative to a normal distribution. Kurtosis = 0.0, signifies a distribution that is similar to a normal distribution in height. When a distribution is more peaked than a normal distribution, kurtosis > 0.0; when less peaked, kurtosis < 0.0. Kurtosis is generally not as important for describing distributions as other statistics, and hence is not emphasized here.

RELATIONSHIPS BETWEEN STATISTICS

Skew and Central Tendency

The mean and median are equal when a distribution of scores is symmetrical. When skew > 0.0, the mean > median. The mean < median when skew < 0.0.

Distributions of individual income often have skew > 0.0. Relatively few individuals have very large incomes and these "pull" the mean above the median. In contrast, distributions of employee performance evaluations in organizations often have skew < 0.0. Most employees obtain middle or high evaluations. The few employees who receive low evaluations "pull" the mean below the median. When a distribution is markedly skewed, it is informative to report both the mean and median.

Skew and Variability

When a distribution is symmetrical, the number or percentage of scores one standard deviation above the mean is the same as the number or percentage of scores one standard deviation below. Thus, 34 percent of scores are between the mean and +1 standard deviations and 34 percent of scores are between the mean and -1 standard deviations in normal distributions.

Not so when the distribution is skewed. To illustrate, visual inspection of Exhibit 9.9 (skew > 0.0) suggests that a larger percentage of scores falls in a given negative area close to the mean (= 136.55 pounds). However, as one gets further from the mean, a greater percentage falls within positive standard deviation intervals. The process is reversed if skew < 0.0 (see Exhibit 9.10, where $\mu_{X2} = 5.11$).

Thus, the standard deviation (and variance) provide more equivocal information as a distribution becomes more asymmetrical.

SUMMARY

Understanding characteristics of scores on single variables is a valuable first step in data analysis. A *frequency table* showing variable scores at different levels, or level intervals, is one way to obtain information about single variables. Another way is to graph score distributions. Graphs of discrete variables are called *bar charts*; graphs of continuous variables are called *histograms.*

Statistics can also summarize distributions of scores on single variables. The *median* and *mean* are two ways to describe *central tendency. Standard deviations* and *variances* represent *variability.*

Scores often approximate a *normal distribution,* which is symmetrical and has a known number of scores fall within any specified distance on a continuous scale (e.g., ±1 standard deviations). *Distribution shapes* that are not normal may be symmetrical or asymmetrical. *Skew* is a statistic that indicates a distribution's symmetry or asymmetry. *Kurtosis* is a statistic that indicates a distributions degree of peakedness or flatness relative to a normal distribution.

When distributions are asymmetrical, the mean and median no longer provide the same central tendency value. Further, standard deviations and variance statistics provide ambiguous information when distributions are asymmetrical, because the number of scores above and below the mean are no longer equal.

FOR REVIEW

Terms to Know

Frequency table. Provides a summary of cases' scores from a data matrix by reporting the number (and/or percentage) of cases at each level of a discrete variable, or within each interval of a continuous variable.

Bar chart. Reports the values of a discrete variable on one axis and the frequency (number and/or percentage) of cases with scores at each value on the other.

Histogram. Reports values of a continuous variable placed in intervals.

Central tendency. The middle of a distribution of scores.

Mean. The sum of the values of each score divided by the number of scores.

Median. The middle score in a distribution (or if there are an even number of scores, the sum of the two middlemost scores divided by 2).

Mode. The most frequent score in a distribution of discrete values.

Variability. The spread in a distribution of scores.

Standard deviation. The average variability of scores around the mean.

Variance. The standard deviation squared.

Distribution shape. Degree to which a distribution is symmetrical or asymmetrical and the degree to which it is peaked or flat. These characteristics are defined by *skew* and *kurtosis.*

Normal distribution. A distribution of a continuous variable that is unimodal, symmetrical around its middle, and has 68.3 percent of scores falling within ± one standard deviation of the mean, 95.5 percent of scores falling within ± two standard deviations, and 99.7 percent of scores falling within ± three standard deviations.

Standard normal distribution. A normal distribution with a mean = 0.0 and a standard deviation = 1.0.

Skew. Describes the symmetry or asymmetry of a distribution relative to a normal distribution. When a distribution is symmetrical, skew = 0.0. When the distribution is asymmetrical and the tail is toward the right, skew > 0.0; when the tail is to the left, skew < 0.0.

Kurtosis. Describes the flatness or peakedness of a distribution relative to a normal distribution. Kurtosis > 0.0 when a distribution is more peaked than a normal distribution. Kurtosis < 0.0 when a distribution is less peaked than a normal distribution.

Formulas to Use

Mean

$$\mu_x = \frac{\Sigma x_i}{N} = \frac{(x_1 + x_2 + \ldots x_i + \ldots + x_N)}{N} \tag{9.1}$$

where x_i = score of the ith subject
N = number of subjects

Standard deviation

$$\sigma_x = \sqrt{\frac{\Sigma(x_i - \mu_x)^2}{N}} \tag{9.2}$$

Variance

$$\sigma^2 x = \frac{\Sigma(X_i - \mu_x)^2}{N} \tag{9.3}$$

Questions for Review

1. Explain why it is important to study characteristics of scores on single distributions even though as a researcher you are more interested in relationships between variables.
2. For what types of variables are bar charts appropriate? Histograms?

3. Using Formulas 9.1 and 9.2, calculate the mean and standard deviation for the variable x.

x	$x_i - \mu_x$	$(x_i - \mu_x)^2$
$\overline{6}$		
6		
6		
1		
6		
$\overline{\Sigma}$	____	____
μ		
σ		

4. How does a standard normal distribution differ from other normal distributions? How is it the same?

Issues to Discuss

1. Be prepared to discuss whether skew and kurtosis are related to the relationship between the mean and median, and if so, how.
2. Be prepared to discuss what implications skew has for the interpretation of the standard deviation.

10

Analysis Applications:
Simple Correlation and Regression

Chapter Outline

- *Graphical Representation*
- *Simple Correlation*
  - *Correlation Formulas*
  - *Variance Explained*
- *Simple Regression*
  - *Regression Model*
  - *Regression Formulas*
- *Nominal Independent Variables*
- *Summary*
- *For Review*

Empirical research investigates relationships between scores on operational variables. This chapter begins the "good stuff" from a data analysis perspective. It introduces two procedures that generate statistics to describe relationships among variables, correlation, and regression.

Correlation and regression are attractive because they are appropriate any time a research problem involves a dependent variable that is measured at a nearly interval level or better and has one or more independent variables. This is a sweeping claim—intendedly so. Consider the following studies:

- A large clinic sends a questionnaire to all recent patients to investigate, among other things, whether patients' satisfaction with medical services depends on the time they must wait before obtaining an appointment.
- A manufacturing firm conducts a study to see whether employees who are trained subsequently perform at higher levels than a comparable (control) group of employees who are not trained.
- A college graduate program reviews its records to determine whether student grade point average (GPA) is related to undergraduate GPA and residence status in the state.
- A state human services office randomly samples from census data to see if residents' income levels differ by county.
- A foundation research team performs a study expecting to learn that participants' behavior on computer tasks depends on a multiplicative relation between participants' motivation and ability to do the task.

EXHIBIT 10.1. Independent variables in the hypothetical studies

Study	Number	Scale	Other
Large clinic	1	Interval	
Manufacturing firm	1	Nominal	Two levels
Graduate program	2	Interval and nominal	
State services office	1	Nominal	Many levels
Foundation research team	2	Interval	Nonlinear relation

All these studies have a dependent variable that is measured at a nearly interval to ratio level. However, as Exhibit 10.1 summarizes, the studies differ widely regarding independent variables. The clinic, business firm, and state services office studies have just one independent variable. The graduate program and foundation studies have two. Independent variables are measured at an interval level in the clinic and foundation studies, they are nominal in the business firm and state services studies. The graduate program has both

RESEARCH HIGHLIGHT 10.1

The Designs Also Differ

If you have read Part III, you'll recognize that the designs of the studies also differ. The clinic and college graduate program are field studies, the state human services office, a survey. The business firm study is an experiment or quasi-experiment, depending on how employees are assigned to training and control groups. Finally, the foundation study may be a field study, if both ability and motivation are measured as characteristics of the participants. On the other hand, it is an experiment or quasi-experiment if levels of motivation participants experience are established by the research team.

By itself, research design has few implications for the type of data analysis method used.

an interval (GPA) and nominal (residence) variable. Finally, a nonlinear relationship is expected in the foundation research team study.

There are correlation and regression procedures suitable to analyze the data in all of the studies described. (The examples actually understate the generality of correlation and regression. In particular, if the number of participants warrant, there can be any number of independent variables.) This and the next chapter describe many of these procedures.

This chapter focuses on simple linear correlation and regression. *Simple* means that only two variables are involved—one dependent and one independent. *Linear* means that only a relationship that conforms to a straight line is identified. Hereafter, *correlation* and *regression* mean *simple linear correlation and regression,* unless otherwise stated.

Most of the chapter deals with relationships when both the dependent and independent variables are measured at a nearly interval, interval, or ratio level. It begins by showing how such relationships can be demonstrated graphically. It then describes correlation followed by regression. The chapter also describes correlation and regression when the independent variable is measured at a nominal level.

GRAPHICAL REPRESENTATION

Exhibit 10.2 shows scores and descriptive statistics from seven participants on a dependent (Y) and five independent (Xj) variables. All are measured at a nearly interval level and summarized as discrete variables. For example, they might represent an opinion scale ranging from 1, "Strongly Disagree," to 7, "Strongly Agree."

EXHIBIT 10.2. Scores and descriptive statistics on six interval variables

Case	Y	X1	X2	X3	X4	X5
1	2	2	6	4	1	1
2	2	3	3	2	7	1
3	2	4	5	1	4	1
4	4	4	5	7	4	4
5	6	3	4	6	1	7
6	6	4	2	4	4	7
7	6	6	3	4	7	7
	—	—	—	—	—	—
μ	4.00	3.71	4.00	4.00	4.00	4.00
σ	1.85	1.16	1.31	1.93	2.27	2.78

It is often informative to begin an investigation of a relationship between two variables by plotting their scores in two dimensions. Exhibits 10.3 and 10.4 show plots of scores on Y and $X1$ and $X2$ (from Exhibit 10.2), respectively. It is conventional to represent the dependent variable on the vertical axis and the independent variable on the horizontal axis as shown.

Visual inspection suggests that scores on $X1$ are positively related to scores on Y in Exhibit 10.3. Scores on Y are larger as scores on $X1$ are larger.

EXHIBIT 10.3. Scatter plot Y and $X1$

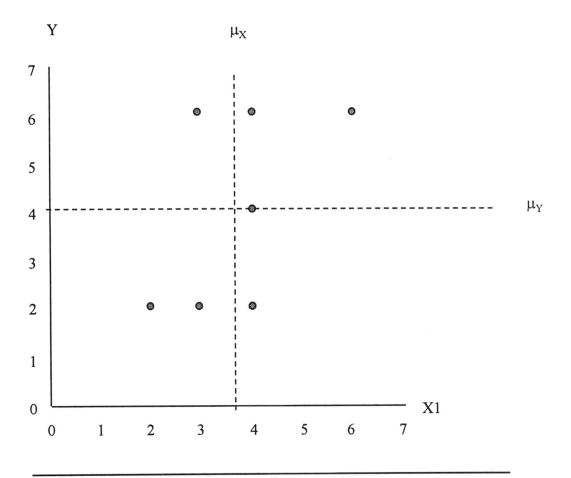

Alternatively, the relationship is negative in Exhibit 10.4; scores on Y are smaller as scores on $X2$ are larger.

Correlation and regression provide statistics that add to visual inspection by describing such relationships quantitatively.

SIMPLE CORRELATION

It is often attractive to study relationships between scores on variables without concern for the scale values or variability of the scores involved. For example, one may want to know whether the relationship between individuals'

EXHIBIT 10.4. Scatter plot Y and $X2$

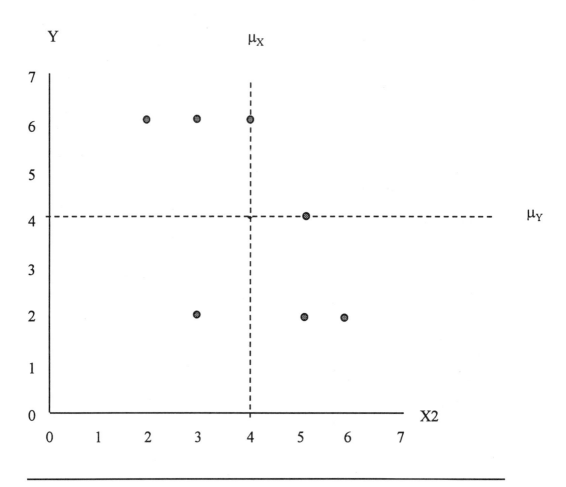

age and income is larger or smaller than the relationship between their height and weight. Time, dollars, length, and weight all represent different scales that must be accounted for if a comparison is to be made.

It is also often desirable to obtain the same relationship regardless of how any one variable is scaled. For example, one may want a measure of relationship between age and income that does not change whether age is recorded in years, months, or some other time unit.

A *correlation coefficient* provides such information; it is a statistic that describes the degree of relationship or association between two variables in standardized form. It can range between ± 1.00.

RESEARCH HIGHLIGHT 10.2

Other Correlation Coefficients

There are other correlation coefficients. Three of these provide PM correlation coefficients using different computational procedures. A *phi coefficient* is sometimes calculated when both Y and X are dichotomous variables—variables that can take on only two values. A *point-biserial correlation* may be calculated when Y or X is dichotomous and the other is not. A *rho coefficient* may be calculated when variables are measured at an ordinal level.

The computational formulas for these correlation coefficients are less demanding than for the PM coefficient, which may explain their use before the widespread availability of statistical software on computers. With statistical software, there is little need for these coefficients, since they are all variations on the basic PM formula (10.2a or 10.2b).

The sign of the correlation coefficient signals the direction of the relationship between the two variables. A positive sign means that as values of one variable increase, so, too, do values of the other. A negative sign means that as values of one variable get larger, values of the other get smaller.

The size of the coefficient signals the degree of relationship. A perfect linear relationship has a value of ± 1.00. Scores on the two variables (after standardization) are identical. A correlation coefficient of 0.00 indicates no linear relationship between the two variables. The degree of relationship gets stronger as correlation coefficients move from 0.00 toward ± 1.00.

The product moment (PM) correlation procedure is described here. *Correlation* hereafter means *PM correlation* unless otherwise designated.

Correlation Formulas

There are many algebraically equivalent ways to calculate correlation coefficients. Two are shown here to help you understand what is accomplished.

Covariance.   One way to think about correlation coefficients extends the notion of variability discussed in Chapter 9. *Covariance* is a statistic that provides information about how values of two variables go together. It is given by:

$$CoVar_{YX} = \frac{\Sigma(Y_i - \mu_Y)*(X_i - \mu_X)}{N} \qquad (10.1)$$

where $CoVar_{YX}$ = covariance of Y and X, the average cross-product of the deviations about their respective means of Y and X

μ_Y and μ_X = means (Formula 9.1), of Y and X, respectively

N = number of cases

Covariance provides information about a relationship in the original units of the variables; it must be standardized to provide a correlation coefficient. This is accomplished by dividing the covariance by the product of the respective standard deviations.

Covariance is standardized to provide correlation coefficient

$$\rho_{YX} = \frac{CoVar_{YX}}{\sigma_Y * \sigma_X} \qquad (10.2a)$$

where ρ_{YX} = correlation coefficient between scores on Y and X

σ_Y and σ_X = standard deviations (Formula 9.2) of Y and X, respectively

Exhibit 10.5 summarizes steps to calculate the simple correlation coefficient of Y and $X1$ using Formulas 10.1 and 10.2a. Deviation scores are first calculated for both Y and $X1$. Then, in the last column each case's deviation scores are multiplied together and divided by N. The sum of this column is the covariance (CoVar = 1.14) from Formula 10.1. The correlation coefficient is then obtained using Formula 10.2a ($\rho_{YX1} = .53$).

EXHIBIT 10.5. Covariance method to calculate a simple correlation coefficient: Y and $X1$ (Exhibit 10.2)

Case	Y	X1	$(Y - \mu_Y)$	$(X1 - \mu_{X1})$	$(Y - \mu_Y) * (X1 - \mu_{X1}) / N$
1	2	2	-2	-1.71	0.49
2	2	3	-2	-0.71	0.20
3	2	4	-2	0.29	-0.08
4	4	4	0	0.29	0.00
5	6	3	2	-0.71	-0.20
6	6	4	2	0.29	0.08
7	6	6	2	2.29	0.65
Σ					1.14
μ	4.00	3.71			
σ	1.85	1.16			

$\rho_{YX1} = \text{CoVar} / (\sigma_Y * \sigma_{X1}) = 1.14 / (1.85 * 1.16) = .53$

Standard Scores. Another way to obtain correlation coefficients is to work with scores that are already standardized. A ***standard score*** is the deviation of a score from its mean divided by the standard deviation. It is given by:

$$Z_{Xi} = \frac{(x_i - \mu_x)}{\sigma_x} \qquad (10.3)$$

where Z_{Xi} = standard score of the ith case on variable X

Exhibit 10.6 illustrates how standard scores are generated from the Y scores in Exhibit 10.2. A deviation score distribution is calculated by subtracting the mean of the Y scores from each case score ($y_i - \mu_Y$). This creates a distribution with $\mu_Y = 0.00$ and a standard deviation of the original distribution. The deviation score distribution is then transformed to a standard score distribution by dividing each deviation score by the original standard deviation, σ_Y. A *standard score distribution* thus has a transformed mean, $\mu_{zY} = 0.00$, and a transformed standard deviation, $\sigma_{zY} = 1.00$. (Standard scores do not change the symmetry or asymmetry of the original distribution.)

EXHIBIT 10.6. Transformation of Y scores (Exhibit 10.2) to standard scores

Case	Y	$Y - \mu_y$	z_y
1	2	−2	−1.08
2	2	−2	−1.08
3	2	−2	−1.08
4	4	0	0
5	6	2	1.08
6	6	2	1.08
7	6	2	1.08
	—	—	—
μ	4.00	0.00	0.00
σ	1.85	1.85	1.00

Standard scores create a scale in standard deviation units. Case 1 has a score 1.08 standard deviations below the mean; Case 7 has a score 1.08 standard deviations above the mean.

A correlation coefficient can be obtained from standard scores by:

$$\rho_{YX} = \frac{\Sigma(z_{Yi} * z_{Xi})}{N} \qquad (10.2b)$$

where ρ_{YX} = simple linear PM correlation coefficient between **Y and X**

z_{Yi} and z_{Xi} = standard scores of the ith case on Y and X, respectively

N = number of cases

Exhibit 10.7 shows correlation computations for the variables Y and $X1$ in Exhibit 10.2 using the standard score formulas. The means and standard deviations of Y and $X1$ are first standardized. The product of each pair of standardized scores is summed and divided by the number of participants. The resulting correlation coefficient from Formula 10.2b, the average product of the standardized scores is, $\rho_{YX1} = .53$.

EXHIBIT 10.7. Standard score method to calculate a simple correlation coefficient: Y and $X1$ (Exhibit 10.2)

Case	Y	$X1$	z_Y	z_X	$z_Y * z_X$
1	2	2	−1.08	−1.47	1.59
2	2	3	−1.08	−.61	.66
3	2	4	−1.08	.25	−.27
4	4	4	0.00	.25	.00
5	6	3	1.08	−.61	−.66
6	6	4	1.08	.25	.27
7	6	6	1.08	1.97	2.13
	—	—	—	—	—
Sum	28.0	26.0	0.0	0.0	3.72
μ	4.00	3.71	0.00	0.00	.53
σ	1.85	1.16	1.00	1.00	

$\rho_{YX1} = 3.72 / 7 = .53$

Variance Explained

The PM correlation coefficient is attractive for the reasons specified. Nevertheless, the definition, standardized degree of relationship, may lack intuitive meaning. A closely related statistic provides greater intuitive understanding. The *coefficient of determination* represents the proportion of variance in Y that is accounted for (explained by) some X variable. It can range from 0.00 to 1.00 and is given by:

$$\rho^2{}_{YX} = \left[\frac{\Sigma(z_{Yi} * z_{Xi})}{N} \right]^2 \qquad (10.4)$$

where $\rho^2{}_{YX}$ = coefficient of determination

The coefficient of determination for Y and $X1$ is $.53^2 = .28$.

One way to think about $\rho^2{}_{YX}$ (usually called *r square*) is to understand that a relationship between variables indicates that scores on one variable provide information about scores on the other. The coefficient of determination provides such information in terms of proportions.

The extreme values of $\rho^2{}_{YX}$ are shown in Exhibit 10.8a and 10.8b where Y is plotted with $X4$ and $X5$ from Exhibit 10.2. Because Y is the same in both cases, its variability is the same in both. Y ranges from 2 to 6 and has a standard deviation of 1.85.

In Exhibit 10.8a information about $X4$ scores provides no information about Y scores. The entire range of Y scores occurs with every $X4$ score. For example, if $X4 = 1$, Y ranges from 2 to 6. It also ranges from 2 to 6 if $X4 = 7$. The coefficient of determination is $\rho^2{}_{YX4} = 0.00$.

Alternatively, knowledge of $X5$ scores in Exhibit 10.8b provides exact information on Y scores. If $X5 = 1$, $Y = 2$; if $X5 = 7$, $Y = 6$. All Y variation is accounted for by knowing the values of $X5$; the coefficient of determination is $\rho^2{}_{YX5} = 1.00$.

Another way to think about the coefficient of determination is to represent the variability in Y and X with circles. Exhibit 10.9 illustrates this using Y and $X1$ from Exhibit 10.2. Each circle represents 100 percent of the variability in the scores for that variable. The overlap shows $\rho^2{}_{YX1} = .28$, the proportion of variance that is common to the two variables.

EXHIBIT 10.8a. Scatter plot *Y* and *X*4

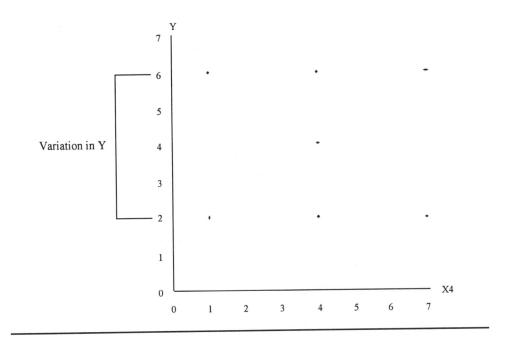

EXHIBIT 10.8b. Scatter plot *Y* and *X*5

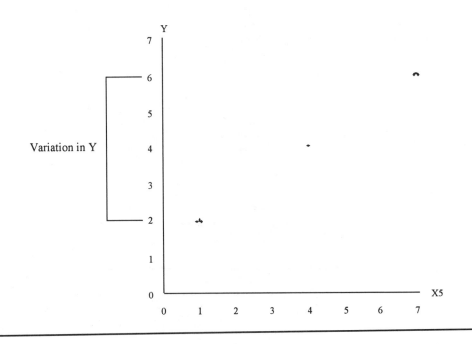

SIMPLE REGRESSION

The correlation coefficient and its informative relative, the coefficient of determination, provide information about a relationship in standardized form. It is also often useful to describe a relationship in the original units of the variables.

Suppose an interest in a relationship between annual income (Y) and years of education (X). Among many participant groups, this relationship is positive, ρ_{YX} and $\rho^2_{YX} > 0.0$. However, one may also want to know how changes in years of education relate to changes in level of annual income. For example, what is the average effect of an additional year of education on level of income?

Regression Model

Regression statistics answer questions of this latter sort. *Regression* describes relationships between a dependent and independent variable in the scale values of the variables. It does so by expressing Y scores as a straight line (linear) function of X scores. This is called the regression line. Y scores can be determined by:

EXHIBIT 10.9. ρ^2_{YX} **explained with circles**

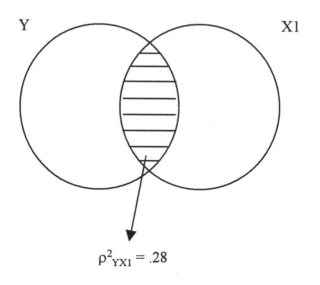

$$\rho^2_{YX1} = .28$$

$$Y_i = \alpha + B_{YX}X_i + \varepsilon_i$$

where α = regression intercept, where the regression line intersects the vertical line describing Y when $X = 0$

B_{YX} = regression coefficient, the slope of the line representing the change in Y for a unit change in X

ε_i = ± error in Y predicted by the regression line and the actual Y value for the ith case

The regression prediction model is:

$$\hat{Y} = \alpha + B_{YX}X \qquad (10.5)$$

where $\hat{Y}$ = **predicted value of Y given x**

Formula 10.5 has no subscripts for individual values because it applies to all scores obtained jointly on Y and X. It has no error term, though it will be in error unless $\rho_{YX} = \pm 1.00$. The dependent variable, Y, thus includes a superscript, ^, to denote it is predicted, not actual. The **regression intercept,** α, in the prediction model refers to the predicted value of Y when $X = 0$. The **regression coefficient,** B_{YX}, refers to the predicted change in Y for a unit change in X.

Exhibit 10.10 (as Exhibit 10.3) shows a plot of Y and $X1$ scores from Exhibit 10.2. Exhibit 10.10 adds a regression prediction line with an intercept, α, and regression coefficient, B_{YX}. Errors, ε_i, in the prediction of Y scores for Cases 2 and 6 are also shown.

The intercept and regression coefficient are set using the **Least Squares Criterion,** which establishes α and B_{YX} so that the sum of the squared deviations (errors) between actual Y_i and the value predicted from the regression line, $\hat{Y}_i$, is minimized.[1]

$$\Sigma(\varepsilon_i)^2 = \Sigma(y_i - \hat{Y}_i)^2 = minimum$$

---

[1]The value of the PM correlation coefficient is established using this same criterion.

Thus, the Least Squares Criterion provides an estimated regression line that provides the best linear fit between Y and X overall—taking all scores into account.

EXHIBIT 10.10. Scatter plot Y and $X1$

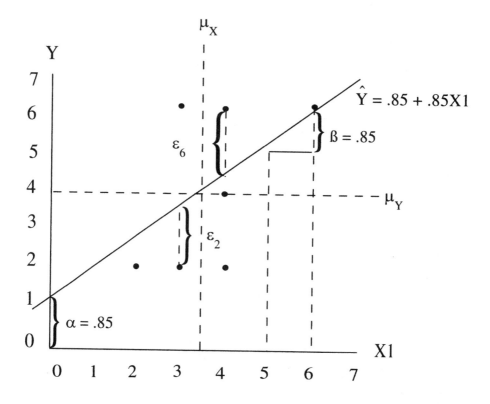

Regression Formulas

One formula for B_{YX} is obtained by transforming the standardized correlation coefficient into a slope coefficient with the original score variability of both Y and X.

$$B_{YX} = \frac{\rho_{YX} * \sigma_Y}{\sigma_X} \qquad (10.6)$$

where B_{YX} = simple regression coefficient for X

A formula for α is:

$$\alpha = \mu_Y - \mu_X * B_{YX} \qquad (10.7)$$

where α = regression intercept

NOMINAL INDEPENDENT VARIABLES

So far correlation and regression have been described in situations in which the dependent and independent variables represent at least nearly interval variables. However, the procedures are equally appropriate when the independent variable represents a nominal variable. Values of nominal variables mean that cases with identical values are similar, cases with different values are dissimilar; no order is implied by the numbers.

The case in which a nominal independent variable has just two values (a dichotomy) is considered here. (Situations in which an independent variable has three or more nominal categories, or in which there are two or more nominal variables, are considered in the next chapter.) Many variables are dichotomous or can be made dichotomous. Examples include responses to a test question (correct or incorrect), gender (female or male), production sector (manufacturing or other), race (majority or minority), type of educational institution (public or private), and assignment in a training intervention (trained group or control group).

RESEARCH HIGHLIGHT 10.3

Nominal Dependent Variables

PM correlation and regression are not appropriate when the dependent variable is nominal and has three or more values. Meaningful interpretation of correlation and regression coefficients is not possible unless such dependent variables have values that are ordered. There are alternative statistical techniques, such as discriminant analysis, that may be appropriate when the dependent variable has more than two nominal values.

PM correlation and regression are conditionally acceptable when the dependent variable is a nominal dichotomy. There are no problems with the use of correlation when the purpose is to describe a set of scores as emphasized in this chapter. There are some problems for both correlation and regression when used to make statistical inferences (see Part V and Chapter 19).

Regression with a dichotomous nominal Y variable can also be used to describe a set of scores. However, Y values predicted by the regression equation may be outside the dummy variable range of 0 and 1. Logit or probit regression models are more appropriate than PM regression in this situation. They predict values within the 0 and 1 range and are more suitable when statistical inferences are desired.

Although any two numbers are permissible, it is convenient to create *dummy variables* for dichotomous variables. Dummy variables are two-level nominal variables assigned values of one or zero. Thus, correct responses might be assigned 1 and incorrect responses assigned 0 for a test question.

Exhibit 10.11 shows a data matrix with an ordered Y variable and a dummy coded nominal X variable. Descriptive, correlation, and regression statistics are also shown.

Nominal coding of an independent variable does not change how the correlation and regression statistics are computed or the way they are interpreted. Thus, the correlation coefficient tells that the mean product of standard scores for Y and X is .55. The coefficient of determination ($.55^2$ =.30) means that 30 percent of the variability in Y is explained by variability in X. The intercept shows that the predicted value of Y when $X = 0$ is 4.00, and the regression coefficient signals that a unit change in X is associated with a predicted increase of 1.00 in predicted Y.

However, the intercept and regression coefficient have additional meaning, because X is dummy coded. Not only do they provide information about predicted Y values, they also provide information about average (mean) Y values. Specifically, the intercept is also equal to mean Y when $X = 0$.

$$\alpha = \mu_{Y|X=0}$$

Furthermore, the intercept plus the regression coefficient is equal to mean Y when $X = 1$.

$$\alpha + B_{YX} = \mu_{Y|X=1}$$

Exhibit 10.12 shows the plot of Y and X scores from Exhibit 10.11. The regression prediction line is also shown. This line intersects the Y axis at 4.00, $\mu_{Y|X=0}$. It increases by 1.00 as X goes from 0 to 1 (a unit change) and thus goes through a line drawn perpendicular to $X = 1$ at $Y = 5$, $\mu_{Y|X=1}$. Thus, dummy coding of independent variables provides bonus information.

SUMMARY

Correlation and regression are statistical procedures appropriate for identifying relationships between a dependent variable and one or more independent variables. This chapter describes correlation and regression methods to identify linear relations among one dependent and one independent variable (simple linear correlation and regression).

It is often useful to plot Y scores (on the vertical axis) and X scores (on the horizontal axis) before calculating correlation or regression statistics. Visual inspection can give insight to the relationship between the two variables.

A *correlation coefficient* is a statistic that provides a standardized measure of a relationship between two variables. Its permissible limits range between ± 1.00. Values near the extremes indicate a strong positive (+) or negative (-) relationship. Values close to zero indicate little relationship.

**EXHIBIT 10.11. Scores and descriptive statistics on an ordered
    Y and a two-value nominal variable**

Case	Y	X
1	6.00	1
2	4.00	1
3	5.00	0
4	4.00	0
5	3.00	0
6	5.00	1
7	4.00	0
μ	4.43	.43
σ	.90	.49
ρ_{YX}		55
α		4.00
B		1.00
$\mu_{Y|X}=0$,		4.00
$\mu_{Y|X}=1$		5.00

The ***coefficient of determination*** is the square of the correlation coefficient. It is defined as the proportion of variance in the dependent variable
that is explained by variation in the independent variable. It can range from
0.00, X scores provide no linear information about Y scores, to 1.00, X scores
provide exact information about Y scores.

  Regression statistics describe a relationship between Y and X in the original scores of the variables. Scores on Y are described as a linear function of
scores in the regression prediction model. That model has an ***intercept,*** the
predicted value of Y when $X = 0.0$; it also has a ***regression coefficient,*** the
predicted change in Y for a unit change in X.

RESEARCH HIGHLIGHT 10.4

Correlation/Regression and Conceptual Relationships

Researchers hope that the strength of the relationship between X and Y constructs is the major influence on the size of the correlation and regression coefficients obtained from research studies. Further, this does not always imply that the coefficients should be large. The degree of relationship should conform to the conceptual model, large or modest, if the model is valid.

However, correlation or regression coefficients obtained may misrepresent the underlying conceptual relationships for several reasons. Unreliability and other sources of construct invalidity can seriously distort relationships observed from those that apply at a conceptual level (see Chapter 17). The observed relationship may also be distorted if the research design has inadequate controls for other independent variables that influence the dependent variable (see Chapters 5 and 19). Inappropriate sampling, in which variability among the participants studied does not reflect variability among the participants one wants to generalize to, is yet another problem for observed relationships (see Part V).

In short, correlation, regression, and any other statistics of relationships can provide good estimates of conceptual relationships only when other characteristics of research design and measurement are also good. Statistics become increasingly necessary to identify relationships between scores on variables as the number of cases become large. However, statistics alone are never sufficient to establish relationships between constructs.

Correlation and regression statistics are calculated using the *Least Squares Criterion.* This criterion results in statistics that provide the best overall linear fit between Y and X. It does so by minimizing the sum of the squared deviations between predicted and actual Y values.

EXHIBIT 10.12. Scatter plot Y and dummy coded X

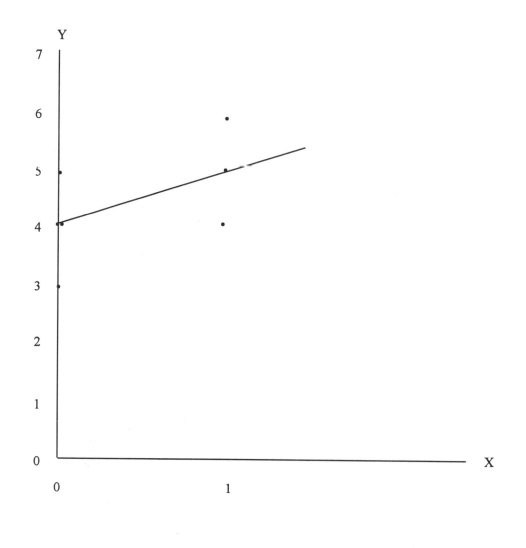

Simple correlation and regression are also appropriate when the independent variable represents a nominal variable with two values. **Dummy variables** are a convenient way to create such variables; one value is assigned 0, the other, 1. When dummy coded, the correlation and regression statistics have the same definitions as when X represents an ordered variable. However, in addition, the intercept and regression coefficient can be used to obtain information about mean Y values for the two groups of cases being studied.

FOR REVIEW

Terms to Know

Correlation coefficient. A statistic that describes the degree of linear relationship between two variables in a standardized form ranging from ± 1.00.

Phi coefficient. A correlation coefficient, sometimes calculated when both variables are dichotomous.

Point-biserial correlation coefficient. A correlation coefficient, sometimes calculated when one variable is ordered and one has two values.

Rho coefficient. A correlation coefficient, sometimes calculated when the variables represent only rank order.

Covariance. A statistic that provides information about how values of two variables go together. It is the average cross-product of the deviations of the values of each variable about its respective mean.

Standard score. A score that results by subtracting its distribution mean and dividing the result by the distribution standard deviation.

Standard score distribution. A distribution of scores on a variable that have been transformed to a mean = 0.0 and standard deviation = 1.0.

Coefficient of determination. The square of the correlation coefficient. A statistic that reports the proportion of linear variance in one variable that is explained or associated with variance in another variable.

Regression. Describes relationships between a dependent and independent variable in the scale values of the variables.

Regression intercept. A statistic that reports the predicted value of the dependent variable when the independent variable is equal to 0.0.

Regression coefficient. A statistic that reports the predicted change in the value of the dependent variable for a unit change (change of 1.0) in the independent variable.

Least Squares Criterion. A rule that establishes the regression line so that the sum of the squared deviations between the actual dependent variable values and the values predicted are minimized.

Dummy variable. A nominal variable with two values coded 0 and 1.

Formulas to Use

Covariance

$$CoVar_{YX} = \frac{\Sigma(Y_i - \mu_Y)*(X_i - \mu_X)}{N}$$

(10.1)

where μ_Y and μ_X are the means of Y and X, respectively

N = Number of cases

Standard score

$$Z_{Xi} = \frac{(x_i - \mu_x)}{\sigma_x}$$

(10.3)

where σ_X is the standard deviation of X

Correlation coefficient

$$\rho_{YX} = \frac{CoVar_{YX}}{\sigma_Y * \sigma_X}$$

(10.2a)

where σ_Y is the standard deviation of Y

$$\rho_{YX} = \frac{\Sigma(z_{Yi} * z_{Xi})}{N}$$

(10.2b)

Coefficient of determination

$$\rho^2_{YX} = \left[\frac{\Sigma(z_{Yi} * z_{Xi})}{N}\right]^2$$

(10.4)

Regression prediction model

$$\hat{Y} = \alpha + B_{YX}X$$

(10.5)

where $\hat{Y}$ is the predicted value of Y

α is the intercept, $\hat{Y}$ when $X = 0.0$

B_{YX} is the regression coefficient, the predicted change in Y for a unit change in X

Regression coefficient

$$B_{YX} = \frac{\rho_{YX} * \sigma_Y}{\sigma_X}$$ (10.6)

Regression intercept

$$\alpha = \mu_Y - \mu_X * B_{YX}$$ (10.7)

Questions for Review

1. Contrast a standard normal distribution (Chapter 9) with a standard score distribution (Chapter 10). How are they similar? How do they differ?

2. Use Formula 10.2a to calculate a correlation coefficient between Y and $X2$. Now, use Formula 10.2b to calculate the same coefficient. Your answers should be the same.

3. Assume that the variable sex (female or male) is dummy coded, that females earn less than males, and that the correlation between sex and income is positive. How has sex been coded?

4. State verbally how the slope of the regression line, B_{YX}, can be increased when ρ_{YX} is held constant.

5. Assume the regression coefficient is 1.0 and the correlation coefficient is .25 when years of experience is regressed on age in years. What can you say about the regression coefficient if age was coded in months instead of years? What about the correlation coefficient?

6. Use Formulas 10.6 and 10.7 to calculate the estimated regression prediction model (Formula 10.5) with Y as the dependent variable and $X2$ as the independent variable. Repeat, only this time treat $X2$ as the dependent variable and Y as the independent variable. Why does it make a difference which is treated as the dependent variable in regression?

7. Other things equal, what happens to the regression intercept, α, when there is an increase in μ_Y? What happens to the intercept, other things equal, if there is an increase in the regression coefficient, B_{YX}?

8. In the matrix below, Y is dependent and X is a dummy coded independent variable. From your knowledge of the bonus information provided by regression in this situation, what is μ_Y for the group coded zero? What is the intercept? What is the regression coefficient?

Y	X
12	0
14	0
13	1
09	1
11	1

Issue to Discuss

1. Simple linear correlation and regression both address relationships between two variables. If you can use one, you can use the other. What are conditions that would lead you to recommend using correlation rather than regression? Regression rather than correlation?

11

Analysis Applications:
Multiple Correlation and Regression

Chapter Outline

- *Graphical Representation*
- *Multiple Correlation*
    - *Multiple Coefficient of Determination*
    - *Examples of the Multiple Coefficient of Determination*
- *Multiple Regression*
    - *Intercept and Partial Regression Coefficients*
    - *Partial Beta Coefficients*
    - *Examples of Multiple Regression*
- *More Than Two Independent Variables*
- *Nominal Independent Variables*
    - *One Nominal Variable With More Than Two Values*
    - *Other Independent Variables*
- *Summary*
- *For Review*
- *Appendix 11A: Contributions of Single Independent Variables in Multiple Correlation*
- *Appendix 11B: Another Way to Think About Partial Coefficients*
- *Part IV: Suggested Readings*

Chapter 10 characterized simple correlation and regression as "good stuff," because it addresses relationships between variables. In that spirit, this chapter addresses "really good stuff." "Really good" because researchers believe that variation in a dependent variable usually depends on more than one independent variable. Multiple correlation and regression are designed to address just such research issues.

Both are straightforward extensions of simple correlation and regression. This chapter focuses on linear (straight line) relationships between a dependent variable, Y, and two or more independent variables, $X1, X2, \ldots, Xk$. Most of the chapter emphasizes cases in which there are just two independent variables; multiple correlation and regression are easiest to understand when only two independent variables are involved. Fortunately, the logic extends intuitively to more than two independent variables.

The chapter first introduces multiple correlation and regression graphically for two ordered independent variables. More detail is then provided on the two independent variable multiple correlation case. Emphasis is placed on how multiple correlation can be thought of in variance explained terms. This is followed by a description of multiple regression with two independent variables.

The chapter then discusses issues in extending multiple correlation and regression to situations in which there are more than two independent variables. Generalization of multiple correlation and regression to independent variables that are measured at a nominal level is also described.

Two appendixes follow the chapter. The first provides information on ways contributions of individual independent variables can be assessed in a multiple correlation framework. The second describes an alternative way to interpret coefficients in multiple correlation and regression.

GRAPHICAL REPRESENTATION

Data introduced in the last chapter (Exhibit 10.2) are repeated at the top of Exhibit 11.1. The bottom of the Exhibit reports means, standard deviations, and simple correlation coefficients between these variables. Only these latter statistics are needed to calculate multiple correlation and regression output.

A relationship between a dependent and two independent variables can be graphed as illustrated in Exhibit 11.2. It shows a scatter plot of the dependent variable, Y, and two independent variables, $X1$ and $X2$ from Exhibit 11.1. A linear relationship among these three variables is expressed by a plane that originates at Y. Exhibit 11.2 shows that the plane increases as $X1$ increases and decreases as $X2$ increases.

EXHIBIT 11.1. Scores and statistics of six ordered variables

Case	Y	X1	X2	X3	X4	X5
1	2	2	6	4	1	1
2	2	3	3	2	7	1
3	2	4	5	1	4	1
4	4	4	5	7	4	4
5	6	3	4	6	1	7
6	6	4	2	4	4	7
7	6	6	3	4	7	7

| | μ | σ | _Simple Correlation Coefficients_ | | | | | |
			Y	X1	X2	X3	X4	X5
Y	4.00	1.85	1.00					
X1	3.71	1.16	.53	1.00				
X2	4.00	1.31	−.59	−.47	1.00			
X3	4.00	1.93	.56	.00	.11	1.00		
X4	4.00	2.27	.00	.65	−.58	−.39	1.00	
X5	4.00	2.78	1.00	.53	−.59	.56	.00	1.00

The general problem for multiple correlation and regression is to establish a plane to best "fit" Y scores from the two X variable scores. The Least Squares Criterion is used for this purpose just as in simple correlation and regression. Multiple correlation and regression statistics are established so that the sum of the squared deviations of actual Y minus Y values predicted by the plane is minimized, $\Sigma(y_i - \hat{Y}_i)^2 = minimum$. Furthermore, just as in the simple case, multiple correlation provides statistics that describe the relationship in standardized form; multiple regression describes the relationship in numerical units of the dependent variable, Y.

EXHIBIT 11.2. Scatter plot of Y, X1, and X2

MULTIPLE CORRELATION

A multiple correlation coefficient, P, describes the degree of linear relationship between one ordered dependent variable and two or more independent variables in standardized form. It ranges from 0.0, indicating no linear relationship, to 1.0, indicating a perfect linear relationship. P is always as large or larger than the absolute value of the largest simple correlation between the dependent and any independent variable. It is also always expressed in positive terms, even though one or more simple correlation coefficients with Y may be negative.

Multiple Coefficient of Determination

The square of P, the ***multiple coefficient of determination,*** P^2, represents the proportion of variance in Y that is jointly accounted for by the independent variables. The multiple coefficient of determination also ranges from 0.0 (no linear variance in Y is explained by the X variables) to 1.0 (all linear variance in Y is explained jointly by the X variables).

Researchers usually report and discuss P^2 rather than P; the explanation here focuses on P^2, which is usually called P *square*. Where there are two independent variables, one formula for P^2 is:

$$P^2{}_{Y \cdot X1X2} = \frac{\rho^2{}_{YX1} + \rho^2{}_{YX2} - 2 * \rho_{YX1} * \rho_{YX2} * \rho_{X1X2}}{1 - \rho^2{}_{X1X2}} \qquad (11.1)$$

where $P^2{}_{Y \cdot X1X2}$ = multiple coefficient of determination of Y and two independent variables, $X1$ and $X2$

$\rho^2{}_{YX1}$ = simple coefficient of determination between Y and $X1$ (and likewise for the other variables)

ρ_{YX1} = simple correlation coefficient between Y and $X1$ (and likewise for the other variables)

The simple coefficients of determination between Y and each X contribute to $P^2{}_{Y \cdot X1X2}$ through the first two terms in the numerator. Other things equal, the higher the simple coefficients of determination between each X and Y, the higher $P^2{}_{Y \cdot X1X2}$.

However, if $X1$ and $X2$ are also correlated, the second part of the numerator generally reduces $P^2{}_{Y \cdot X1X2}$.[1] The larger the correlation coefficient between the independent variables, the smaller $P^2{}_{Y \cdot X1X2}$, other things equal.

A simple correlation between independent variables is called ***multicollinearity.*** Some of the variance that each independent variable explains in Y is redundant when there is multicollinearity. The redundant portion must be removed so that the amount of Y variance explained jointly by

---

[1]It is possible that the signs of the coefficients can lead the second part of the numerator to increase $P^2{}_{Y \cdot X1X2}$. For example, this would occur if ρ_{YX1} and $\rho_{YX2} > 0.0$ and $\rho_{X1X2} < 0.0$. This is an unlikely empirical outcome.

*X*1 and *X*2 is not overstated. (See Appendix 11A for a description of the contribution of single independent variables to the explanation of *Y* variance and Chapter 18, for more detail on multicollinearity.)

Examples of the Multiple Coefficient of Determination

Formula 11.1 can be used to calculate $P^2_{Y \cdot X_i X_j}$ between *Y* and any two independent variables. For example, use *X*1 and *X*2 from Exhibit 11.1:

$$P^2_{Y \cdot X1 X2} - (.53^2 \; | \; -.59^2 - 2 \; * \; .53 \; * \; -.59 \; * \; -.47) \, / \, (1 - -.47^2) = .43$$

Forty-three percent of the variance in *Y* is explained jointly by *X*1 and *X*2. This is less than the sum of the simple coefficients of determination, $(.53^2 + -.59^2 = .63)$, because some of the *Y* variance that *X*1 and *X*2 explain separately is redundant.

Exhibit 11.3 illustrates the outcome of Formula 11.2 using circles to show variance in the variables as introduced in the last chapter. Each circle represents 100 percent of the variability in the scores of its variable.

EXHIBIT 11.3. Variance in *Y* explained by *X*1 and *X*2

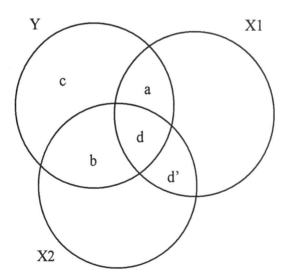

The area designated by a shows the proportion of Y variance explained by $X1$ that is not redundant with $X2$; the area b shows the analogous proportion of Y for $X2$. The area d shows the proportion of Y explained by both $X1$ and $X2$. (The square of the multicollinearity between $X1$ and $X2$ is shown by $d + d'$.) $P^2_{Y \cdot X1X2}$ is shown in Exhibit 11.3 as:

$$(a + b + d) / (a + b + c + d), \text{ or } (1 - c) / (a + b + c + d).$$

Another example from Exhibit 11.1 uses $X1$ and $X3$,

$$P^2_{Y \cdot X1X3} = (.53^2 + .56^2 - 2 * .53 * .56 * .00) / (1 - .00^2) = .59$$

Fifty-nine percent of the variance in Y is explained jointly by $X1$ and $X3$. This is greater than the Y variance explained by $X1$ and $X2$ even though the simple correlation coefficient of Y and $X2$ is greater than of Y and $X3$. Why is this so?

The explanation can be found in multicollinearity. $X1$ and $X2$ are correlated (multicollinear), $X1$ and $X3$ are not. Exhibit 11.4 shows the linear variance in Y explained by $X1$ and $X3$; there is no redundant explanation:

$$P^2_{Y \cdot X1X3} = (a + b) / (a + b + c), \text{ or } (1 - c) / (a + b + c)$$

In field and survey research, independent variables are usually correlated, not only with Y, but with each other. Thus, typically, $P^2_{Y \cdot XiXj} < \rho^2_{YXi} + \rho^2_{YXj}$ because of multicollinearity. However, in experiments and some quasi-experiments, researchers may assign cases to levels of independent variables so that there is no multicollinearity. In such cases, Formula 11.1 shows that $P^2_{Y \cdot XiXj}$ simplifies to $\rho^2_{YXi} + \rho^2_{YXj}$.

EXHIBIT 11.4. Variance in Y explained by $X1$ and $X3$

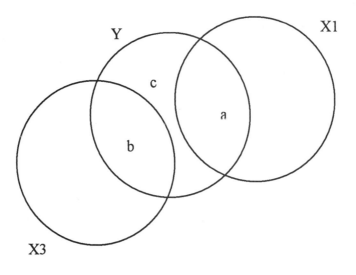

MULTIPLE REGRESSION

Multiple regression describes relationships between a dependent and two or more independent variables in units of the dependent variable. It does so by expressing Y scores as a linear function of two or more X scores.

Where there are two independent variables, $X1$ and $X2$, the dependent variable scores can be determined by:

$$Y_i = \alpha + B_{YX1 \cdot X2} * X1_i + B_{YX2 \cdot X1} * X2_i + \varepsilon_i$$

where α = regression intercept, where the regression plane intersects the vertical line describing Y when $X1 = X2 = 0.0$

$B_{YX1 \cdot X2}$ = partial regression coefficient, the change in Y for a unit change in $X1$ controlling for $X2$, and analogously for $B_{YX2 \cdot X1}$

ε_i = error, the deviation between the Y score predicted by the regression plane and the actual Y value for the ith case

---

RESEARCH HIGHLIGHT 11.1

Suppressor Variables

Occasionally a researcher finds a suppressor variable as defined in Chapter 5; it is a collinear independent variable that has only a small (often negative) or no relationship with the dependent variable. $X4$ is a suppressor variable in Exhibit 11.1. Use data from Table 11.1 to show:

$$P^2_{Y \cdot X1X4} = (.53^2 + .00^2 - 2 * .53 * .00 * .65) / (1 - .65^2) = .48.$$

Only Y variance explained by $X1$ contributes to the numerator, $.53^2 = .28$. The latter part of the numerator drops out because $\rho_{YX4} = 0.00$. However, the denominator is less than 1.0 by virtue of the multicollinearity. Consequently, $P^2_{Y \cdot X1X4} = .48 > .28$. The suppressor variable takes away irrelevant variance from an independent variable ($X1$ in this case) and thus increases the proportion of the remaining $X1$ variance that explains Y. In the language of Chapter 5, $X4$ serves as a noise variable, not with respect to Y, but with $X1$.

The multiple regression prediction model for these two independent variables is:

$$\hat{Y}_{X1X2} = \alpha + B_{YX1 \cdot X2} * X1 + B_{YX2 \cdot X1} * X2 \qquad (11.2)$$

where $\hat{Y}_{X1X2}$ = predicted value of Y given $X1$ and $X2$

As with the prediction model for simple regression (Formula 10.5), Formula 11.2 has no subscripts, because it applies to all scores obtained jointly on Y, $X1$ and $X2$. It has no error term, though it will be in error unless $P^2_{Y \cdot X1X2} = 1.0$. The dependent variable, Y_{X1X2}, again includes a superscript, $\hat{Y}$, to denote it is predicted, not actual. The **multiple regression intercept,** α, is now the predicted value of Y when both $X1$ and $X2 = 0.0$. A **partial regres-**

sion coefficient, $B_{YX1 \cdot X2}$ $(B_{YX2 \cdot X1})$ refers to the predicted change in Y for a unit change in $X1$ $(X2)$, holding $X2$ $(X1)$ constant. (See Appendix 11B for another interpretation of partial regression coefficients.)

Intercept and Partial Regression Coefficients

Formulas for partial regression coefficients for the two independent variable cases are:

$$B_{YX1 \cdot X2} = \frac{\sigma_Y}{\sigma_{X1}} * \frac{\rho_{YX1} - \rho_{YX2} * \rho_{X1X2}}{1 - \rho^2_{X1X2}} \qquad (11.3a)$$

$$B_{YX2 \cdot X1} = \frac{\sigma_Y}{\sigma_{X2}} * \frac{\rho_{YX2} - \rho_{YX1} * \rho_{X1X2}}{1 - \rho^2_{X1X2}} \qquad (11.3b)$$

where $B_{YX1 \cdot X2}$ and $B_{YX2 \cdot X1}$ = the partial regression coefficient of $X1$ and $X2$, respectively

σ_Y and σ_{Xj} = standard deviation of Y and Xj, respectively

A formula for the intercept when there are two independent variables is:

$$\alpha = \mu_Y - B_{YX1 \cdot X2} * \mu_{X1} - B_{YX2 \cdot X1} * \mu_{X2} \qquad (11.4)$$

where α = intercept

μ_Y and μ_{Xj} = mean of Y and Xj, respectively

Partial Beta Coefficients

$B_{YX1 \cdot X2}$ and $B_{YX2 \cdot X1}$ are unstandardized partial regression coefficients because they are expressed in the original units of the variables. They are attractive for just this reason.

However, researchers sometimes transform regression coefficients to a standardized form. **Beta coefficients** are regression coefficients standardized so that the means of Y and Xj = 0.0 and standard deviations = 1.0.

In simple regression, beta coefficients are identical to correlation coefficients. This is not true of partial beta coefficients in multiple regression if there is multicollinearity among the independent variables. Formulas for partial beta coefficients in the two independent variable case are:

$$Beta_{YX1 \cdot X2} = B_{YX1 \cdot X2} * \frac{\sigma_{X1}}{\sigma_Y} \qquad (11.5a)$$

$$Beta_{YX2 \cdot X1} = B_{YX2 \cdot X1} * \frac{\sigma_{X2}}{\sigma_Y} \qquad (11.5b)$$

where $Beta_{YX1 \cdot X2}$ and $Beta_{YX2 \cdot X1}$ = partial beta coefficients of $X1$ and $X2$, respectively

Partial beta coefficients are an attractive way to express multiple regression results when researchers are interested in assessing the relative contribution of different independent variables to the explanation of the dependent variable. Because they are standardized, beta coefficients can be compared directly to see which has the largest impact on Y, holding other independent variables constant.

Examples of Multiple Regression

From Exhibit 11.1, the partial regression coefficients when Y is regressed on $X1$ and $X2$ are (Formulas 11.3a and 11.3b):

$$B_{YX1 \cdot X2} = (1.85 / 1.16) * [(.53 - -.59 * -.47) / (1 - .22)] = .52$$

$$B_{YX2 \cdot X1} = (1.85 / 1.31) * [(-.59 - .53 * -.47) / (1 - .22)] = -.62$$

Y is predicted to increase .52 for a unit change in $X1$ when $X2$ is held constant; it is predicted to decrease .62 for a unit change in $X2$ when $X1$ is held constant.

The multiple regression intercept in this case is (Formula 11.4):

$$\alpha = 4.00 - (.52 * 3.71) - (-.62 * 4.00) = 4.55$$

The predicted Y value when $X1 = X2 = 0.0$ is 4.55.

RESEARCH HIGHLIGHT 11.2

Simple and Partial Regression Coefficients

Y regressed on $X1$ to $X3$ in three separate simple equations, Formula 10.6 ($B_{YX} = \rho_{YX} * \sigma_Y / \sigma_X$) yields simple regression coefficients, $B_{YX1} = .85$, $B_{YX2} = -.83$, and $B_{YX3} = .54$. Compare these with the partial regression coefficients in the two example prediction models.

When Y is regressed on $X1$ and $X2$, the partial regression coefficients differ from their respective simple regression coefficients. This happens because of multicollinearity. $X1$ and $X2$ are correlated; the coefficient resulting from a simple regression of Y on either X alone is biased (see Chapter 5). However, if there is no correlation between the independent variables, as is true of $X1$ and $X3$, the partial and simple regression coefficients are identical.

Putting these together, the regression prediction model (Formula 11.2) for $X1$ and $X2$ is:

$$\hat{Y}_{X1X2} = 4.55 + .52 * X1 - .62 * X2$$

The standardized partial (beta) coefficients are (Formulas 11.5a and 11.5b):

$$Beta_{YX1 \cdot X2} = .52 * (1.16 / 1.85) = .33$$

$$Beta_{YX2 \cdot X1} = -.62 * (1.31 / 1.85) = -.44$$

Use $X1$ and $X3$ as another example:

$$B_{YX1 \cdot X3} = (1.85 / 1.16) * [(.53 - .56 * .00) / (1 - .00)] = .85$$

$$B_{YX3 \cdot X1} = (1.85 / 1.93) * [(.56 - .53 * .00) / (1 - .00)] = .54$$

$$\alpha = 4.00 - (.85 * 3.71) - (.54 * 4.00) = -1.31$$

and

$$\hat{Y}_{X1X3} = -1.31 + .85 * X1 + .54 * X3$$

In this example the partial beta coefficients are:

$$\text{Beta}_{YX1 \cdot X3} = .85 * (1.16 / 1.85) = .53$$

$$\text{Beta}_{YX3 \cdot X1} = .54 * (1.93 / 1.85) = .56$$

Compare the relative size of the unstandardized and standardized partial regression coefficients of $X1$ and $X3$. The results using the standardized formulas 11.5a and 11.5b show $X3$ contributes more to the explanation of Y than $X1$. The difference between the unstandardized and standardized results is found in the standard deviations of the independent variables. The standard deviation of $X3$ is greater than $X1$. When these are equalized by standardization, $X3$ contributes relatively more than $X1$ to the explanation of Y.

MORE THAN TWO INDEPENDENT VARIABLES

Multiple correlation and regression can be performed with any number of independent variables.[2] Although the formulas become more complex, the meaning of the statistics extends intuitively from the two independent variable case. An appeal to intuition is made with an example using Y and $X1$ to $X3$ from Exhibit 11.1.

Multiple correlation and regression statistics are shown in Exhibit 11.5.[3] The coefficient of determination, $P^2_{Y \cdot X1X2X3} = .81$, indicates the proportion of Y variance that is jointly explained by $X1$, $X2$, and $X3$. Exhibit 11.6 shows this proportion as $(a + b + c + d_1 + d_2) / (a + b + c + d_1 + d_2 + e)$ or $(1 - e) / (a + b + c + d_1 + d_2 + e)$.

EXHIBIT 11.5. Multiple correlation and regression output with three independent variables

Variable	$B_{YXi \cdot XjXk}$	$Beta_{YXi \cdot XjXk}$
X1	.45	.28
X2	−.74	−.53
X3	.59	.62
α	2.90	
$P^2_{Y \cdot X1X2X3}$	.81	

---

[2]The number of cases must exceed the number of variables in the model.

[3]SPSS for Windows™, a statistical software package, was used to calculate all multiple correlation and regression statistics involving three or more independent variables here and elsewhere in the book.

EXHIBIT 11.6. Variance in Y explained by $X1$, $X2$, and $X3$

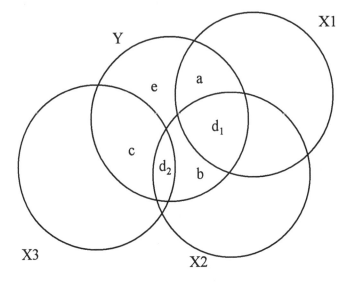

Area d_1 represents Y variance redundantly explained by $X1$ and $X2$; d_2 represents Y variance redundantly explained by $X2$ and $X3$. ($X1$ and $X3$ are not collinear, so their explanations of Y variance do not overlap.) The multicollinearity implied by those two areas signals that $P^2_{Y \cdot X1X2X3}$ is smaller than the sum of the simple coefficients of determination ($.53^2 + -.59^2 + .56^2 = .94$).

Exhibit 11.5 also shows regression output for the three independent variables. The intercept, $\alpha = 2.90$, is the value of Y predicted when $X1$, $X2$, and $X3 = 0.0$. A partial regression coefficient represents the predicted change in Y for a unit change in one X, holding the other two X variables constant. For example, Y is predicted to change .45 for a unit change in $X1$ if $X2$ and $X3$ do not change. Standardized partial (beta) coefficients are also shown.

NOMINAL INDEPENDENT VARIABLES

Chapter 10 showed how a nominal independent variable with two values can be analyzed using simple correlation and regression. This is done by creating a dummy variable with values 0 or 1. This valuable procedure can be generalized several ways in multiple correlation and regression.

One Nominal Variable With More Than Two Values

When a nominal independent variable has more than two values, its information can be captured for multiple correlation and regression by creating more than one dummy variable. For example, Exhibit 11.7 shows the dependent variable, Y, used to illustrate simple correlation and regression. However, this time the independent variable has three values: A, B, and C. For example, these might represent three levels of marital status: A = never married, B = currently married, and C = formerly but not currently married.

Two dummy variables are needed to capture the information of a three-value nominal variable as shown by $X1$ and $X2$. (In general, k values of a nominal variable are captured by $k-1$ dummy variables. Thus, a two-value nominal variable is captured by one dummy variable, $k-1=1$.) $X1$ contrasts the never married group (A) with the other two groups (B and C); $X2$ contrasts the currently married group (B) with the other two. Group C (formerly but not currently married) is assigned zeros in both $X1$ and $X2$. The value assigned zeros to all dummy variables is called the ***omitted category*** in multiple regression and correlation.

Multiple correlation and regression can be performed on these two independent variables in the usual way using the calculating procedures already discussed. Thus, from Formula 11.1, the simple correlation coefficients and their squares can be used to obtain $P^2_{Y \cdot X1X2} = .30$. Thirty percent of Y variance is accounted for by the two dummy variables; the three categories of marital status account for 30 percent of the variance in Y.

Regression output can be calculated with Formulas 11.2 to 11.4. Statistical values from these formulas are shown at the bottom of Exhibit 11.7. The predicted value of Y when $X1$ and $X2 = 0.00$ is $\alpha = 4.00$. The predicted change in Y for a unit change in $X1$ is, $B_{YX1 \cdot X2} = 1.00$ holding $X2$ constant; the predicted change in Y for a unit change in $X2$ is, $B_{YX2 \cdot X1} = 0.00$ holding $X1$ constant. These are the standard interpretations of regression statistics.

EXHIBIT 11.7. Scores and descriptive statistics on an ordered Y and a three-value nominal variable

Case	Y	X	$X1$	$X2$	$X'1$	$X'2$
1	6.00	A	1	0	0	0
2	4.00	A	1	0	0	0
3	5.00	A	1	0	0	0
4	4.00	B	0	1	1	0
5	3.00	C	0	0	0	1
6	5.00	C	0	0	0	1
7	4.00	B	0	1	1	0

			Simple Correlation Coefficients		
	μ	σ	Y	$X1$	$X2$
Y	4.43	.90	1.00		
$X1$	.43	.49	.55	1.00	
$X2$	.29	.45	−.30	−.55	1.00

Multiple Correlation/Regression Output

$P^2_{Y \cdot X1X2} = .30$

$\alpha = 4.00$

$B_{YX1 \cdot X2} = 1.00$

$B_{YX2 \cdot X1} = 0.00$

Note: A = never married, B = currently married, C = formerly, but not currently married.

However, because the two dummy variables are mutually exclusive and exhaustive, bonus information of the sort described in Chapter 10 is also provided. Specifically, the intercept, $\alpha = 4.00$, is also the mean Y value for the omitted Group C (formerly but not currently married). Mean Y for Group A (never married) is given by the sum of $\alpha + B_{YX1 \cdot X2}$, $4.00 + 1.00 = 5.00$; mean Y for Group B (currently married) is given by the sum of $\alpha + B_{YX2 \cdot X1}$, $4.00 + 0.00 = 4.00$.

The coding of the nominal variable is arbitrary, any value can serve for the omitted category. For example, $X'1$ and $X'2$ in Exhibit 11.7 show an alternative way to capture information about marital status with two dummy variables. In this case, Group A constitutes the omitted category. Group B is assigned ones in $X'1$ and Group C is assigned ones in $X'2$.

Which value one chooses for the omitted category depends on the group comparisons of greatest interest. The coding of $X1$ and $X2$ provides a contrast between the mean of Y for Group C (formerly married) with the Y means of Groups A ($B_{YX1 \cdot X2}$) and B ($B_{YX2 \cdot X1}$). Alternatively, the coding of $X'1$ and $X'2$ provides a contrast between the mean of Y for Group A (never married) and the Y means of Groups B ($B_{YX'1 \cdot X'2}$) and C ($B_{YX'2 \cdot X'1}$).[4]

Other Independent Variables

A group of dummy variables representing one nominal independent variable can be included in multiple correlation and regression along with other independent variables. These other independent variables may be ordered, nominal, or a mixture of both.

Exhibit 11.8 illustrates all possibilities. The variables, Y, $X1$, and $X2$ are repeated from Exhibit 11.7. $X3$ is an ordered variable, participants' age. Finally, $X4$ is another nominal variable, gender, dummy coded so males $= 1$, females $= 0$.

Multiple correlation and regression output from data in Exhibit 11.8 are shown in Exhibit 11.9. Results from four regression models are shown. The first repeats the model shown in Exhibit 11.7. It shows the intercept, partial regression coefficients, and multiple coefficient of determination when Y is regressed on just $X1$ and $X2$. As noted, the intercept and partial regression coefficients have the standard interpretation. They also provide bonus information about group means on Y, because $X1$ and $X2$ account for marital status in a mutually exclusive and (when combined in a multiple regression model) exhaustive fashion.

The intercept and partial regression coefficients have only the standard meaning once other independent variables are included with the two variables defining marital status. For example, Model 2 shows results of Y regressed on $X1$ through $X3$ (the ordered independent variable, age). The

---

[4]Contrasts between the mean Y value of the currently married and the other two groups could be obtained by making B the omitted category.

EXHIBIT 11.8. Scores and statistics on an ordered Y and several types of independent variables

Case	Y	X1	X2	X3	X4
1	6.00	1	0	32	0
2	4.00	1	0	28	1
3	5.00	1	0	40	1
4	4.00	0	1	43	0
5	3.00	0	0	40	0
6	5.00	0	0	51	1
7	4.00	0	1	46	1

Simple Correlation Coefficients

	μ	σ	Y	X1	X2	X3	X4
Y	4.43	.90	1.00				
X1	.43	.49	.55	1.00			
X2	.29	.45	−.30	−.55	1.00		
X3	40.00	7.31	−.11	−.79	.39	1.00	
X4	.57	.49	.09	.17	−.09	.20	1.00

Note: $X1 = 1$ if never married; $X2 = 1$ if currently married; $X4 = 1$ if male.

coefficient for $X1$, 2.31, represents the predicted change in Y for a unit change in $X1$ holding $X2$ and $X3$ constant. It no longer necessarily or typically reflects the mean Y value for the group coded 1 on $X1$ (never married), because $X3$ is also in the model. Age values and marital status values are not mutually exclusive. The intercept is now the predicted Y value for formerly married participants age 0.0, which is a nonexistent group in this data set.

The intercept and partial regression coefficients of $X1$ and $X2$ also refer only to predicted Y values if another dummy variable is added. Model 3 shows results when Y is regressed on $X1$, $X2$, and $X4$. Again, the intercept and coefficients cannot be interpreted in terms of mean Y values for marital status groups, because they are not mutually exclusive with gender. The intercept is now the predicted Y value for formerly married females.

Finally, Exhibit 11.9 also shows the model when all four independent variables are entered in Model 4. In each instance, partial regression coefficients represent predicted Y values when (now) three other independent variables are held constant. The intercept is the predicted Y value for formerly married females age 0.0.

EXHIBIT 11.9. Multiple correlation and regression output from Exhibit 11.8

Multiple Regression Models

Variable	(1)	(2)	(3)	(4)
	(Partial Regression Coefficients)			
X1	1.00	2.31	1.00	2.99
X2	.00	.11	.00	.15
X3		.11		.15
X4			.00	−.76
α	4.00	−.89	4.00	−2.58
$P^2Y^{\cdot}$	.30	.58	.30	.70

SUMMARY

Multiple correlation and *regression* generalize simple correlation and regression to cases in which there are an ordered dependent variable and two or more independent variables. The present chapter describes linear multiple correlation and regression and emphasizes situations in which there are just two independent variables.

A *multiple correlation coefficient* describes the degree of linear relationship between one dependent variable and two or more independent variables in a standardized form ranging from 0.0 to 1.0. Its square, the *multiple coefficient of determination,* represents the proportion of dependent variable variance that is jointly accounted for by the independent variables. It ranges from 1.0 (all the dependent variable variance is explained by the independent variables), to 0.0 (no variance is explained by the independent variables).

A *multiple regression* equation describes relationships between a dependent and two or more independent variables in units of the dependent variable. The *multiple regression intercept* of this equation is the predicted value of the dependent variable when all independent variables have a value of zero. A *partial regression coefficient* refers to the predicted change in the dependent variable for a unit change in the independent variable, holding other independent variables constant. A *beta coefficient* is a standardized regression coefficient.

Multicollinearity is represented by nonzero correlation coefficients among independent variables in a multiple correlation or regression model. Interpretation of multiple correlation and regression output becomes more complex when there is multicollinearity.

As with simple correlation and regression, multiple correlation and regression can be performed on independent variables that are measured at a nominal level. When a nominal variable has more than two values, a set of dummy variables can be created for use in multiple correlation and regression; $k - 1$ dummy variables are needed to account for k values of a nominal variable. The nominal value that is scored zero for all of the dummy variables is called the *omitted category.* Mean values of the dependent variables can be obtained from regression coefficients when only the dummy variables representing one nominal variable are included in a multiple regression model. Multiple correlation and regression statistics have standard interpretations when a nominal variable is dummy coded and included with other independent variables.

FOR REVIEW

Terms to Know

Multiple Correlation Coefficient. Describes the degree of linear relationship between one ordered dependent variable and two or more independent variables. It describes the relationship in standardized form and ranges from 0.0 to 1.0.

Multiple coefficient of determination. Describes the proportion of linear variance in one ordered dependent variable that is accounted for jointly by two or more independent variables. It ranges from 0.0 to 1.0.

Multiple regression. Describes relationships between a dependent and two or more independent variables in units of the dependent variable.

Multiple regression intercept. The predicted value of Y when all independent variables = 0.0.

Partial regression coefficient. The predicted value of Y for a unit change in one independent variable when all other independent variables in the equation are held constant.

Beta coefficient. A standardized (mean = 0.0, standard deviation = 1.0 of all variables in the model) regression coefficient. In simple regression, the beta coefficient is identical to the simple correlation coefficient.

Multicollinearity. Nonzero correlation coefficients among independent variables in a multiple correlation or regression context.

Omitted category. The value of a nominal variable assigned zeros to all dummy variables established to account for the nominal variable in multiple correlation and regression.

Squared semipartial (or *part*) *correlation coefficient.* Represents the proportion of the total variance in Y that is uniquely (nonredundantly) explained by an independent variable (see Appendix 11A).

Squared partial correlation coefficient. Represents the proportion of Y variance explained by an independent variable that is not otherwise explained (see Appendix 11A).

Formulas to Use (Text)

Multiple coefficient of determination for two independent variables

$$P^2{}_{Y \cdot X1X2} = \frac{\rho^2{}_{YX1} + \rho^2{}_{YX2} - 2 * \rho_{YX1} * \rho_{YX2} * \rho_{X1X2}}{1 - \rho^2{}_{X1X2}} \qquad (11.1)$$

where ρ^2_{YX1} = simple coefficient of determination between Y and $X1$ (and likewise for the other variables)

ρ_{YX1} = simple correlation coefficient between Y and $X1$ (and likewise for the other variables)

Multiple regression prediction model for two independent variables

$$\hat{Y}_{X1X2} = \alpha + B_{YX1 \cdot X2} * X1 + B_{YX2 \cdot X1} * X2 \qquad (11.2)$$

Partial regression coefficients for two independent variables

$$B_{YX1 \cdot X2} = \frac{\sigma_Y}{\sigma_{X1}} * \frac{\rho_{YX1} - \rho_{YX2} * \rho_{X1X2}}{1 - \rho^2_{X1X2}} \qquad (11.3a)$$

$$B_{YX2 \cdot X1} = \frac{\sigma_Y}{\sigma_{X2}} * \frac{\rho_{YX2} - \rho_{YX1} * \rho_{X1X2}}{1 - \rho^2_{X1X2}} \qquad (11.3b)$$

where σ_Y and σ_{Xi} = standard deviation of Y and Xi, respectively

Intercept when there are two independent variables

$$\alpha = \mu_Y - B_{YX1 \cdot X2} * \mu_{X1} - B_{YX2 \cdot X1} * \mu_{X2} \qquad (11.4)$$

where μ_Y and μ_{Xi} = mean of Y and Xi, respectively

Beta coefficients when there are two independent variables

$$Beta_{YX1 \cdot X2} = B_{YX1 \cdot X2} * \frac{\sigma_{X1}}{\sigma_Y} \qquad (11.5a)$$

$$Beta_{YX2 \cdot X1} = B_{YX2 \cdot X1} * \frac{\sigma_{X2}}{\sigma_Y} \qquad (11.5b)$$

Formulas to Use (Appendix A)

Squared semipartial correlation coefficients when there are two independent variables (see Appendix 11A)

$$s\rho^2_{YX1\cdot X2} = P^2_{Y\cdot X1X2} - \rho^2_{YX2} \qquad \textbf{(11A.1a)}$$

$$s\rho^2_{YX2\cdot X1} = P^2_{Y\cdot X1X2} - \rho^2_{YX1} \qquad \textbf{(11A.1b)}$$

Squared partial correlation coefficients for two independent variables (see Appendix 11A)

$$p\rho^2_{YX1\cdot X2} = \frac{P^2_{Y\cdot X1X2} - \rho^2_{YX2}}{1 - \rho^2_{YX2}} \qquad \textbf{(11A.2a)}$$

$$p\rho^2_{YX2\cdot X1} = \frac{P^2_{Y\cdot X1X2} - \rho^2_{YX1}}{1 - \rho^2_{YX1}} \qquad \textbf{(11A.2b)}$$

Questions for Review

1. Use the descriptive and simple correlation results below to answer the following questions.

			Simple Correlation Coefficients							
			Y	*X1*	*X2*	*X3*	*X4*	*X5*	*X6*	*X7*
Y	100	10	1.00							
X1	5	1	.50	1.00						
X2	10	4	.40	.40	1.00					
X3	7	2	−.30	−.20	−.10	1.00				
X4	8	3	.30	.30	.30	-.30	1.00			
X5	11	5	.20	.10	.00	−.15	.05	1.00		
X6	10	2	.50	1.00	.40	−.20	.30	.10	1.00	
X7	4	1	.00	.30	.20	−.30	.20	.20	.30	1.00

    a. How much variance in Y is explained by $X1$ and $X2$?

    b. How much variance in Y is explained by $X1$ and $X3$?

    c. Consider a regression of Y on $X1$ and $X4$. What is the intercept? What is the partial regression coefficient and partial beta coefficient for $X1$?

    d. Consider a regression of Y on $X6$ and $X4$. What is the intercept? What is the partial regression coefficient and partial beta coefficient for $X6$?

    e. Explain the similarities and differences for the coefficients, $X1$ and $X6$ in answers c and d.

    f. Calculate P^2_{YX1X7}. Explain why this result explains more variance than the simple sum of ρ^2_{YX1} and ρ^2_{YX7}.

    g. From Appendix A, what is $s\rho^2_{YX1 \mid X2}$?

    h. In words, what does your answer to Question g mean?

2. Compare and contrast a partial regression coefficient with a partial beta coefficient.

3. Explain what the Least Squares Criterion accomplishes in multiple regression.

4. From Appendix 11A, compare and contrast a squared semipartial correlation coefficient with a squared partial correlation coefficient. When would they be equal? Which one will generally be larger?

5. A nominal independent variable with three mutually exclusive and exhaustive values (A, B and C) has been recorded into two dummy variables (with C omitted). The resulting regression equation is:

$$Y = 10 + 3 * XA - 4 * XB$$

Write the regression equation (with the appropriate numbers for the intercept and partial regression coefficients) if A was made the omitted category instead of C.

6. An investigator makes three mutually exclusive dummy variables out of race (majority, minority) and gender (female, male) by creating the variables majority males = 1, else 0; majority females = 1, else 0, and minority males = 1, else 0. (Minority females serve as the omitted category). These variables serve as independent variables in a regression equation.

    a. Are the independent variables collinear?

    b. The dependent variable is income and the coefficient for majority males is positive. In words, what does that partial coefficient mean?

APPENDIX 11A:
CONTRIBUTIONS OF SINGLE INDEPENDENT
VARIABLES IN MULTIPLE CORRELATION

Multiple correlation coefficients and multiple coefficients of determination provide information about the relationship between Y and the independent variables combined. It is sometimes also of interest to know how each independent variable contributes to the relationship with Y in correlational terms.

The issue is not straightforward because of multicollinearity. There is no way to adequately partition the collinear variance among the independent variables. Thus, the two standard methods for addressing the contributions of each independent variable ignore Y variance that is explained jointly by the independent variables (e.g., d in Exhibit 11.3). Again, the focus will be on the square of the coefficients to cast the discussion in variance explained terms.

Squared Semipartial Correlation Coefficient

A *squared semipartial* (or *part*) *correlation coefficient* represents the proportion of the total variance in Y that is uniquely (nonredundantly) explained by an independent variable. In the case of $X1$ and $X2$, $s\rho^2_{YX1 \cdot X2}$ is shown by area $a/(a+b+c+d)$ in Exhibit 11.3; $s\rho^2_{YX2 \cdot X1}$ is shown by area $b/(a+b+c+d)$.

Formulas for a two independent variable case are:

$$s\rho^2_{YX1 \cdot X2} = P^2_{Y \cdot X1X2} - \rho^2_{YX2} \qquad \textbf{(11A.1a)}$$

$$s\rho^2_{YX2 \cdot X1} = P^2_{Y \cdot X1X2} - \rho^2_{YX1} \qquad \textbf{(11A.1b)}$$

where $s\rho^2_{YX1 \cdot X2}$ and $s\rho^2_{YX2 \cdot X1}$ = the squared semipartial correlation coefficient of $X1$ and $X2$, respectively

Squared Partial Correlation Coefficient

A *squared partial correlation coefficient* represents the proportion of Y variance explained by an independent variable that is not otherwise explained. In the case of $X1$ and $X2$, $p\rho^2_{YX1\cdot X2}$ is shown by area $a / (a + c)$ in Exhibit 11.3. $p\rho^2_{YX2\cdot X1}$ is shown by area $b / (b + c)$.

Formulas for a two independent variable case are:

$$p\rho^2_{YX1\cdot X2} = \frac{P^2_{Y\cdot X1X2} - \rho^2_{YX2}}{1 - \rho^2_{YX2}} \qquad \text{(11A.2a)}$$

$$p\rho^2_{YX2\cdot X1} = \frac{P^2_{Y\cdot X1X2} - \rho^2_{YX1}}{1 - \rho^2_{YX1}} \qquad \text{(11A.2b)}$$

where $p\rho^2_{YX1\cdot X2}$ and $p\rho^2_{YX2\cdot X1}$ = the squared partial correlation coefficient of $X1$ and $X2$, respectively

The numerator of 11A.2a (11A.2b) is the same as for the squared semipartial correlation coefficient, 11A.1a (11A.1b). The difference is in the denominators. In 11A.1a (11A.1b) the denominator is (implied) 1.0. Variance accounted for by $X1$ ($X2$) is the proportion of all Y variance.

In Formula 11A.2a (11A.2b) the denominator is 1.0 minus the variance accounted for uniquely and redundantly by $X2$ ($X1$). Thus, the square of the partial correlation coefficient tells how much of the otherwise unexplained Y variance is accounted for by $X1$ ($X2$). Because the denominator of 11A.2a (11A.2b) is smaller than 11A.1a (11A.1b), the squared partial correlation of $X1$ ($X2$) is larger than the squared semipartial correlation coefficient of $X1$ ($X2$).[5]

Examples

Consider again the scores on the variables in Exhibit 11.1. The squared semipartial correlation coefficients for $X1$ and $X2$ are,

$$s\rho^2_{YX1\cdot X2} = .43 - .35 = .08$$

$$s\rho^2_{YX2\cdot X1} = .43 - .28 = .15$$

---

[5]Unless $X2$ ($X1$) is uncorrelated with Y. Then $s\rho^2_{YX1} = p\rho^2_{YX1}$ ($s\rho^2_{YX2} = p\rho^2_{YX2}$).

Eight percent of Y variance is uniquely explained by $X1$; 15 percent by $X2$. The unique contributions of the two do not sum to the total variance explained in Y by $X1$ and $X2$ because of multicollinearity.

The square of the partial correlation coefficients for $X1$ and $X2$ are:

$$p\rho^2_{YX1 \cdot X2} = (.43 - .35) / (1 - .35) = .13$$

$$p\rho^2_{YX2 \cdot X1} = (.43 - .28) / (1 - .28) = .21$$

Thirteen percent of the variance in Y that is unexplained by $X2$ is explained by $X1$. Twenty-one percent of the variance in Y that is unexplained by $X1$ is explained by $X2$. The square of the partial correlation coefficient of $X1$ ($X2$) is greater than the square of the semipartial correlation coefficient of $X1$ ($X2$) because $\rho^2_{YX2} > 0.0$ ($\rho^2_{YX1} > 0.0$).

Consider $X1$ and $X3$ as another example from Exhibit 11.1.

$$s\rho^2_{YX1 \cdot X3} = .59 - .31 = .28$$

$$s\rho^2_{YX3 \cdot X1} = .59 - .28 = .31$$

In this case, the squared semipartial correlation coefficients equal their corresponding simple coefficients of determination, because there is no collinearity between $X1$ and $X3$. The sum of the squared semipartial correlation coefficients also sum to $P^2_{Y \cdot X1X3} = .59$.

The square of the partial correlation coefficients in this example are:

$$p\rho^2_{YX1 \cdot X3} = (.59 - .31) / (1 - .31) = .41$$

$$p\rho^2_{YX3 \cdot X1} = (.59 - .28) / (1 - .28) = .43$$

Forty-one percent of Y variance not explained by $X3$ is explained by $X1$. Forty-three percent of Y variance not explained by $X1$ is explained by $X3$.

Neither of these two methods of expressing the effect of a single independent variable on Y is inherently superior. The appropriate measure of the effect of an independent variable depends on the causal model being investigated (see Chapter 19).

APPENDIX 11B:
ANOTHER WAY TO THINK ABOUT
PARTIAL COEFFICIENTS

In general, partial regression or correlation coefficients are defined as showing the contribution of one independent variable holding other independent variables in the model constant. For example, a partial regression coefficient is the predicted change in Y for a unit change in an independent variable holding other independent variables constant. This is useful since it correctly indicates the predicted change in Y for a unit change in an independent variable if there were no changes in other independent variables in the multiple regression model.

However, if there is multicollinearity, a change in values on one independent variable means that values of collinear independent variables must also change. Thus, although the definition is technically correct, it is of limited value unless the independent variables are uncorrelated.

There is another way to think about partial regression and correlation coefficients. This alternative is illustrated with a partial regression coefficient, although it also can be applied to the partial or semipartial correlation coefficient and their squares. Specifically, a partial regression coefficient also approximates the weighted average simple regression coefficient across all values of other independent variables in the model.

To illustrate, consider a case in which Y scores are regressed on $X1$ and $X2$ as shown in Exhibit 11B.1. Y and $X1$ are ordered variables, $X2$ is a dummy variable. A regression of Y on $X1$ and $X2$ produces (from Formula 11.2):

$$\hat{Y}_{X1X2} = 1.62 + .77 * X1 - .13 * X2$$

A unit change in $X1$ leads to a predicted change of .77 in Y holding $X2$ constant.

Now subgroup on $X2$ and calculate simple regressions of Y on $X1$ for each subgroup. From Formula 10.6, $B_{YX1|X2=0} = .50$ and $B_{YX1|X2=1} = 1.20$. The weighted (by the number of cases) average of these simple regression coefficients approximates the partial regression coefficient [(10 * .50 + 5 * 1.2) / 15 = .73].

Thinking of a partial regression coefficient as a weighted average of simple regression coefficients helps to understand its limited value when a rela-

EXHIBIT 11B.1. **Scores and statistics for partial regression coefficients examples**

Case	Y	X1	X2	X3	X4
01	3	5	0	1	0
02	7	4	0	5	0
03	2	1	0	3	0
04	7	2	0	5	0
05	6	2	0	2	0
06	4	4	0	3	0
07	1	1	0	3	0
08	2	3	0	1	0
09	1	2	0	1	0
10	4	3	0	2	0
11	4	3	1	3	1
12	2	1	1	5	1
13	5	5	1	1	1
14	7	4	1	2	1
15	1	2	1	3	1

| | μ | σ | Simple Correlation Coefficients | | | | |
			Y	X1	X2	X3	X4
Y	3.73	2.17	1.00				
X1	2.80	1.32	.47	1.00			
X2	.33	.47	.02	.11	1.00		
X3	2.67	1.40	.27	-.40	.07	1.00	
X4	.33	.47	.02	.11	1.00	.07	1.00

tionship between Y and Xi varies substantially depending on the values of Xj.[6] For example, consider the regression of Y on $X3$ and the dummy variable $X4$ from Exhibit 11B.1. The multiple regression prediction model is:

$$\hat{Y}_{X3X4} = 2.67 + .40 * X3 + .02 * X4$$

The partial regression coefficient indicates a predicted increase in Y of .40 for a unit increase in $X3$ holding $X4$ constant. Subgrouping on $X4$ provides a different picture. The simple regression coefficients are $B_{YX3|X4=0} = 1.02$, while $B_{YX3|X4=1} = -1.04$. The $YX3$ relationship is positive when $X4 = 0$, but negative when $X4 = 1$. The weighted average ($10 * 1.02 + 5 * -1.04 = .33$) approximates the partial regression coefficient of .40. However, neither is informative about the relationship within each $X4$ subgroup.[7]

PART IV: SUGGESTED READING

The topics covered in Part IV in no way exhaust basic statistics. If you have used a basic statistics book you are probably best off returning to it for issues not covered here. Cryer and Miller (1993) and Hays (1988) are my personal favorites. Both are a little demanding as introductory books, but both are very competent.

There are also many books available just on multiple regression and correlation (e.g., Bobco, 1995; Cohen & Cohen, 1983; Frees, 1996; Pedhazur, 1982). I especially like two of these. Cohen and Cohen's data analysis as opposed to statistical approach parallels the viewpoint taken here. They do an especially good job explaining the use of multiple regression and correlation for testing different kinds of conceptual models (see also Chapter 19). I also like Frees' treatment of multiple regression for causal analysis, and his coverage of the use of regression for time series analyses.

---

[6] That is, when the YXi relationship is moderated by Xj see Chapter 5.

[7] Chapter 19 shows another way that multiple regression can be performed to account for moderator variables.

V

STATISTICAL VALIDATION

12

Statistical Inference Foundations

Chapter Outline

- *Probability*
  - *Random Variables*
  - *Independent Random Variables*
- *Probability Distributions*
  - *Discrete Probability Distributions*
  - *Continuous Probability Distributions*
- *Sampling Distributions*
  - *Statistics and Parameters*
  - *Sampling Distribution of the Mean*
  - *Other Sampling Distributions*
- *Summary*
- *For Review*

Part IV discussed the use of statistics to describe scores on variables and to identify the strength and direction of relationships between variables. Statistics applied in this way help describe characteristics of cases studied in research. In terms of the research model introduced in Chapter 2, statistics used this way help establish empirical relationships linking scores on independent and dependent variables.

But Chapter 2 additionally pointed out that statistics are also used to help make two types of inference. ***Statistical inference*** uses probability theory to draw conclusions that transcend the relationships between variables, per se. One of these involves inferences about whether or not an observed relationship is due to chance or coincidence. For example, a study is conducted in which a group of young students are randomly assigned to one of two reading programs. One program includes explicit parental involvement including scheduled sessions in which parents read to their children at home. The other group is taught reading at school in the standard way with no special effort to obtain parental participation. Reading achievement test scores are administered at the end of the school year, and it is found that the students whose parents participated score higher, on average, than students taught in the standard way.

Internal statistical validation procedures are used to infer whether a difference between the two groups is large enough to conclude that it is due to the difference in reading programs rather than to chance differences in reading achievement that might be expected between any two groups of randomly selected students. Statistical inferences of this sort are typically made in experimental studies in which cases (students in the example) are randomly assigned to levels of an independent variable (reading program).

A second type of statistical inference is made in survey research in which a probability sample is drawn from some identifiable population. For example, a polling agency conducts a probability sample of adult citizens in a metropolitan area. Sample members are asked to state preferences between two mayoral candidates. Candidate A is preferred to Candidate B among sample members. Statistical generalization validation procedures are used to infer whether or not it is reasonable to also conclude that Candidate A is preferred in the population from which the sample was drawn.

Exhibit 12.1 illustrates these two types of inference. Internal statistical inference refers to conclusions made about statistical differences or relationships observed in the cases studied. External statistical inference refers to conclusions made about a probable population statistic based on a sample statistic.

Exhibit 12.1 also indicates that both types of inference employ procedures that rely on knowledge developed about chance phenomena. In the first example, it is possible that the group of students attaining higher reading achievement scores would have done so regardless of whether or not they had been assigned to the parental involvement group. By the luck of the draw, students that form this group may simply have greater reading aptitude than the other group. Analogously, the sample of citizens drawn from the population may not be representative of that population. Sample preferences for Candidate A may not reflect citizen opinions in the population where Candidate B may be preferred.

EXHIBIT 12.1. Two types of statistical inference

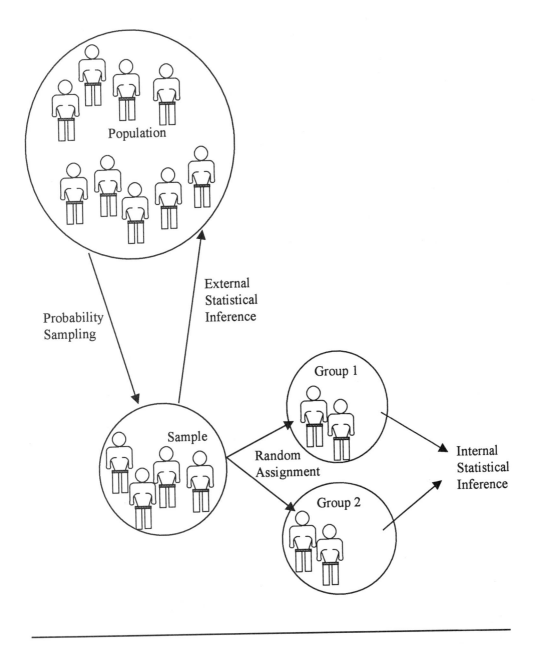

Thus, the validity of both internal and external statistical inference is uncertain. Validation procedures that account for such uncertainty are described in Chapter 13. These procedures allow researchers to quantify the
risks they confront when making statistical inferences.

However, use of these procedures requires that you first understand how uncertainty operates in statistical validation contexts. This chapter introduces issues that underlie statistical validation. Briefly, statistical validation requires knowledge of probability distributions and sampling distributions. These, in turn, require knowledge of random variables and probability. Accordingly, the chapter begins with a discussion of probability and random variables; it then describes probability distributions and sampling distributions.

It turns out that these probability issues and distributions play the same role for both internal and external statistical validity. Thus, to simplify the discussion, examples and illustrations focus only on external statistical validation. Implications of the ideas developed in this chapter for internal statistical validation are developed in Chapter 13.

PROBABILITY

The most fundamental building block in statistical validation is probability. *Probability* (P_r) specifies the likelihood that a particular value of a variable will be obtained. Probability can range from 0.0 (the value is certain not to occur), to 1.0 (the value is certain to occur). When P_r is greater than (>) 0.0, but less than (<) 1.0 there is uncertainty about whether the value will occur.

There are many types of probability and interesting issues associated with them. However, the objective here is modest; only probability topics needed to understand basic statistical inference issues are addressed.

Random Variables

Statistical inferences are made about values of variables. For example, an inference is made about the proportion of citizens' preferring Candidate A in the population. A proportion is a variable that can take on different values. This population value cannot be known exactly based on a sample proportion. However, it will be shown that when a sample is chosen in particular ways the population proportion can be known probabilistically. In such cases, the population proportion becomes a *random variable.* The values of the variable are not known exactly, but they are described by probability.

Consider a simple illustration. The outcome of a coin toss is a random variable that can take on two values, heads or tails. It is a random variable because each value is determined by its probability. If the coin is tossed many times it will land heads about half the time, P_r (heads) = 0.50, and tails about half the time, P_r (tails = 1.00 – 0.50) = .50. Although the outcome of any one toss is unknown, the probability is known. Statistical inference capitalizes on this type of probabilistic knowledge.

Values of random variables are **mutually exclusive** meaning that if one value occurs then another value cannot, and vice versa. For example, one toss of a coin can produce either a head or a tail, but not both. They are also **exhaustive** meaning that one value must occur. A toss of a coin must produce a head or a tail. When values of a random variable are mutually exclusive and exhaustive, they must sum to P_r = 1.0. For example, the probability of a head or tail following a coin toss:

$$P_r \text{(head or tail)} = P_r \text{(head)} + P_r \text{(tail)} = (0.5) + (1.0 - 0.5) = 1.0$$

Independent Random Variables

One additional property of probability, **independence,** is needed to understand how probability and sampling distributions are developed. Two different random variables are independent if the probabilities associated with values of one provide no information about the probabilities of values of the other. Consider the outcome of each of two coin tosses as variables. The variables are independent if the probabilities of the values obtained on the second toss remain the same regardless of the value obtained on the first toss. Probabilities of values of two or more random variables that are independent are multiplicative. For example:

$$P_r \text{(toss 1} = \text{head and toss 2} = \text{head)} = P_r \text{(toss 1} = \text{head)} * P_r$$
$$\text{(toss 2} = \text{head)} = (0.5) * (0.5) = .25$$

PROBABILITY DISTRIBUTIONS

A **probability distribution** summarizes probabilities associated with values of a random variable. Exhibit 12.2 shows the generic form of such distributions. Probability is represented on the vertical axis and values of the random variable are represented on the horizontal axis. The specific form depends on whether the probability distribution is of a discrete or continuous variable (Chapter 8).

RESEARCH HIGHLIGHT 12.1

Variables That Are Independent and Independent Variables

Researchers use the term *independent* in two distinctly different
ways. Independent means that two variables have no connection
in probability theory. The expected correlation coefficient between two variables that are independent is 0.00. Alternatively, in
causal models as described in Chapter 2, independent variables
are assumed to influence dependent variables; there is an expected
relationship. The correlation coefficient between an independent
and dependent variable in the latter context is assumed to be
greater or less than 0.00.

Discrete Probability Distributions

Discrete random variables have a countable number of identifiable values.
Accordingly, a *discrete probability distribution* has a probability associated
with each value of the random variable. To illustrate, create a random variable by counting the number of heads after three tosses of a coin. Four discrete values of this random variable are possible: 0, 1, 2, or 3 heads. These
four values are mutually exclusive (only one value can occur following three
tosses) and exhaustive (one of the values must occur).

Exhibit 12.3 shows all possible outcomes of this variable in a probability
tree. For example, the first toss might result in a tail ($P_r = 1.0 - 0.5$), the second a head ($P_r = 0.5$), and the third a head ($P_r = 0.5$). Since outcomes of each
toss are independent, the probability of this sequence of values (t, h, h) is:

$$P_r \text{ (tails)} * P_r \text{ (heads)} * P_r \text{ (heads)} =$$
$$(1.0 - 0.5) * (0.5) * (0.5) = .125$$

Exhibit 12.3 shows that there are eight possible outcome sequences. Because the probability of a head or tail on each toss is equal, each outcome following three tosses has an equal probability of occurring.

The results shown in the probability tree of Exhibit 12.3 can be combined
and summarized in a discrete probability distribution, a bar chart, as shown
in Exhibit 12.4. This distribution shows each value of a random variable on
the horizontal axis and the probability of each value on the vertical axis.

EXHIBIT 12.2. Generic probability distribution

Probability

Values of a Random Variable

In the example, $P_r(0 \text{ heads}) = .125$, there is only one combination of values that leads to zero heads, all tails (the left-most set of branches in Exhibit 12.3). Alternatively, there are three combinations that lead to one head:

P_r (toss 1 = head, and toss 2 = tail, and toss 3 = tail) +

P_r (toss 1 = tail, and toss 2 = head, and toss 3 = tail) +

P_r (toss 1 = tail, and toss 2 = tail, and toss 3 = head) =
.125 + .125 + .125 = .375

This discrete probability distribution illustrates a ***binomial probability distribution,*** a distribution of values from a set of trials in which:

EXHIBIT 12.3. Probability tree

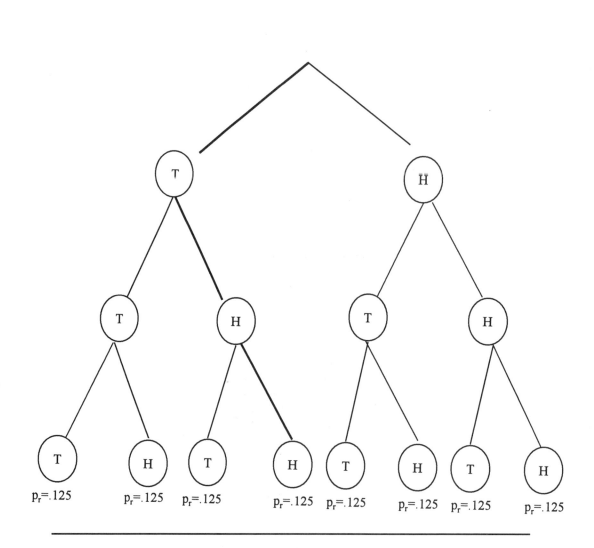

1. The values of trials are independent.
2. Each trial can lead to one of two values.
3. The probability of each value is constant across trials.

In the example, each coin toss represents a trial. Each toss can lead to one of two values, heads or tails. Finally, the probability remains constant across tosses.

Binomial probability distributions are widely applicable in research, because many situations approximate a binomial probability process. For ex-

EXHIBIT 12.4. Discrete probability distribution

RESEARCH HIGHLIGHT 12.2

Probabilities are Conceptual Constructions

A probability distribution reports the proportion of values to expect in an infinitely long series of trials; in the example, an infinitely long series of three coin tosses. If one were to actually toss three coins many times, recording the number of heads that appeared each time, an empirical frequency distribution can be obtained. This frequency distribution shows outcomes of tossing actual coins. Although frequencies of values in this distribution are expected to converge on the probabilities associated with each value as the number of tosses increases, they may never match the probabilities exactly.

ample, transactions recorded by a discount store scanning device can be characterized as correct or incorrect. Job applicants can be characterized as having prior work experience or not. Products coming off an assembly line can be characterized as satisfactory or unsatisfactory. All these examples illustrate a binomial probability process as long as the probabilities remain constant from trial to trial.

Continuous Probability Distributions

Continuous variables and continuous random variables are infinitely divisible between any two values. For example, chronological age can be reported in years. But years can be subdivided into months, days, hours, and so forth. Age values can be infinitely divided into smaller values.

Continuous probability distributions summarize probabilities associated with continuous random variables. However, the infinite divisibility of continuous random variables presents a small problem for continuous probability distributions. Since continuous variables are infinitely divisible between any two values, a probability cannot be assigned to specific values. As a consequence, probabilities are assigned to regions of a continuous probability distribution, just as frequencies are assigned to regions of histograms when distributions of continuous variables are described generally (Chapter 9).

EXHIBIT 12.5. A normal probability distribution

Probability

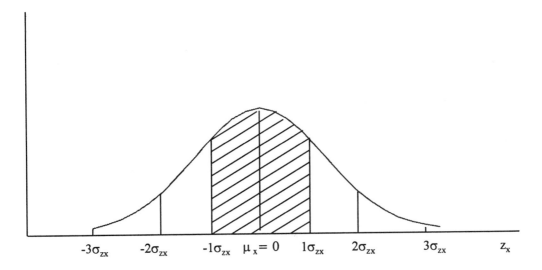

A *normal probability distribution* that shows probabilities associated with a normal distribution is shown in Exhibit 12.5 to illustrate a continuous probability distribution. Probabilities are assigned to regions under the normal probability curve. In a normal distribution, 68.3 percent of the cases fall between ± 1.0 standard deviations of the mean. Consequently, the probability distribution shows that 68.3 percent of cases fall between ± 1.0 standard deviations of the mean.

Normal probability distributions are widely useful in research. Many processes, natural and otherwise, produce continuous probability distributions that approximate a normal distribution. Furthermore, some discrete distributions, such as the binomial, also approximate a normal distribution as the number of trials become large.

RESEARCH HIGHLIGHT 12.3

Sampling Distributions Are Also Conceptual Constructions

Sampling distributions are conceptual just as probability distributions are. Researchers do not actually draw all possible probability samples from a population. To do so would be far more laborious than including all population cases in a study.

Rather, researchers estimate key characteristics of sampling distributions from statistics obtained on the sample drawn and from knowledge of what sampling distribution applies to a particular sample statistic. They use such information to estimate characteristics of the sampling distribution. These estimated characteristics of sampling distributions, in turn, are used to make statistical inferences.

SAMPLING DISTRIBUTIONS

Sampling distributions are probability distributions with two special characteristics:

1. They apply to random variables that are sample statistics. For example, the variable may be a mean or a regression coefficient.
2. The probabilities assigned values (discrete variables) or regions (continuous variables) are those that occur from the calculation of a statistic on all possible probability samples of a given size (n) that have been drawn from a population.

In *probability samples* the likelihood that each case in the population is chosen for the sample is known. There are several ways to obtain probability samples. Explanations of statistical validation typically use a simple random sample to illustrate probability sampling. In a *simple random sample,* each unique sample (of some given size) in a population has an equal chance of being selected. Randomness depends solely on the process for selecting cases; the actual probability of being selected in the sample may be large or small. A simple random sample requires only that the probability of one unique sample being selected is the same as the probability for any other unique sample.

EXHIBIT 12.6. Symbols for statistics and parameters

Variable	Statistic	Parameter
Number of cases	n	N
Mean	X_{Bar}	μ_x
Standard deviation	SD_x	σ_x
Variance	SD^2_x	σ^2_x
Correlation coefficient	r_{YX}	ρ_{YX}
Coefficient of determination	r^2_{YX}	ρ^2_{YX}
Regression coefficient	b_{YX}	B_{YX}
Regression intercept	a	α
Multiple correlation coefficient	$R_{Y.X1X2}$	$P_{Y.X1X2}$
Multiple coefficient of determination	$R^2_{Y.X1X2}$	$P^2_{Y.X1X2}$
Partial regression coefficient	$b_{YX1.X2}$	$B_{YX1.X2}$
Partial beta coefficient	$beta_{YX1.X2}$	$Beta_{YX1.X2}$

Note. Multiple correlation and regression statistics are illustrated with two independent variables.

Statistics and Parameters

In Part IV, statistics were described assuming that the data at hand exhausted a researcher's interest; cases were treated as a population, no inferences were involved. Now it is useful to distinguish between statistics calculated on the scores investigated in a study from statistics representing the inferences one wants to make. Accordingly, the term *statistic* is now reserved to summarize numerical information about the scores studied. When a statistic is used to make an inference it is called a ***parameter.*** Different symbols are also used to distinguish statistics that are calculated from parameters estimated. These are summarized in Exhibit 12.6.

Sampling Distribution of the Mean

Issues associated with sampling distributions are illustrated using a sampling distribution of the mean. A sampling distribution of the mean is a distribution created by calculating means for all possible probability samples of a given size. Suppose a researcher is interested in the average height of adult males in a metropolitan area. (Height is a continuous variable requiring a continuous sampling distribution.) Though unknown to the researcher, the population distribution of height (as shown in Exhibit 12.7a) is near normally distributed with mean, $\mu_Y = 5.70$ feet, and standard deviation, $\sigma_X = .25$ feet.

The researcher draws one simple random sample of five male participants from the population. Each sample member's height is measured, and the sample mean height, X_{Bar}, and standard deviation, SD_X, are calculated.

The researcher's best estimate of the population mean, μ_X, is the sample mean, X_{Bar}. But it is unlikely that the two are equal. X_{Bar} is probably greater or smaller than μ_X because of sampling error. **Sampling error** is the deviation between a sample statistic and population parameter that results because the sample size, n, is smaller than the population, N. Most random samples of five participants also yield means above or below μ_X because of sampling error.

Think now of drawing all possible random samples ($n = 5$) from the population, measuring participants' height in each sample and calculating X_{Bar}. These means represent values of a new variable, sample means of height. It is a random variable, because mean values of the samples result from a random sampling process. The probability of any region of this distribution is given under the curve of the sampling distribution of the mean as illustrated in Exhibit 12.7b.

This distribution has several noteworthy characteristics. First, the mean of the sampling distribution (the mean of the sample means of all samples ($n = 5$) is equal to μ_X.

Second, there is variability in this distribution, because there is variation in the amount of sampling error from sample to sample. Some samples consist of cases that mirror the population height distribution and hence produce means close to μ_X. Some, however, consist of a disproportionate number of cases with height values at the high or low end of the population height distribution. Such samples result in means that deviate from μ_X to a greater or lesser degree.

EXHIBIT 12.7. Population and sampling distributions

(a) Distribution of Height in the Population

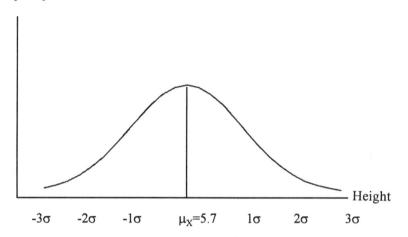

Frequency

-3σ $\quad$ -2σ $\quad$ -1σ $\quad$ μ_X=5.7 $\quad$ 1σ $\quad$ 2σ $\quad$ 3σ

Height

(b) Sampling Distribution of Mean Height: n = 5

Probability

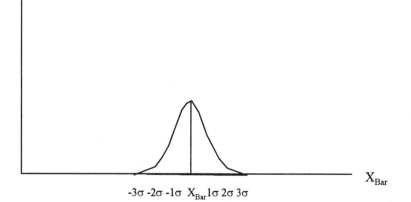

-3σ -2σ -1σ X_{Bar} 1σ 2σ 3σ

X_{Bar}

Nevertheless, there is less variability in the sampling distribution of the means than there is in the population distribution. This is illustrated with an example. Suppose the population of male adults is rank ordered by height and the 10 tallest are shown in Exhibit 12.8. The largest sample value in the population is 7.30 feet. However, in the sampling distribution ($n = 5$), the sample with the tallest adults must include the first five tallest participants. Thus, the largest mean value in the sampling distribution is only 6.89 feet.

EXHIBIT 12.8. Ten tallest participants in the population

Participant	Height
1	7.30 feet
2	7.05
3	6.81
4	6.73
5	6.54
6	6.46
7	6.35
8	6.33
9	6.28
10	6.21

Finally, as the sample size increases, variability in the sampling distribution of the mean decreases. Exhibit 12.8 also illustrates this characteristic. If the sample size is 10, the largest sample mean must include all participants in Exhibit 12.8. The largest sampling distribution value ($n = 10$) is 6.61 feet.

Variability can be addressed for sampling distributions just as it can be addressed for any other distribution. The standard deviation of sampling distributions is an especially important measure of variability, because it is needed to make statistical inferences. The standard deviation of a sampling distribution of the mean is:

$$SE_{XBar} = \frac{\sigma_X}{\sqrt{n}} \qquad (12.1a)$$

where SE_{XBar} = **standard deviation of a sampling distribution of the mean**

σ_X = **standard deviation of X in the population**

n = **number of cases in the sample**

Because the population standard deviation is typically unknown, SE_{XBar} is typically estimated using the sample standard deviation:

$$SE_{XBar} = \frac{SD_X}{\sqrt{n}} \qquad (12.1b)$$

where SD_X = **standard deviation of X in the sample**

Standard deviations of sampling distributions are called ***standard errors.*** The ***standard error of the mean*** is the standard deviation of a sampling distribution of the mean, sample size = n. (The ***standard error of the correlation coefficient*** is the standard deviation of the sampling distribution of the correlation coefficient, and so on for other statistics.)

The formula for SE_{XBar} has sample size in the denominator. This indicates that a sampling distribution of the mean has less variability than the population distribution, as suggested by the examples using Exhibit 12.8. Furthermore, the larger the size of the sample, the smaller the standard error. The relationship between sample size and standard error is important for statistical inference, since it correctly suggests that estimates of parameters improves as sample sizes become larger.

The sampling distribution of the mean shown in Exhibit 12.7b is symmetrical and is approximately normal. When the population is normally distributed, the sampling distribution of the mean is normally distributed. Moreover, even if the population is not normally distributed, the sampling distribution of the mean will approach the normal distribution as the sample becomes large. This follows from the ***Central Limit Theorem***; it states that as sample sizes randomly obtained become larger, the sampling distribution of the mean becomes less variable and more normally distributed.

Other Sampling Distributions

The shape of a particular sampling distribution depends on the probability sampling procedure and the statistic under consideration. A normal distribution represents the sampling distribution for some statistics, but not all. Indeed, two other distributions better characterize the sampling distributions for most statistics used in research.

    Students' t Distributions.   ***Students' t distributions*** are symmetrical (skew = 0.0), and have a mean = 0.0, just as a standard normal distribution. However, they have greater variability than the standard normal distribution (kurtosis < 0.0).

    A *t* distribution, rather than a standard normal distribution, is usually appropriate when making inferences about simple correlation coefficients and simple and partial regression coefficients. It is also appropriate for inferences about a mean when the standard deviation of the population must be estimated from the sample.

    F Distributions.   Students' *t* distributions were developed to address inferential problems involving the mean of a distribution. Other distributions are applicable to inferential issues involving variability in distributions. ***F distributions*** are sampling distributions designed to make inferences about the equality of two variances. These are important for statistical inference using either multiple regression or multiple correlation. Researchers make statistical inferences in multiple regression and correlation by comparing the variance in the dependent variable that is explained by the independent variables to the total variance in the dependent variable using *F* distributions.

SUMMARY

Researchers use statistical validation procedures to make inferences about population parameters and to make inferences about whether relationships observed are meaningfully greater than what might be expected by chance or coincidence. Inferences appropriately made require that statistics be combined with probabilistic processes. These are probability sampling for statistical generalization validity or random assignment for internal statistical validity.

Probabilities range from 0.0 to 1.0 and indicate the likelihood that a particular value of a variable will be obtained. Probabilities are characteristics of *random variables,* variables whose values are not known exactly but are described by probability. Random variables possess *mutual exclusivity* (when the occurrence of one value precludes the occurrence of other values, and vice versa). A random variable is *exhaustive* (when one value must occur). The probability of mutually exclusive and exhaustive values must sum to 1.0.

Two or more random variables are independent when the values of one variable provide no information about the probabilities of the values of the other(s). The probability that specific values will occur among two or more independent variables is multiplicative.

Probability distributions are formed with values from random variables. Such distributions may be *discrete,* if there are a countable number of mutually exclusive values, or *continuous,* if the values are infinitely divisible into smaller values.

Sampling distributions are probability distributions that describe statistics obtained from probability sampling. The standard deviations of such distributions are called *standard errors.* For example, the *standard error of the mean* is the standard deviation of the sampling distribution of the mean for a given sample size.

Three distributions that describe probability distributions and sampling distributions are *normal probability distributions, Students' t distributions,* and *F distributions.* Student *t* distributions are similar to a standard normal distribution but are more variable. Normal probability and *t* distributions are used to make inferences about means. Students' *t* distributions are also used to make inferences about simple and partial regression and correlation coefficients. *F* distributions address the equality of variances and are used to make inferences in multiple correlation and regression.

FOR REVIEW

Terms to Know

Statistical inference. Use of statistics and probability theory to draw conclusions about population parameters or the likelihood that observed relationships (differences) are due to chance.

Probability (P_r). Specifies the likelihood that a particular value of a variable will be obtained. It can range from 0.0 to 1.0.

Random variable. A variable whose values are not known exactly but are described by probability.

Mutually exclusive values. When the presence of one value precludes the presence of another value, and vice versa.

Exhaustive values. When one of the values on a variable must result.

Independence. Two variables are independent when information about the value on one variable provides no information about the probability of values on the other variable.

Probability distribution. A distribution that summarizes probabilities associated with values of a random variable.

   Discrete probability distribution. Probability distribution has a probability associated with each value of the discrete random variable.

   Binomial probability distribution. Discrete probability distribution that results from a set of trials where the values of each trial is independent, the probability remains constant from trial to trial, and each trial can lead to one of two values.

   Continuous probability distribution. Probability distribution where probabilities are assigned to regions of the continuous random variable.

   Normal probability distribution. Continuous probability distribution where probabilities assigned to regions conform to a normal distribution.

   Sampling distribution. A probability distribution of a sample statistic obtained on all possible probability samples of a given sample size.

Probability sample. Obtained when the likelihood of each case chosen for the sample is known.

   Simple random sample. A probability sample where every unique sample of a given size from a population has an equal chance of being selected.

Parameter. Statistic that describes a statistical inference drawn by a researcher.

Sampling distribution of the mean. A sampling distribution created by calculating means for all possible probability samples of a given size.

Sampling error. The difference between a sample statistic and population parameter brought about because the sample size is smaller than the population. The size of this error can be estimated when probability sampling is used.

Standard error. Standard deviation of a sampling distribution.

Standard error of the mean. Standard deviation of a sampling distribution of the mean.

Standard error of the correlation coefficient. Standard deviation of a sampling distribution of the correlation coefficient.

Central Limit Theorem. States that as sample sizes randomly obtained become larger, the sampling distribution becomes less variable and more normally distributed. Applies to several, but not all, sampling distributions.

Students' t distributions. A set of symmetrical sampling distributions that are shaped as a standard normal distribution but more variable. Students' *t* distributions become more like a standard normal distribution as the sample size gets larger.

F distributions. A set of asymmetrical sampling distributions with positive skew. *F* distributions are designed to test the equality of variances from two populations.

Formulas to Use

Standard error of the mean

$$SE_{XBar} = \frac{\sigma_X}{\sqrt{n}} \qquad \textbf{(12.1a)}$$

$$SE_{XBar} = \frac{SD_X}{\sqrt{n}} \qquad \textbf{(12.1b)}$$

where σ_X and SD_X = the standard deviation of the population and sample, respectively

Questions for Review

1. How do the objectives of statistical generalization validity differ from internal statistical validity?
2. How are standard deviations and standard errors similar? How are they dissimilar?
3. Compare and contrast statistics and parameters.
4. Compare and contrast the t distribution with the standard normal distribution.
5. A coin is biased so that P_r (head) = .60 and P_r (tail) = .40. Create a probability tree resulting from three tosses of this biased coin. Given the bias, develop the probability distribution for the possible values, 0, 1, 2, or 3 heads.
6. Political party affiliation is a random variable that has four mutually exclusive values. Assign a probability (P_r) to "other" to make this variable exhaustive.

$$P_r \text{ (Republican)} = .25; \ P_r \text{ (Democrat)} = .30; \ P_r \text{ (Independent)}$$
$$= .30; \ P_r \text{ (Other)} = \underline{\quad} ?$$

Issues to Discuss

1. Explain why the sample mean in a sampling distribution of the mean is a random variable.
2. What is the parameter when statistical inference is used to make an external statistical inference? An internal statistical inference?
3. What characteristic(s) of the sampling distribution of the mean is influenced by sample size? What characteristic(s) is not?

13

Statistical Inference Applications

Chapter Outline

The probability and sampling distributions described in Chapter 12 provide a foundation for making external and internal statistical inferences. This chapter describes two procedures researchers use to make such inferences. These two, statistical hypothesis testing and confidence intervals, are intimately related; they are simply different ways of addressing the same objectives.

245

However, the objectives for hypothesis testing and confidence intervals differ depending on whether a researcher is interested in statistical generalization validity or in internal statistical validity. When statistical generalization validity is of interest, hypothesis testing and confidence intervals are used to estimate a population parameter from a statistic calculated on a sample that has been drawn from the population. When internal statistical validity is of interest, the two procedures are used to estimate whether a statistic observed on cases is large enough to rule out chance as its explanation.

Both types of inference use probability and sampling distributions. In statistical generalization, this requires that a probability sample be drawn from the population. Internal statistical validation requires that cases be randomly assigned to levels of an independent variable.

However, except for the way that probability is used to produce statistics that meet probability distribution assumptions, hypothesis testing and confidence interval procedures are otherwise identical. Thus, to simplify the presentation, hypothesis testing and confidence intervals are described assuming that only statistical generalization validity is of interest. Issues associated with internal statistical validity are discussed after the procedures are described.

The chapter also contains an appendix. This appendix identifies procedures to calculate statistical hypothesis tests and confidence intervals on the statistics described in this book.

STATISTICAL HYPOTHESIS TESTING

Statistical hypothesis testing is designed to estimate whether a relationship (or difference) observed on the cases studied suggests there is a relationship (or difference) among the population from which the sample was drawn. It may address whether the sample results suggest that there is any population relationship or difference. For example, a sample correlation coefficient may be assessed to decide whether any relationship exists among cases in the population. Alternatively, the research hypothesis may address a directional issue, whether a relationship is positive or negative, or whether a difference favors one group over another. For example, a sample correlation coefficient may be assessed to decide whether it suggests the population relationship is positive.

EXHIBIT 13.1. Statistical hypothesis testing sequence of steps

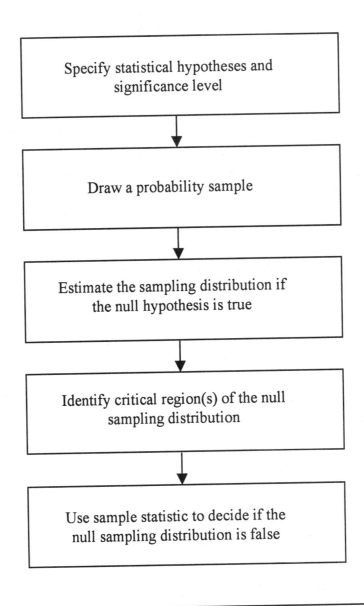

Hypothesis Testing Logic and Procedures

Hypothesis testing involves the same five steps whether for internal or external statistical inference. These steps are summarized in Exhibit 13.1. Each is explained in detail below.

Specify Statistical Hypotheses and Significance Levels.   Hypothesis testing involves two statistical hypotheses. The ***research hypothesis (H_1)*** represents an investigator's expectation about what is true of the population parameter. For example, a research hypothesis may be that salary level is positively related to years of work experience, or it may be that the average age of women in a population differs from the average age of men.

Research hypotheses are evaluated against a ***null hypothesis (H_0)***, the hypothesis of no association or no difference. (The null hypothesis does not have to specify there is literally no relationship (or difference) in the population. However, it is unlikely that you will see the null hypothesis stated any other way.) The null hypothesis for the salary level–years of work experience example is that there is no relationship between the two, or that the relationship is negative. If the research and null hypotheses are tested by regressing salary level (Y) on years of work experience (X) then:

$$\text{research hypothesis, } H_1 \; B_{YX} > 0.0$$

$$\text{null hypothesis, } H_0 \; B_{YX} \leq 0.0$$

The research hypothesis is directional since it anticipates a positive relationship between salary level and years of work experience. A directional research hypothesis is called ***one-tailed.***

In the second example, the research hypothesis is that the average age of women (W) is different from that of men (M). The null hypothesis is that the average age of women and men are the same:

$$\text{research hypothesis, } H_1 \; \mu_W \neq \mu_M$$

$$\text{null hypothesis, } H_0 \; \mu_W = \mu_M$$

In this example, the research hypothesis is nondirectional. It does not suggest that women are younger or older than men, only that the average age of the two groups differ. A nondirectional research hypothesis is called ***two-tailed.***

At this stage, researchers should also establish a ***statistical significance level,*** which refers to the risk they take of accepting the research hypothesis (H_1) when the null hypothesis (H_0) is true. Probability sampling involves uncertainty. The probability sample drawn from a population may not be representative of that population. The conclusion drawn from the sample may thus be in error. For example, the sample regression coefficient may support the research hypothesis that salary level is related to the years work experience. Yet, in the population no such relationship may exist.

Researchers set a statistical significance level so that the risk of erroneously concluding H_1, when H_0 is true, is small. Typically, researchers use significance levels of $p = 0.05$ or $p = 0.01$. In the salary example, a significance level of, $p = 0.05$, means that the researcher has established a risk of erroneously concluding a relationship between salary and years experience of 5 percent when the null hypothesis is true in the population.

The choice of a significance level is arbitrary in the absence of information about the costs and benefits of incorrect and correct decisions. The levels of 0.05 and 0.01 are merely conventions widely used by researchers. As Rosnow and Rosenthal (1989) said, "surely, God loves the .06 nearly as much as the .05" (p. 1277).

Draw a Probability Sample. The researcher next draws a sample from the population. This must be a probability sample so that the sampling distribution estimated in the next step has the shape, variability, and central tendency assumed for it. A researcher has no way of knowing these sampling distribution characteristics unless a probability sample is used. The procedures described here assume that the probability sample is a simple random sample.

Estimate the Sampling Distribution If the Null Hypothesis Is True.

Here is a critical point of hypothesis testing: Researchers estimate a sampling distribution assuming the null (H_0) hypothesis is true. Of course, a researcher doesn't really believe this; the researcher believes that H_1 is true. The null distribution is created only to serve as a criterion against which the research hypothesis (H_1) is evaluated. This criterion distribution is used to protect researchers from erroneously concluding support for the research hypothesis in the event that the null hypothesis is really true.

A sampling distribution contains sample statistics from all possible samples of a given sample size. It thus must follow that the sample statistic calculated in a research study comes from the null sample distribution if the null hypothesis is true in the population. H_0 is rejected in favor of H_1 only if it is unlikely ($p < 0.05$ or $p < 0.01$) that the sample statistic obtained comes from the null sampling distribution. Alternatively, H_0 is not rejected if the sample plausibly comes from the null distribution. It is in this sense that statistical hypothesis testing establishes a low risk of erroneously concluding H_1 when H_0 is true.

The null sampling distribution must be estimated because a researcher draws one sample, not all possible samples, of a given sample size. Since a distribution is defined by its central tendency, variability, and shape, researchers must estimate these three characteristics of null sampling distributions.

1. *Central tendency.* The central tendency of the distribution is established assuming the null hypothesis is true. Thus, the sampling distribution is assumed to have a mean of zero.
2. *Variability.* The variability in the sampling distribution is usually estimated using information obtained from the sample. Formulas for sample estimates of variability (sampling errors) vary by parameter estimated but typically include the sample size and/or the variability in the sample. For example, the standard error of the mean is estimated using both (see Formula 12.2).
3. *Shape.* Researchers draw on knowledge provided by statisticians to decide the shape of the sampling distribution for a given statistic. As noted in Chapter 12, the standard normal distribution, Students' *t* distributions, and *F* distributions frequently approximate the shape of sampling distributions for the statistics used in research.

Identify Critical Region(s) of the Null Sampling Distribution.   Information about the sampling distribution estimated given the null and the significance level established are combined to identify the region(s) of the distribution where a sample statistic is unlikely if the null hypothesis is true. Exhibit 13.2 shows values identifying several critical regions for one- and two-tailed tests involving *t* distributions with varying degrees of freedom. *Degrees of freedom (d.f.)* refer to the amount of information available to estimate population parameters from sample statistics. They are more accurate for this purpose than is sample size, though the two are closely connected. The number of degrees of freedom available to conduct tests of statistical inference has been identified by statisticians.

To identify the critical value(s) in Exhibit 13.2 you must know whether the research hypothesis is one- or two-tailed, the significance level, and the degrees of freedom. For example, suppose the test is one-tailed, $p < 0.05$, and the degrees of freedom equal 25. Exhibit 13.2 shows that the critical *t* distribution value is 1.71. Less than 5 percent of the sample statistics drawn from a population if the null hypothesis is true will have *t* distribution values greater than 1.71.

Use Sample Statistic to Decide If the Null Sampling Distribution Is False. In the last step of statistical hypothesis testing, a researcher transforms the sample statistic to a scale value on the null sampling distribution and compares it with the critical value established in the previous step. If the transformed sample statistic falls in the critical region, the researcher concludes that the sample drawn actually comes from a distribution other than the null distribution. The researcher rejects H_0 and accepts H_1. In the example just given, a researcher concludes H_1 if the transformed sample statistic is greater than 1.71. The researcher does not reject H_0 if the transformed sample statistic is 1.71 or less.

Hypothesis Testing Example

The steps in statistical hypothesis testing are illustrated using the example of the research hypothesis that salary level (Y) is positively related to years of work experience (X) among a population of working adults. The research hypothesis is one-tailed. The researcher establishes a significance level of 0.01 and intends to test the hypothesis by calculating a simple correlation coefficient on salary and work experience scores from a simple random sample of 27 adults chosen from the population. The research and null hypotheses are:

$$\text{research hypothesis, } H_1 \; P_{YX} \geq 0.0$$

$$\text{null hypothesis, } H_0 \; P_{YX} \leq 0.0$$

In this situation the null sampling distribution has a mean equal to zero, $p_{YX} = 0.0$, a shape approximated by a t distribution with $n-2$ degrees of freedom,[1] and a standard error:

$$SEr_{YX} = \frac{1}{\sqrt{n-1}} \qquad (13.1)$$

where SEr_{YX} = standard error of the correlation coefficient
when $p_{YX} = 0.0$

---

[1] When $p_{YX} \neq 0.0$, the sampling distribution is no longer symmetrical, hence it no longer assumes the shape of a t distribution and the appropriate statistical test is a little more complicated.

EXHIBIT 13.2. Values identifying critical regions of *t* distributions

Two-Tailed

One-Tailed

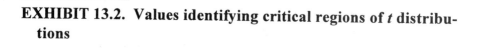

| | Critical value | Critical value | | Critical value |

| Two-Tailed | .100 | .050 | .020 | .010 |
| One-Tailed | .050 | .025 | .010 | .005 |

d.f.				
1	6.31	12.70	31.80	63.70
2	2.92	4.30	6.96	9.92
3	2.35	3.18	4.54	5.84
4	2.13	2.78	3.75	4.60
5	2.02	2.57	3.36	4.03
10	1.81	2.23	2.76	3.17
15	1.75	2.13	2.60	2.95
20	1.72	2.09	2.53	2.85
25	1.71	2.06	2.49	2.79
30	1.70	2.04	2.46	2.75
40	1.68	2.02	2.42	2.70
60	1.67	2.00	2.39	2.66
120	1.66	1.98	2.36	2.62
∞ Standard Normal	1.64	1.96	2.33	2.58

RESEARCH HIGHLIGHT 13.1

A Legal Analogy

Hypothesis testing logic is analogous to the logic for determining a defendant's guilt or innocence in the American judicial system. The null hypothesis is accepted as provisionally true; the defendant is provisionally assumed to be innocent. The null hypothesis is rejected and the research hypothesis accepted only if it is improbable that the null hypothesis is true; the assumption of innocence is rejected and a decision of guilt is accepted only if the defendant is found guilty beyond a reasonable doubt.

Both decision rules are asymmetrical, and for the same reason. The cost of erroneously concluding a relationship when none exists is seen as greater than the cost of erroneously missing a relationship that does exist. The cost of erroneously convicting an innocent defendant is seen as greater than the cost of erroneously letting a guilty defendant go free.

The standard error of the correlation coefficient depends only on the sample size when $p_{YX} = 0.0$. The larger the sample size, the more tightly clustered are the sample correlation coefficients around the population correlation coefficient.

The critical region for this null sampling distribution is found in Exhibit 13.2. It shows that a critical region for a one-tailed test, $p < 0.01$, with $n - 2 = 25$ d.f. begins at 2.49.

The researcher draws a sample, obtains salary and years of experience scores, and calculates a simple correlation coefficient, $r_{YX} = 0.55$. This correlation coefficient is transformed to a t distribution value by:

$$t_{cc} = r_{YX} * \frac{\sqrt{n-2}}{\sqrt{1 - r_{YX}^2}} \tag{13.2}$$

where t_{cc} = location of the sample correlation coefficient on a t distribution with $n - 2$ degrees of freedom

From the example:

$$t_{cc} = .55 * \sqrt{27-2} / \sqrt{1-.55^2} = 3.29.$$

This value, 3.29, is greater than the value of 2.49 that identifies the beginning of the critical region. Consequently, H_0 is rejected and H_1 is accepted.

The sample correlation coefficient of .55 suggests there is a positive relationship between salary level and work experience in the population as hypothesized.

This conclusion is modest because of the way it is tested. The null hypothesis states that there is a negative or no (zero) relationship in the population. Thus, to reject H_0 and accept H_1, given a directional one-tailed test, only permits a conclusion that some positive relationship probably exists in the population. The actual population relation may be less than $r_{YX} = .55$, or greater.

Hypothesis Testing Outcomes

Research and null hypotheses pertain to parameters. A researcher draws inferences about these parameters based on evidence obtained from a sample. These inferences and parameters are shown in Exhibit 13.3 as a two-by-two table.

Exhibit 13.3 shows that a researcher can make two correct inferences. A correct inference is drawn when H_1 is accepted and H_1 is true of the parameter. A correct inference is also made when a researcher fails to reject H_0 and H_0 is the true parameter value.

Two errors are also possible. An α or **Type I error** is made if a researcher concludes H_1 but H_0 is true in the population. Alternatively, a B or **Type II error** is made if H_1 is true in the population but a researcher fails to reject H_0.

Hypothesis testing is designed to protect against Type I error, an error of concluding a relationship in the population when none exists. As noted, it does so by specifying the likelihood that a sample statistic comes from a population with no relationship. This likelihood is usually set low ($p < 0.05$ or $p < 0.01$) so that it is unlikely that H_1 is accepted from the sample when H_0 is true in the population.

While unlikely, it is not impossible. For example, suppose a significance level, $p < 0.05$, is established, and H_0 is true in the population. Further, suppose many, many samples are drawn and a sample statistic is calculated on each. About 5 percent of the time, these statistics will fall in the improbable

EXHIBIT 13.3. **Outcomes of statistical hypothesis tests**

Inference	Parameter	
	H_0	H_1
H_0	Correct	B (Type II)
H_1	α (Type I)	Correct

region of the null sampling distribution, leading to the erroneous conclusion that a relationship exists in the population when it does not. This illustrates how hypothesis testing controls the risk of a Type I error, but doesn't eliminate its possibility.

Further, hypothesis testing does not protect against Type II error, an error of failing to accept H_1 from a sample statistic when H_1 is true of the population parameter. This latter issue is addressed by statistical power.

Statistical Power

Statistical power refers to the likelihood of concluding H_1 from a sample statistic when H_1 is true of the population parameter. It is equal to 1 - Type II error. Power thus addresses the second error that can be made in statistical hypothesis testing. Statistical hypothesis testing addresses Type I error—the error of erroneously concluding a relationship (difference) when there is none. Statistical power addresses Type II error—the error of failing to detect a relationship (difference) in the population when it exists. The two procedures are best used together.

Exhibit 13.4 illustrates statistical power using a one-tailed directional hypothesis test for a correlation coefficient. The null sampling distribution on the left assumes $\rho_{YX} = 0.0$, a critical value ($p < 0.01$), and a particular sample size.

However, assume now that the null hypothesis is really false. H_1 is true, $\rho_{YX} > 0.0$, as represented by the distribution to the right in Exhibit 13.4. Any sample a researcher draws must be from the sampling distribution centered over the true parameter ($\rho_{YX} > 0.0$). Statistical power is shown by the proportion of this distribution that is to the right of the critical value established for the null distribution. It is the proportion of the total population sampling dis-

RESEARCH HIGHLIGHT 13.2

Don't Accept the Null Hypothesis

Only the risk of erroneously accepting the research hypothesis is known in hypothesis testing. The risk of erroneously accepting the null hypothesis is not known (i.e., the risk of erroneously concluding there is no relation in the population). Consequently, in hypothesis testing H_0 should never be accepted unless one also knows the power of a statistical test.

tribution with diagonal lines. This follows because a researcher concludes H_1 (correctly in this case) for any sample drawn that results in a sample correlation coefficient to the right of the critical value. Any sample from the distribution around the population parameter resulting in a correlation coefficient to the left of the critical value results in a Type II error.

Statistical Power Conventions. Statistical treatments of power usually emphasize four factors. One factor influencing statistical power is whether the research hypothesis is one- or two-tailed. Exhibit 13.2 shows that a one-tailed test locates the critical region farther to the right (left if a negative relationship is hypothesized) than a two-tailed test, other things equal. This means that the critical region of the null distribution reaches further into the true sampling distribution. Statistical power is thus lower given a one-tailed hypothesis test compared to a two-tailed hypothesis test.

A second factor influencing power is the statistical significance level established as illustrated in Exhibit 13.5. For example, as the significance level is relaxed from 0.01 (top panel) to 0.05 (bottom panel), power increases. The proportion of sample correlation coefficients in the sampling distribution around the population parameter that fall to the right of the critical value increases as statistical significance is relaxed from 0.01 to 0.05. Thus, increases in the risk of Type I error decrease the risk of Type II error (and vice versa).

A third factor influencing power is the sample size. Exhibit 13.6 shows that power increases as sample size increases. An increase in the sample size has two effects, both increase power (compare the top and bottom panels). First, the larger sample size decreases the variability (standard error) in the

EXHIBIT 13.4. Power of a test of a simple correlation coefficient

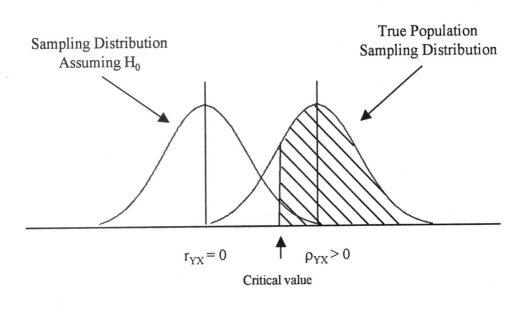

sampling distribution given H_0. This pulls the critical value closer to the mean of the null sampling distribution and further from the mean of the sampling distribution around the population parameter. Second, the increase in sample size also decreases the standard error of the sampling distribution around the population parameter, pulling more sample correlation coefficients away from the null distribution.

Finally, the power of a statistical test increases as the population relationship increases. The bottom panel in Exhibit 13.7 shows that the entire population sampling distribution is shifted to the right (compared to the top panel) as ρ_{YX} increases. This pulls more of the population sampling distribution above the critical value established for the null sampling distribution.

The relative contribution of the latter three factors is illustrated in Exhibit 13.8. It shows the power of two-tailed statistical tests of sample correlation coefficients for two population relationships ($\rho_{YX} = .10$, and $\rho_{YX} = .40$) and two levels of significance ($p < 0.05$, and $p < 0.01$) across sample sizes ranging to 500.

Exhibit 13.8 shows that power is low, even for large sample sizes, when the relationship in the population is small. The statistical power ($p < 0.05$,

EXHIBIT 13.5. Power increases as risk of Type I error increases

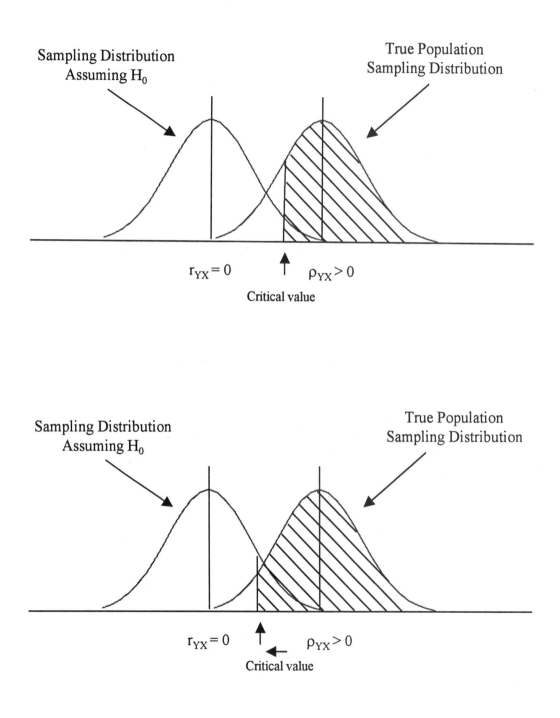

EXHIBIT 13.6. Power increases as sample size increases

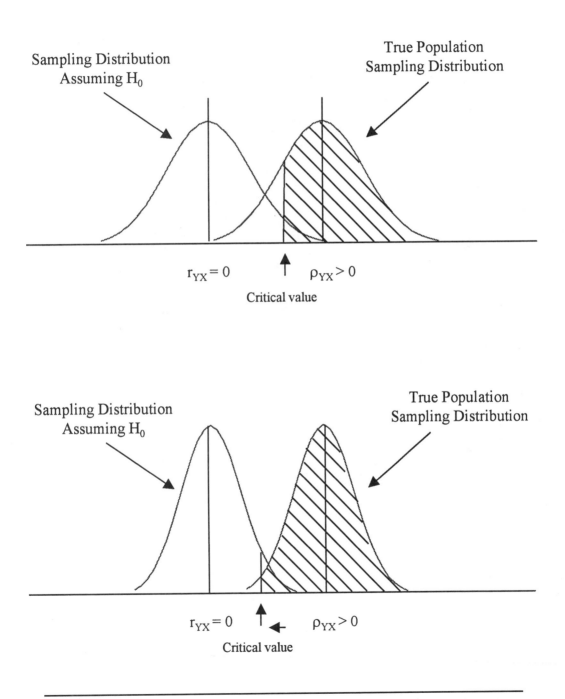

EXHIBIT 13.7. **Power increases as relationship in population increases**

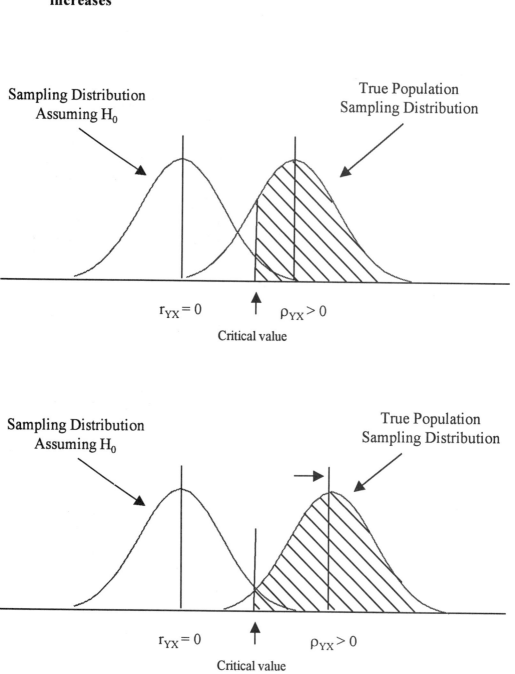

$r_{YX} = 0$ $\rho_{YX} > 0$

Critical value

$r_{YX} = 0$ $\rho_{YX} > 0$

Critical value

two-tailed) to detect $\rho_{YX} = 0.10$ is less than 0.50 until a sample size reaches almost 400. Alternatively, power quickly becomes high as the sample size increases when $\rho_{YX} = 0.40$. A sample of 100 has statistical power of 0.95 to detect $\rho_{YX} = 0.40$ ($p < 0.01$, two-tailed).

Other Power Determinants. The four power determinants just identified receive most attention. However, the utility of such knowledge for improving power is limited. Although two-tailed statistical tests are more powerful, researchers typically seek to formulate one-tailed tests, because they provide more substantive information. A researcher has no control over the size of the relationship that exists in the population. Increasing power by relaxing statistical significance levels pits one desirable feature (low Type II error) against another (low Type I error). Of the three determinants identi-

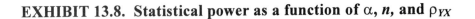

EXHIBIT 13.8. Statistical power as a function of α, n, and ρ_{YX}

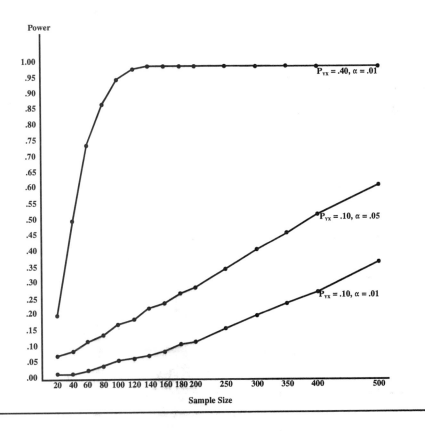

fied, only increases in sample size are unambiguously attractive and potentially within the control of a researcher.

However, there are other ways researchers can increase power of statistical tests. One involves measurement. Chapter 17 shows that unreliability tends to attenuate (reduce) observed relationships compared to relationships obtained with reliable measurement. Increasing the reliability of measures serves to increase statistical power.

Good research designs can also help improve the power of statistical tests. Design activities that serve to control nuisance variables (see Chapters 5 and 19), in particular, can help strengthen the power to detect population relationships or differences.

CONFIDENCE INTERVALS

Statistical hypothesis testing begins with an assumption that the null (no relationship or difference) hypothesis is the true parameter. This is the hypothesis that a researcher expects to reject in favor of a research hypothesis that there is a relationship (difference). Researchers using confidence intervals begin with a different perspective. They assume that the best estimate of the parameter is the sample statistic. Thus, the sampling distribution estimated is not centered over 0.0, it is centered over the value of the sample statistic. Researchers estimate this sampling distribution to create a *confidence interval* representing a range around a sample statistic that likely includes its population parameter. The probabilistic logic underlying confidence intervals parallels that of hypothesis testing. However, the logic is used differently, and the procedure is carried out using different steps as summarized in Exhibit 13.9 and developed more fully in the following section.

Confidence Interval Logic and Procedures

Set Confidence Level. A *confidence level* refers to the likelihood that a range created around a sample statistic includes the population parameter. Any level may be established, but researchers usually set confidence levels at 95 percent or 99 percent. These are the inverse of statistical significance levels of 0.05 and 0.01, respectively. Like statistical significance levels, confidence levels refer to the process being employed, not to a specific interval created based on one sample. A confidence interval based on one sample

RESEARCH HIGHLIGHT 13.3

When Statistical Power Analysis is Essential

There are times when researchers want to claim that a relationship (difference) in the population does not exist. For example, a researcher wishes to combine two samples into one for purposes of analysis. The researcher performs a statistical hypothesis test to determine whether the two samples differ on some characteristic(s) of the cases; for example, age. If H_0 is not rejected at some level of significance the researcher reasons that the two samples do not differ and hence combines them.

There are several problems with such a procedure. Here note only the problem for statistical inference. Hypothesis testing protects against Type I error—the risk of concluding there is a relationship or difference in the population when there is none. However, in this example, the researcher should be concerned with Type II error—the risk of not finding a relationship (difference) when it exists. Statistical power, not hypothesis testing, addresses Type II risk.

either includes the population parameter or it does not. Likelihood refers to the process, not to the outcome from any one sample.

Draw a Probability Sample and Calculate Sample Statistic. The second step, as in statistical hypothesis testing, is to draw a sample. This must also be a probability sample so that a sampling distribution can appropriately be estimated. The sample statistic of interest is then calculated.

Estimate Sampling Distribution Assuming the Statistic Represents the Parameter. Here is where confidence intervals and hypothesis testing differ most dramatically. As noted, the sampling distribution for confidence intervals is centered over the sample statistic. In hypothesis testing, it is centered over the null hypothesis value. The other characteristics of the sampling distribution do not differ between hypothesis testing and confidence intervals. The shape of the distribution is again determined by knowledge provided by statisticians. The variability in the sampling distribution is typically estimated from the sample as in hypothesis testing.

EXHIBIT 13.9. Confidence interval sequence of steps

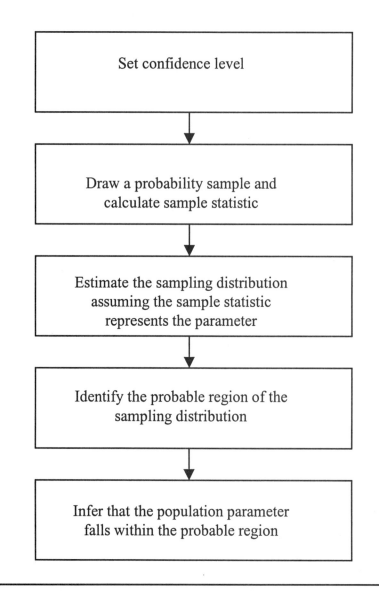

Identify Probable Region of the Sampling Distribution.   Since it is assumed that the sample statistic estimates the population parameter, the sampling distribution is now centered over the sample statistic. The most probable region of this sampling distribution is identified. As noted, the most probable 95 percent or 99 percent of this distribution is typically located.

Infer That the Population Parameter Falls Within the Probable Region.
The researcher concludes that the population parameter falls within the most probable region from the procedure above. In doing so, the researcher runs a risk that is exactly analogous to the risk of a Type I error in hypothesis testing. In this case, the risk is that the parameter may not actually fall within the interval created.

Confidence Interval Example

Consider again the example in which a researcher is interested in the relationship between salary level (Y) and years of work experience (X). However, instead of testing a hypothesis that the relationship between these variables is greater than zero, the researcher now develops a 95 percent confidence interval around the sample regression coefficient, b_{YX}, calculated on a probability sample of 27 participants.

The top of Exhibit 13.10 shows the true but unknown population sampling distribution. Assume its mean (which is equal to the population regression coefficient, B_{YX}) equals $800.00. In the population, there is a positive relationship between income and years of experience. Each additional year of work experience leads to a predicted increase in income of $800.00. Assume the standard error of this distribution, $SEb_{YX} = 80.00, for $n = 27$.

The researcher draws a probability sample, calculates the sample regression coefficient, $b_{YX} = 750, and estimates the standard error of the regression coefficient, $SEb_{YX} = 100, from:

$$SEb_{YX} = \frac{SD_{Y \cdot X}}{SD_X \sqrt{n-1}} \qquad (13.3)$$

where SEb_{YX} = standard error of the regression coefficient, and

$$SD_{Y \cdot X} = \frac{n-1}{n-2} * SD^2{}_Y (1 - r^2{}_{YX}) \qquad (13.4)$$

where $SD_{Y \cdot X}$ = standard error of estimate of Y on X, estimate of the standard deviation of the residual errors in the population.

EXHIBIT 13.10. Population sampling distribution of ρ_{YX} and three sample confidence interval estimates

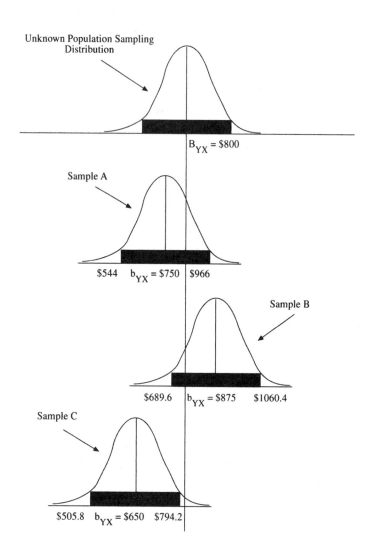

Unknown Population Sampling Distribution

$B_{YX} = \$800$

Sample A

$\$544$ $b_{YX} = \$750$ $\$966$

Sample B

$\$689.6$ $b_{YX} = \$875$ $\$1060.4$

Sample C

$\$505.8$ $b_{YX} = \$650$ $\$794.2$

The standard error of the regression coefficient has a t distribution with $n - 2$ degrees of freedom. The 95 percent confidence interval is found from:

$$CI = b_{YX} \pm SEb_{YX} * t_{95} \qquad (13.5)$$

where $t_{95} = 2.06$ when d.f. = 25 (see Exhibit 13.2)

Thus, from Sample A:

$$CI = 750.00 \pm 100.00 * 2.06 = 750.00 \pm 206.00 = 544.00 \leftrightarrow 956.00$$

The researcher concludes the population regression coefficient likely falls within the range $544.00 to $956.00. Given the assumption about the population parameter in this illustration, $B_{YX} = \$800.00$, the researcher's conclusion is correct.

Suppose instead that the researcher had drawn probability Sample B shown in Exhibit 13.10. The sample regression coefficient, $b_{YX} = \$875.00$ and $SEb_{YX} = \$90.00$. Given these values,

$$CI = 875.00 \pm 90.00 * 2.06 = 875.00 \pm 185.40 = 689.60 \leftrightarrow 1060.40$$

Given this sample, the researcher concludes the population regression coefficient likely falls within the range $689.60 to $1,060.40. Again the conclusion is correct.

Finally, suppose the researcher draws Sample C shown at the bottom of Exhibit 13.10. The sample regression coefficient, $b_{YX} = \$650.00$ and $SEb_{YX} = \$70.00$. Given these values:

$$CI = 650.00 \pm 70.00 * 2.06 = 650.00 \pm 144.20 = 505.80 \leftrightarrow 794.20$$

Given Sample C, the researcher concludes that the population regression coefficient likely falls within the range $505.80 to $794.20. This time the researcher is incorrect, as is expected about 5 percent of the time if many, many samples are drawn and 95 percent confidence intervals are established each time.

CONFIDENCE INTERVALS VERSUS HYPOTHESIS TESTING AND POWER

Confidence intervals and statistical hypothesis testing are two ways to make statistical inferences from a sample statistic. Both rely on exactly the same probability processes and logic to generate inferences. Both share risks that inferences made are incorrect. However, because the probability processes are known, the likelihood of the risks is known and can be controlled.

The procedures differ in the type of inference made and hence the form that the risks take. Statistical hypothesis testing is set up to identify the risks of erroneously concluding there is a parameter relationship or difference if none exists. Statistical hypothesis testing does not provide information about the risk of missing a parameter relationship or difference. Statistical power analysis must be performed to assess that risk.

Alternatively, confidence intervals begin with the assumption that the sample statistic is a researcher's best estimate of a parameter. Thus, an interval is created around the sample statistic that likely includes the parameter. The risk here is that the interval may not include the parameter relationship or difference.

Researchers who conduct organizational research overwhelmingly report inferential results in statistical hypothesis testing form. Research reporting conventions clearly favor statistical hypothesis testing. Furthermore, it is not conventional to report power analyses with statistical hypothesis testing. The risk of failing to recognize a parameter relationship or difference is thus typically unknown.

Although less used, confidence intervals are attractive relative to statistical hypothesis testing in several respects. First, they focus attention on the sample statistic; it is usually a better estimate of the parameter than the null hypothesis value of no relationship or difference. They thus focus attention on the probable strength of the relationship or difference, not just whether any relationship or difference exists as assessed by statistical hypothesis tests.

Second, confidence intervals provide information about statistical power without actually requiring power analysis. Specifically, the narrower the confidence interval, the greater the statistical power. Although confidence intervals do not provide a quantitative estimate of power as is available from formal power analysis, neither does it require that one specify a parameter value to obtain the power estimate.

Finally, confidence intervals can be interpreted so that they provide the same information as a two-tailed hypothesis test. When a confidence interval of 95 (99) percent does not include zero, a two-tailed hypothesis test on the same data set will reject the null hypothesis at $p < .05$ ($p < .01$). If the confidence interval includes zero, a statistical hypothesis test will not reject the null hypothesis. These outcomes follow because the underlying probability logic of the two procedures is identical.

INTERNAL STATISTICAL VALIDITY

Hypothesis testing, statistical power, and confidence interval procedures have so far been described for statistical generalization validity, for generalizing from a sample statistic to a population parameter after drawing a probability sample from that population. However, these same procedures are also used to make internal statistical inferences when cases are randomly assigned to levels of an independent variable. This inference is of a different sort. Internal statistical validation addresses whether a particular relationship or difference is potentially the result of assignment error. *Assignment errors* lead to group differences in values of a dependent variable because of the uncertain outcomes of random assignment.

Consider an example to illustrate assignment error when cases are randomly assigned to two levels of an independent variable. A researcher randomly assigns six students to one of two training methods; three are assigned to Method A and three are assigned to Method B. A standardized achievement test is administered to all students after the training.

Outcomes are shown in Exhibit 13.11. It shows that Individuals C, E, and F are assigned to Method A and that their average achievement score is 17.33. Individuals A, B, and D are assigned to Method B and their average achievement score is 12.67. The difference is 4.67. Should the researcher conclude that Method A results in higher achievement scores than Method B?

Randomization Tests

Statistical hypothesis testing can be used to address this question. Begin with a null hypothesis that there is no difference in the average achievement test performance resulting from the two training methods. A null probability distribution can be developed using a randomization test. A

EXHIBIT 13.11. Training example outcomes

Training Type	Method A	Method B
Individual		
A		10.00
B		12.00
C	14.00	
D		16.00
E	18.00	
F	20.00	
Group Mean	17.33	12.67

randomization test generates a distribution of mean differences from all possible ways that the six students can be assigned to the two training methods in groups of three.

In the example, there are 20 such combinations, as shown in Exhibit 13.12. Also shown are the average achievement test scores and the mean differences in test scores between groups. Exhibit 13.13 shows the distribution created by the mean differences. This distribution has a mean of zero (consistent with the null hypothesis) and is symmetrical. The variability in this distribution reflects assignment error, since it shows differences in results due to different ways that random assignment can combine the six individuals into two groups.

Hypothesis testing can now proceed using the same logic described for statistical generalization. The researcher asks whether the mean difference observed is improbable given the null hypothesis. In the example, the mean difference of 4.67 is the second largest difference favoring Method A. If the null hypothesis is true, there are $2 / 20 = 0.10$ differences as large as those obtained in the study. A probability of 0.10 is larger than the p values 0.05 or 0.01 that are ordinarily regarded as statistically significant. Thus, the researcher would likely be reluctant to conclude that Method A was superior to Method B in this example.

EXHIBIT 13.12. Possible random assignments and outcomes: Six individuals to two groups

Method A	Mean	Method B	Mean	Mean Difference
ABC	12.00	DEF	18.00	−6.00
ABD	12.67	CEF	17.33	−4.67
ABE	13.33	CDF	16.67	−3.33
ABF	14.00	CDE	16.00	−2.00
ACD	13.33	BEF	16.67	−3.33
ACE	14.00	BDF	16.00	−2.00
ACF	14.67	BDE	15.33	−0.67
ADE	14.67	BCF	15.33	−0.67
ADF	15.33	BCE	14.67	0.67
AEF	16.00	BCD	14.00	2.00
BCD	14.00	AEF	16.00	−2.00
BCE	14.67	ADF	15.33	−0.67
BCF	15.33	ADE	14.67	0.67
BDE	15.33	ACF	14.67	0.67
BDF	16.00	ACE	14.00	2.00
BEF	16.67	ACD	13.33	3.33
CDE	16.00	ABF	14.00	2.00
CDF	16.67	ABE	13.33	3.33
CEF	17.33	ABD	12.67	4.67
DEF	18.00	ABC	12.00	6.00

Randomization tests are laborious to construct, the more so as sample sizes increase. Fortunately, as sample sizes increase, internal statistical inference tests can be approximated using the same probability and sampling distributions used for statistical generalization tests. In the example, a t test of mean differences can be used to perform the statistical hypothesis test. Conducting that test on the data in Exhibit 13.11 produces a probability value of 0.13.

EXHIBIT 13.13. Distribution of mean training differences given the null hypothesis

Frequency

```
          X     X   X     X
     X    X     X   X     X   X
 X   X    X  X     X   X   X   X     X   X
-6.0  -4.50  -3.00  -1.50  -0.00  -1.50  3.00  4.50  6.00
```

Concluding Cautions

The similarity of methods used to conduct statistical hypothesis testing, confidence intervals, and statistical power calculations in both internal statistical inference and statistical generalization inferences is a source of potential confusion. Because the methods are similar, there may be a temptation to conclude that the inferences drawn are similar. They are not.

Statistical generalization is appropriate when a probability sample is drawn from a population. Sample statistics are used to make inferences about population parameters subject to sampling error. Internal statistical inference is appropriate when cases are randomly assigned to levels of an independent variable. Statistics generated in such studies are used to make inferences that the results are not due to assignment error.

Sometimes researchers misinterpret their use of internal statistical validation procedures. They obtain statistically significant results using random assignment and then discuss implications of the results as if statistical generalization was addressed. This is an error.

There is a further, more widespread danger. Researchers often use statistical inference techniques without benefit of either probability sampling or random assignment. For example, a researcher surveys all participants in an organization. Statistical hypothesis testing is then performed to determine whether the results are "generalizable." No such statistical generalization is warranted. Without benefit of a probability sample, researchers have no legitimate way to estimate sampling distributions. Without sampling distributions, researchers have no legitimate way to estimate significance levels, confidence intervals, or statistical power.

SUMMARY

There are two closely related methods for using sampling distributions to make inferences about population parameters from statistics calculated on sample cases. *Hypothesis testing* addresses whether a relationship (or difference) observed in a sample suggests a relationship (difference) in the population. Hypothesis testing pits a *research hypothesis (H_1)* against a *null hypothesis (H_0)*. The research hypothesis is the hypothesis of a relationship (difference); the null hypothesis is the hypothesis of no relationship (difference). The research hypothesis is *two-tailed* when only a relationship is hypothesized; it is *one-tailed* when the direction of the relationship (difference) is specified as well.

Hypothesis testing begins by specifying the research and null hypotheses and a significance level. A probability sample is then drawn. Information from this sample is used to estimate the null hypothesis sampling distribution and to calculate the sample statistic. A critical region of the null sampling distribution is identified that serves as the criterion for the researcher's conclusion. Finally, the sample statistic is compared to this critical region that leads to a decision to either reject or not reject the null hypothesis.

Hypothesis testing may lead to two incorrect decisions. A *Type I error* is made if a researcher concludes H_1, but H_0 is true in the population. This is the error that is specified in hypothesis testing and generally kept low (5 percent or 1 percent). Alternatively, a *Type II error* is made if the researcher fails to conclude H_1 when H_1 is true in the population. Hypothesis testing does not provide information about Type II error.

Statistical power refers to the likelihood of correctly concluding H_1 from a sample statistic when H_1 is true in the population. Thus statistical power provides information about the likelihood of making a Type II error. The power of a statistical test generally increases (likelihood of a Type II error decreases) as the (a) sample size increases, (b) likelihood of a Type I error increases, and (c) relationship (difference) in the population increases. The power of two-tailed tests is also higher than the power of one-tailed tests. Measurement reliability and research design can also contribute to more powerful statistical tests.

Confidence intervals use a sample statistic and information about sampling distributions to create a range of values that likely includes the population parameter. Unlike hypothesis testing that begins with the assumption that the null hypothesis is true, confidence intervals are created on the assumption that the sample statistic is the best estimate of the population parameter. The intervals created around this sample statistic are likely to include the population parameter.

Statistical hypothesis testing, typically without power analyses, is reported by researchers more often than confidence intervals. However, confidence intervals are attractive relative to hypothesis testing because they: (a) focus on the strength of the relationship between the variables, (b) provide indirect information on statistical power, and (c) provide the same information as a two-tailed hypothesis test.

These inferential procedures can be used to make internal statistical inferences as well as external generalizations. Internal statistical inference addresses whether a statistic obtained on a group of cases studied is potentially a result of *assignment error.* Assignment errors result because random assignment procedures may not equalize scores on the dependent variable across the groups studied.

Internal statistical validity can be assessed using *randomization tests* that create null probability distributions from all possible combinations of ways that cases can be assigned to levels of an independent variable. However, as sample sizes get larger, results of randomization tests are approximated by distributions used to perform statistical generalization tests.

Although the procedures are identical, internal statistical inferences and statistical generalization inferences are different. Researchers should not confuse these inferences when interpreting research results.

FOR REVIEW

Terms to Know

Statistical hypothesis test. Estimates whether or not a relationship (or difference) observed on a sample of cases suggests there is a relationship (difference) in the population from which the sample was drawn.

Research hypothesis (H₁). Represents a researcher's expectation about what is true of the population parameter.

One-tailed hypothesis. A research hypothesis that is directional; the researcher believes a relationship is positive or negative.

Two-tailed hypothesis. A research hypothesis that is not directional; the researcher believes there is a relationship, but does not speculate on whether it is positive or negative.

Null hypothesis (H_0). The hypothesis of no relationship (or no difference) in the population.

Statistical significance level. Level of risk a researcher takes when rejecting the null hypothesis.

Degrees of freedom (d.f.). The amount of information available to estimate population parameters from sample statistics. Are used to identify the appropriate sampling distribution for statistical hypothesis tests and confidence intervals.

Type I error, also α *error.* In hypothesis testing, the error of concluding a relationship exists in the population when it does not.

Type II error, also β *error.* In hypothesis testing, the error of failing to conclude a relationship exists in the population when it does.

Statistical power. The likelihood that a statistical hypothesis test will lead to the rejection of the null hypothesis when the research hypothesis is true in the population.

Confidence intervals. A range of statistical values that likely include the population parameter.

Confidence level. The likelihood that a confidence interval includes the population parameter.

Assignment error. Results because the random allocation of cases to levels of an independent variable typically does not exactly equalize scores on the dependent variable across groups.

Randomization test. Used to develop a null probability distribution by generating all possible ways that cases may be assigned to levels of the independent variable.

Formulas to Use

Standard error of the correlation coefficient

$$SEr_{YX} = \frac{1}{\sqrt{n-1}} \tag{13.1}$$

where n = sample size

Location of the sample correlation coefficient on a t distribution with n – 2 d.f.

$$t_{cc} = r_{YX} * \frac{\sqrt{n-2}}{\sqrt{1-r_{YX}^2}}$$

(13.2)

Standard error of the regression coefficient

$$SEb_{YX} = \frac{SD_{Y \cdot X}}{SD_X \sqrt{n-1}}$$

(13.3)

where $SD_{Y \cdot X}$ = standard error of estimate of Y on X, estimate of the standard deviation of the residual errors in the population

Standard error of estimate of Y on X

$$SD_{Y \cdot X} = \frac{n-1}{n-2} * SD_Y^2 (1 - r_{YX}^2)$$

(13.4)

Regression coefficient confidence interval (95%), n – 2 d.f.

$$CI = b_{YX} \pm SEb_{YX} * t_{95}$$

(13.5)

where t_{95} is the t distribution value for a 95 percent confidence interval

Questions for Review

1. Use the formulas provided to test a research hypothesis that a simple correlation coefficient between Y and X is not equal to zero in the population. A simple random sample of 62 cases has been drawn from a population and a sample correlation, $r_{YX} = 0.20$, has been calculated. Exhibit 13.2 has needed t-distribution information. What conclusion do you reach?

2. Use the formulas provided to develop a 95 percent confidence interval around a sample regression coefficient, $b_{YX} = 5.00$, obtained on a random sample of 122 cases. Other sample statistics are $SD_Y = 150.00, SD_X = 9.00$, and $r_{YX} = 0.30$. Exhibit 13.2 has needed t-distri-

bution information. What conclusion would you reach if instead of confidence intervals you had tested a two-tailed statistical hypothesis test, $p < .05$?

3. A researcher conducts a statistical hypothesis test in the usual way and concludes that a sample correlation coefficient ($r = .25$) is statistically significant ($p < .05$). What does this statement say about the population correlation coefficient?

4. A researcher conducts a two-tailed statistical hypothesis test in the usual way and makes a Type II error. What can you say about the population parameter, and what can you say about the sample statistic?

5. Be able to discuss how the statistical power of a test is influenced by the strength of the relationship in the population, the significance level, and the sample size.

6. A researcher conducts an experiment by randomly assigning cases to two levels (A or B) of an independent variable. The researcher tests a research hypothesis that the dependent variable is larger on average in Group A than B against a null hypothesis of no difference. The test is correctly performed, and the researcher rejects the null hypothesis at $p < 0.05$.

   In this case, the researcher may make a Type I error. In words, what does a Type I error mean in this situation?

   Assume instead that the statistical test provides a correct outcome. What conclusion should the researcher draw from the statistical test?

7. Compare and contrast sampling error with assignment error.

Issues to Discuss

1. Type I errors have been described in the context of hypothesis testing. Think about them in the context of confidence intervals. Using a simple regression coefficient, describe a population parameter, sample statistic, and confidence intervals that would be comparable to making a Type I error in hypothesis testing.

2. For a given sample statistic, sample size, and so forth, what assumption(s) about the sampling distribution differs in hypothesis testing as compared with confidence intervals? What assumption(s) remains the same?

3. Statistical hypothesis testing and confidence intervals both use probability theory to make internal and external statistical inferences. Researchers usually report one or the other but not both. Discuss your preferences. Why would you prefer one method to the other?

APPENDIX 13A:
FORMULAS FOR STATISTICAL INFERENCE[1]

This appendix provides procedures to compute tests of statistical inference for simple and multiple correlation and regression. Computer programs that calculate statistics usually calculate some, but not all, of the statistical inference values reported here.

SAMPLING DISTRIBUTIONS

Three sampling distributions are needed to perform statistical inference tests for statistics described in this book. These are the standard normal, t, and F distributions.

Exhibit 13.2 (in the body of the chapter) shows values that identify conventional critical regions of the t and standard normal distributions. There are separate t distributions for each number of degrees of freedom (d.f.). Inference tests described next that use t distributions report the number of d.f. to use.

Exhibit 13A.1 shows critical values for F distributions. These distributions are used to make statistical inferences about overall multiple correlation and regression statistics. For example, an F distribution can be used to estimate whether a sample multiple coefficient of determination, obtained from a set of independent variables, suggests that they collectively explain variance in a dependent variable among the population of cases.

F distributions are formed from the ratio of two variances. They thus involve two sets of d.f., one that applies to the numerator, the other to the denominator. There is a separate F distribution for each combination of numerator and denominator d.f. Unlike t and standard normal distribution inferential tests that can be one- or two-tailed, F distribution tests for the statistical significance of multiple correlation and regression are one-tailed.

[1]Linda Brothers' contribution to this appendix is gratefully acknowledged.

EXHIBIT 13A.1. Values identifying critical regions of the *F* distribution

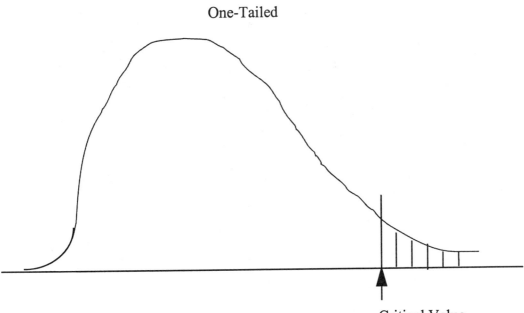

One-Tailed

Critical Value

d.f. denom- inator	d.f. numerator for $p < .05$					d.f. numerator for $p < .01$				
	1	2	3	4	5	1	2	3	4	5
5	6.61	5.79	5.41	5.19	5.05	16.30	13.30	12.10	11.40	11.00
10	4.96	4.10	3.71	3.48	3.33	10.00	7.56	6.55	5.99	5.64
20	4.35	3.49	3.10	2.87	2.71	8.10	5.85	4.94	4.43	4.10
40	4.08	3.23	2.84	2.61	2.45	7.31	5.18	4.31	3.83	3.51
60	4.00	3.15	2.76	2.53	2.37	7.08	4.98	4.13	3.65	3.34
120	3.92	3.07	2.68	2.45	2.29	6.85	4.79	3.95	3.48	3.17
∞	3.84	3.00	2.60	2.37	2.21	6.63	4.61	3.78	3.32	3.02

STATISTICAL INFERENCE TESTS

Simple Correlation Coefficient

Test H_1, $\rho_{YX} \neq 0.0$ (two-tailed) or $\rho_{YX} > 0.0$ (one-tailed) against H_0, $\rho_{YX} = 0.0$

$$t_{cc} = \frac{r_{YX}\sqrt{n-2}}{\sqrt{1-r^2_{YX}}} \qquad \textbf{(13A.1)}$$

where t_{cc} is the sample correlation coefficient transformed to a value on a t distribution with $(n-2)$ d.f.

The hypothesis is tested by comparing the computed value of t_{cc} with the critical value on the t distribution determined by the significance level, test of a two-tailed or a one-tailed hypothesis, and the d.f.

Example. A researcher sets a statistical significance criterion of $p < .05$ for a test of whether a sample correlation coefficient obtained on a sample of 122 participants signals that a relationship in the population is greater than 0.0 (a one-tailed hypothesis). Exhibit 13.2 shows that the value on the t distribution, d.f. = 120, is 1.66. The correlation coefficient obtained on the sample is $r_{YX} = .24$. From Formula 13A.1, $t_{cc} = 2.71$, the researcher concludes H_1, the relationship in the population is greater than 0.0.

Confidence interval for ρ_{YX}

Confidence intervals for simple correlation coefficients require a new statistic, z_r; it is created because the sampling distribution of ρ_{YX} is symmetrical only when $\rho_{YX} = 0.0$. The sampling distribution of z_r, alternatively, is approximately normal for any value of ρ_{YX} and has a standard error of:

$$SE_{z_r} = \frac{1}{\sqrt{n-3}} \qquad \textbf{(13A.2)}$$

To obtain a confidence interval for ρ_{YX}, first establish the confidence level (e.g., 95% or 99% corresponding to significance levels of $p < .05$ or $p < .01$, respectively). Second, find the value of z_r from Exhibit 13A.2 corresponding to the sample value of r_{YX}. Third, determine the confidence interval for z_r from:

EXHIBIT 13A.2. zr transformations of r

r	zr	r	zr	r	zr	r	zr
0.000	0.000	0.300	0.310	0.600	0.693	0.850	1.256
0.010	0.010	0.310	0.321	0.610	0.709	0.855	1.274
0.020	0.020	0.320	0.332	0.620	0.725	0.860	1.293
0.030	0.030	0.330	0.343	0.630	0.741	0.865	1.313
0.040	0.040	0.340	0.354	0.640	0.758	0.870	1.333
0.050	0.050	0.350	0.365	0.650	0.775	0.875	1.354
0.060	0.060	0.360	0.377	0.660	0.793	0.880	1.376
0.070	0.070	0.370	0.388	0.670	0.811	0.885	1.398
0.080	0.080	0.380	0.400	0.680	0.829	0.890	1.422
0.090	0.090	0.390	0.412	0.690	0.848	0.895	1.447
0.100	0.100	0.400	0.424	0.700	0.867	0.900	1.472
0.110	0.110	0.410	0.436	0.710	0.887	0.905	1.499
0.120	0.121	0.420	0.448	0.720	0.908	0.910	1.528
0.130	0.131	0.430	0.460	0.730	0.929	0.915	1.557
0.140	0.141	0.440	0.472	0.740	0.950	0.920	1.589
0.150	0.151	0.450	0.485	0.750	0.973	0.925	1.623
0.160	0.161	0.460	0.497	0.760	0.996	0.930	1.658
0.170	0.172	0.470	0.510	0.770	1.020	0.935	1.697
0.180	0.182	0.480	0.523	0.780	1.045	0.940	1.738
0.190	0.192	0.490	0.536	0.790	1.071	0.945	1.783
0.200	0.203	0.500	0.549	0.800	1.099	0.950	1.832
0.210	0.213	0.510	0.563	0.805	1.113	0.955	1.886
0.220	0.224	0.520	0.576	0.810	1.127	0.960	1.946
0.230	0.234	0.530	0.590	0.815	1.142	0.965	2.014
0.240	0.245	0.540	0.604	0.820	1.157	0.970	2.092
0.250	0.255	0.550	0.618	0.825	1.172	0.975	2.185
0.260	0.266	0.560	0.633	0.830	1.188	0.980	2.298
0.270	0.277	0.570	0.648	0.835	1.204	0.985	2.443
0.280	0.288	0.580	0.662	0.840	1.221	0.990	2.647
0.290	0.299	0.590	0.678	0.845	1.238	0.995	2.994

$$CI_{zr} = z_r \pm (z_{sl} * SE\, z_r) \qquad (13A.3)$$

where z_{sl} is the two-tailed value on the standard normal distribution corresponding to the significance level (see bottom of Exhibit 13.2)

Finally, set the confidence interval for ρ_{YX} by transforming the values of z_r back to correlation coefficient values.

Example. A researcher wants to determine a confidence interval for the population's correlation coefficient at the 99 percent confidence level based on a sample correlation coefficient of $\rho_{YX} = .63$ obtained on a sample of 67 participants. From Exhibit 13A.2, $z_r = .741$, and by Formula 13A.2, $SEz_r = .125$. Formula 13A.3 then shows that $.419 < CI_{zr} < 1.064$. Finally, after transforming the values of z_r back to correlation coefficient values (use Exhibit 13A.2), the researcher finds that $.40 < CI\rho_{YX} < .79$.

Test H_1, $\rho_{YXa} \neq \rho_{YXb}$ (two-tailed), or $\rho_{YXa} > \rho_{YXb}$ (one-tailed) against H_0 $\rho_{YXa} = \rho_{YXb}$, where a and b refer to two different populations. (This test also requires z_r.)

$$z_{cc} = \frac{z_{rYXa} - z_{rYXb}}{\sqrt{\dfrac{1}{n_a - 3}} + \sqrt{\dfrac{1}{n_b - 3}}} \qquad (13A.4)$$

where z_{cc} = is a transformed value of the sample statistic on a standard normal distribution, z_{rYXa} and z_{rYXb} refer to the z_r transformations of r_{YXa} and r_{YXb} for samples from populations a and b, respectively, and n_a and n_b refer to the sample sizes selected from populations a and b, respectively

The hypothesis is tested by comparing the computed value of z_{cc} with the value on the standard normal distribution determined by the significance level and whether the test is of a two-tailed or a one-tailed hypothesis.

Example. A researcher hypothesizes that the relationship between income level and financial contributions to a political party is greater among the population of registered Democrats than among the population of registered Republicans. This is a one-tailed hypothesis and a significance level of $p < .05$ is established. Probability samples are obtained of 112 registered Democrats (Population A) and of 128 registered Republicans (Population

B). The correlation coefficients obtained on these samples are $r_{YXa} = .36$ and $r_{YXb} = .29$. From Exhibit 13A.2, $z_{rYXa} = .377$ and $z_{rYXb} = .299$. From Formula 13A.4, $z_{cc} = 0.60$. Comparing this value to the value of 1.64 obtained from Exhibit 13.2 leads to the conclusion that the hypothesis test fails to reject the null hypothesis that $\rho_{YXa} = \rho_{YXb}$ at a significance level of $p < .05$.

Test H_1, $\rho_{YX1} \neq \rho_{YX2}$ (two-tailed), or $\rho_{YX1} > \rho_{YX2}$ (one-tailed) against H_0, $\rho_{YX1} = \rho_{YX2}$, when computed for the same population

$$t_{cc} = r_{YX1} - r_{YX2} \sqrt{\frac{n - 3(1 + r_{X1X2})}{2 * (1 - r^2_{X1X2} - r^2_{YX1} - r^2_{YX2}) + \left(2 * r_{X1X2} * r_{YX1} * r_{YX2}\right)}}$$

(13A.5)

where t_{cc} is a transformed value of the sample statistic on a t distribution with $(n - 3)$ d.f.

The hypothesis is tested by comparing the computed value of t_{cc} with the value on the t distribution determined by the significance level, test of a two-tailed or a one-tailed hypothesis, and the d.f.

Example. A researcher hypothesizes that the relationship between job pay (Y) and years of work experience $(X1)$ is greater than the relationship between Y and age $(X2)$ in a population of employees. This is a one-tailed hypothesis and the researcher establishes a statistical significance level of $p < .01$. An employee sample of 83 is obtained. The correlation coefficients determined for this sample are $r_{YX1} = .73$, $r_{YX2} = .57$, and $r_{X1X2} = .68$. From Formula 13A.5, $t_{cc} = 2.65$, the researcher concludes that $\rho_{YX1} > \rho_{YX2}$ at a significance level of $p < .01$ after comparing this value to the value of 2.38 obtained from Exhibit 13.2 (d.f. = 80).

Simple Regression Coefficient

Test H_1 $B_{YX} \neq 0.0$ (two-tailed) or that $B_{YX} > 0.0$ (one-tailed) against H_0 $B_{YX} = 0.0$

$$t_{cc} = \frac{b_{YX}}{SEb_{YX}} \qquad (13A.6)$$

where t_{cc} is a transformed value of the sample statistic value on a t distribution with $(n - 2)$ d.f. and SEb_{YX} is the standard error of the regression coefficient defined as:

$$SEb_{YX} = \frac{SD_{Y \cdot X}}{SD_X \sqrt{n-1}} \qquad (13A.7)$$

and $SD_{Y \cdot X}$ is the standard error of estimate of Y on X which is defined as:

$$SD_{Y \cdot X} = \sqrt{\frac{n-1}{n-2}} * SD^2_Y (1 - r^2_{YX}) \qquad (13A.8)$$

The hypothesis is tested by comparing the computed value of t_{cc} with the value on the t distribution determined by the significance level, test of a two-tailed or a one-tailed hypothesis, and d.f. $(n-2)$.

Example. A researcher hypothesizes that changes in levels of job satisfaction predict changes in levels of absenteeism. This is a two-tailed hypothesis and a significance level of $p < .05$ is established. The researcher obtains a sample of 32 employees. Exhibit 13.2 shows that the value on the t distribution, d.f. = 30, is 2.04.

Sample statistics required to test H_1 are $SD_X = 0.5$, $SD_Y = 3.0$, $r_{YX} = 0.20$, and $b_{YX} = 1.20$. From Formula 13A.8, $SD_{Y \cdot X} = 2.99$; from Formula 13A.7, $SEb_{YX} = 1.07$; and from Formula 13A.6, $t_{cc} = 1.11$. The researcher concludes that the hypothesis test based on the sample regression coefficient fails to reject the null hypothesis that $B_{YX} = 0.0$.

Confidence interval for B_{YX}

$$\mathbf{CI = b_{YX} \pm (t_{sl} * SEb_{YX})} \qquad (13A.9)$$

where t_{sl} is the the t distribution value with $(n-2)$ d.f. corresponding to the two-tailed significance level

Example. From the preceding illustration, assume the researcher instead wants to determine the confidence interval for the regression coefficient of the population. The researcher establishes a confidence interval of 95 percent. From Formula 13A.9, $-0.98 < CI \; B_{YX} < 3.35$.

Multiple Coefficient of Determination

Test H_1, $P^2_{YXiXj} > 0.0$ (one-tailed only) against H_0, $P^2_{YXiXj} = 0.0$ [2]

---

[2]This is the same statistical test to determine whether $P_{YXiXj} > 0.0$.

$$F_{cc} = \frac{R^2_{YXiXj}/(n-k-1)}{(1-R^2_{YXiXj})/k} \qquad \text{(13A.10)}$$

where k is the number of independent variables (two shown in this case) and F_{cc} is a transformed value of the sample statistic on a F distribution with $[k$ and $(n-k-1)]$ d.f.

The hypothesis is tested by comparing the computed value of F_{cc} with the value on the F distribution determined by the significance level and the $[k$ and $(n-k-1)]$ d.f.

Example. A researcher hypothesizes that variance in the rate of turnover of companies in the same industry will be explained by differences in average employee income level, level of employer-provided benefits, and perceived job alternatives. The researcher establishes a significance level of $p <$ .01 for the test and obtains data on a sample of 24 companies. The multiple coefficient of determination obtained on the sample is $R^2_{YX1X2X3} = .45$. From Formula (13A.10), $F_{cc} = 5.45$. Comparing this to the value of 4.94 obtained from Exhibit 13A.1, the researcher concludes that $P^2_{YX1X2X3} > 0.0$ at a significance level of $p < .01$.

Partial Beta Coefficients[3]

Test hypothesis that $Beta_{YXi \cdot Xj} \neq 0.0$ (two-tailed) or that $Beta_{YXi \cdot Xj} > 0.0$ (one-tailed)

$$SEbeta_{YXiXj} = \sqrt{\frac{1-R^2_{YXiXj}}{n-k-1}} \sqrt{\frac{1}{1-r^2_{YXj}}} \qquad \text{(13A.11)}$$

$$t_{cc} = \frac{beta_{YXi \cdot Xj}}{SEbeta_{YXi \cdot Xj}} \qquad \text{(13A.12)}$$

where t_{cc} is a transformed value of the sample statistic value on a t distribution with $(n-k-1)$ d.f., and k is the number of independent variables

---

[3]The same test establishes the statistical significance of the corresponding unstandardized partial regression coefficients.

The hypothesis is tested by comparing the computed value of t_{cc} with the value on the t distribution determined by the significance level, test of a two-tailed or a one-tailed hypothesis, and the d.f.

Example. A researcher hypothesizes that satisfaction with life depends on job satisfaction ($X1$) and gender ($X2$). These are two-tailed hypotheses and significance levels of $p < .05$ are established for each independent variable. The researcher obtains a sample of 63 employees. Exhibit 13.2 shows that the value on the t distribution, d.f. = 60, is 2.00. The statistics obtained on the sample are $R^2_{YX1X2} = .49$; $r^2_{YX1} = .41$; $r^2_{YX2} = .20$; $beta_{YX1 \cdot X2} = .35$; $beta_{YX2 \cdot X1} = .27$; $SD_Y = .92$; $SD_{X1} = .85$; $SD_{X2} = .50$; and, by Formula 13A.11, $SEbeta_{YX1 \cdot X2} = .10$ and $SEbeta_{YX2 \cdot X1} = .12$. From Formula 13A.12, $t_{cc} = 3.50$ and 2.25. Comparing these values to 2.00, the researcher concludes that $Beta_{YX1 \cdot X2} \neq 0.0$ (or $B_{YX1 \cdot X2} \neq 0.0$) and that $Beta_{YX2 \cdot X1} \neq 0.0$ (or $B_{YX2 \cdot X1} \neq 0.0$) at a significance level of $p < .05$.

Confidence interval for $Beta_{YXi \cdot Xj}$ ($B_{YXi \cdot Xj}$)

$$CI = beta_{YXi \cdot Xj} \pm (t_{sl/2} * SEbeta_{YXi \cdot Xj}) \qquad \text{(13A.13a)}$$

$$CI = b_{YXi \cdot Xj} \pm (t_{sl/2} * SEb_{YXi \cdot Xj}) \qquad \text{(13A.13b)}$$

where $t_{sl/2}$ is the value on the t distribution with ($n - k - 1$) d.f. corresponding to the significance level divided by two ($sl/2$).

Example. Using information from the previous example, assume the researcher instead wants to determine the confidence intervals for the partial beta coefficients of the population. The researcher establishes a confidence level of 95 percent. From Formula 13A.13a and 13A.13b, $.15 < CI\ Beta_{YX1 \cdot X2} < .55$ ($.16 < CI\ B_{YX1 \cdot X2} < .60$) and $.03 < CI\ Beta_{YX2 \cdot X1} < .51$ ($.06 < CI\ B_{YX2 \cdot X1} < .94$).

Incremental R^2

Test hypothesis that addition of an independent variable(s) adds to variance explained in Y.

$$F_{cc} = \frac{(R^2_{YB} - R^2_{YSA})/(B - A)}{(1 - R^2_{YB})/(n - B - 1)} \qquad (13A.14)$$

where Fcc is a transformed value of the sample statistic on a F distribution with [(B-A) and (n-B-1)] d.f. B is the total number of independent variables, A is the number of initial independent variables, and (B-A) is the number of independent variables added.

The hypothesis is tested by comparing the computed value of F_{cc} wih the value on the F distrubution determined by the significance level and [(B - a) and (n - B - 1)] d. f.

Example. A researcher hypothesizes that incremental variance in income will be explained by race and gender after controlling for age, years of work experience and years of education; A = 3, B = 5, and B - A = 2. A statistical significance level of p < .05 is extablished. A probability sample of 126 participants is drawn from a population; R^2_{YA} = .25 and R^2_{YB} = .28. The addition of race and gender add three percent to the explanation of income variance after the control variables are accounted for. F_{cc} from formula 13A - 15 = 2.50. Comparing this value to the value of 3.07 obtained from Exhibit 13A-1, the reasearcher concludes that the hypothesis test based on the sample multiple coefficients of determination fails to reject the null hypotheses that P^2_{YXB} - P^2_{YXA} = 0.0 at a significance level of p < .05.

PART V: SUGGESTED READING

A substantial number of statistical hypothesis testing and confidence interval procedures are provided in the Appendix to Chapter 13 for correlation and regression. Standard statistics textbooks also typically include hypothesis testing and confidence interval procedures for other statistics such as means and proportions.

However, standard textbooks may not have much to say about statistical power. Cohen and Cohen (1983) have the most complete discussion of power regarding correlation and regression that I'm familiar with. In addition, Cohen (1988) has a book devoted to statistical power issues and methods for calculating it.

Abelson (1995) offered an interesting perspective on statistics and especially statistical inference. He emphasized contributions that probability and statistics can make to the generalization of understandings from research. The book is easy to understand.

Statistical inference is a topic that has generated a substantial amount of controversy in the social sciences. Contentious issues involve when significance testing is appropriate, preferences for statistical hypothesis testing versus confidence intervals, and contributions of significance testing to the advancement of knowledge. Although some of this controversy arises because of misunderstandings about basic issues covered in this book, some revolve around more subtle issues. Readers interested in obtaining more detailed knowledge on these topics may read books by Oakes (1986) and Morrison and Henkel (1970). Cohen (1994), Hagen (1997), and Schmidt (1996) have written recent papers that address these issues from very different perspectives.

VI

GENERALIZATION: ADDRESSING EXTERNAL VALIDITY

14

External Validity

Chapter Outline

- *External Generalization Challenges*
- *Generalizing from Single Studies*
- *Replication*
  - *Replication Roles*
  - *Narrative Reviews of Replications*
- *Meta-Analysis*
  - *Example*
  - *Evaluation*
- *Summary*
- *For Review*
- *Part VI: Suggested Reading*

A training manager in an investment firm hypothesizes that knowledge about investment derivatives will help a firm's investment counselors recommend more profitable investment choices to clients. (An *investment derivative* is a security whose value depends on the price of some other security. A stock option is an example; the value of the option depends on the price of the stock.) A training program is developed, and a sample of investment counselors is trained. Client investment performance is then compared between the trained counselors and a sample of untrained counselors over a 12-month period following the training. As expected, the manager finds that clients of the trained counselors obtain a higher investment return.

No generalization issues are involved if the manager is simply curious about the relationship between counselor training and client investment performance in the group studied. However, research is seldom conducted for such a limited purpose; researchers and research consumers are almost always interested in generalizing research results.

The following questions illustrate ways a researcher may wish to generalize the observed relationship:

- Does the relationship found among sample counselors suggest a relationship in the firm's population of counselors?
- Does the relationship suggest that clients who worked with trained counselors will continue to obtain superior investment performance in the next 12 months?
- Should another firm conclude investment performance will improve if its counselors are given the same training?
- Will investment performance improve if the training program is modified to be less expensive?
- Will investment performance improve if the training focuses on another type of investment instrument?

The external statistical validation procedures described in Part V provide information only on the first question. During the previous 12 months, was there a relationship between training and investment performance in the population of firm counselors? Furthermore, statistical generalization procedures address this question correctly only if the sample drawn is representative of the population of counselors in the firm.

External statistical validation receives separate status largely because there are elegant procedures available. It is not necessarily more important than the other kinds of generalization suggested by these questions; often it is not as important.

This chapter discusses issues associated with other types of research generalization that interest researchers and consumers who rely on research results. It begins by discussing challenges confronting such generalization. It then describes contributions of repeating research studies to address generalization. Finally, it discusses two procedures for evaluating research repetitions and generalizing from them.

EXTERNAL GENERALIZATION CHALLENGES

Empirical research studies are conducted on a specific group of cases at a particular moment in time. However, researchers are almost always interested in generalizing the findings beyond that group and time period. For example, it is almost certain that an investment training manager is not particularly interested in a relationship between training and client investment performance observed in the past. The manager wants to know if the relationship can be expected in the future. Is it reasonable to suppose that future client investment performance will improve relative to untrained counselors if the same training were implemented with a group of counselors now?

This illustrates one of the greatest challenges facing research—change. Research findings obtained at one time often do not generalize to findings at another time. In the illustration, economic climates change, so it is likely that successful investment strategies change. As a consequence, strategies involving investment derivatives that are successful during a time period studied may not be successful in the future.

Research investigations that ask for opinions about topical issues are particularly susceptible to changes that may invalidate generalizations to other time periods. For example, survey studies designed to predict election outcomes are conducted before citizens actually vote. Questions to a probability sample of prospective voters are often prefaced with, "If the election were held today, . . ."

Results of such surveys often accurately reflect voter population sentiment at the time taken; sampling error as discussed in Part V is small. Yet the sample estimate may not predict the election outcome. Voter opinions in the population change between the date the survey is conducted and the date the election is held. The research results, even though statistically valid, do not generalize to the relevant time period.

So, change resulting from the passage of time is one important dimension of external generalization. Another important dimension involves the cases in which research results are applicable. Researchers often are interested in generalizing results from a group(s) studied to groups not studied. For example, if the derivative training is successful among counselors in one investment firm, will it also be successful among counselors in other investment firms? Will it be successful among trust department counselors in commercial banks?

Statistical generalization procedures are not designed to address questions of this sort. Inferences using sampling distributions as described in the last chapter require that generalization be made only to the population from which the probability sample was drawn. Generalizations beyond that specific population transcend what statistical generalization can deliver.

GENERALIZING FROM SINGLE STUDIES

There is no systematic or verifiable method to conduct external validation based solely on a single investigation of a research relationship. By definition, external generalization is aimed at cases and environments that transcend the boundaries of the study and hence cannot be addressed within it. Nevertheless, researchers are usually interested in ways their results likely generalize as noted.

As a consequence, researchers typically address external validity in the discussion section of research reports. When done well, this section is the product of the thoughtful identification of similarities and potentially important differences between the cases and environment studied with other cases and environments to which the results may also apply. Simply put, results from any one study are most likely to generalize to similar cases and environments.

The quality of this type of generalization depends on a researcher's knowledge of important characteristics (variables) that may influence results from one research setting to another. In the language of Chapter 5, researchers must be able to identify probable moderator variables. Relationships generalize across research environments, such as time, as long as the new environments do not represent different values of moderator variables that change the nature of the relationship(s) observed.

To illustrate, under what conditions might the investment derivative training not generalize? One potential moderator may be the investment sophistication of the counselors trained. A group of counselors markedly less sophisticated than those studied may not acquire the necessary knowledge and hence not provide appropriate investment advice even though they are trained. Or, the counselor payment system may serve as a moderator. The counselors trained in the illustration may be paid incentives for improving client investment returns. Training may be ineffective among counselors who are not paid in the same way.

Exhibit 14.1 shows a simple representation of the issues involved. Research investigates a relationship between *X* and *Y*. These variables are inside the ellipse to signal that their relationship is actually studied by a researcher. Outside the circle are potential moderator variables (*M*1 to *Mk*), potential limits or boundaries to generalization.

EXHIBIT 14.1. Limits on generalization

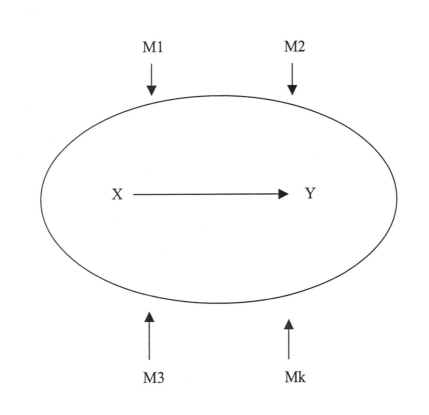

REPLICATION

Researchers conducting single studies can only speculate about conditions that may apply outside the domain of the variables studied. Judgmental claims of generalization, therefore, must be provisional. Whether results actually generalize across potential moderator variables to other cases or environments can only be established by replication. A ***replication*** is a research study that investigates a research issue that has already been studied; it repeats a previous study.

Replication Roles

Replications permit external generalization of a more rigorous sort if they differ from previous research on values of potential moderator variables. Although neither the original study nor its replication has variation in a moderator variable (e.g., $M1$ in Exhibit 14.1), the two taken together may bring the moderator into the ellipse. For example, a comparison of the original training study with replication using less sophisticated counselors provides information about whether the training generalizes across levels of sophistication.

Some researchers argue that the word *replication* should be reserved for studies that are identical to a study replicated. In this view, replications are often seen as superior to *partial replications* or *constructive replications,* terms recommended if the studies are not identical.

This view misses the point that a replication always differs from a prior study. The time period must be different even in the unlikely event that the cases and measures are identical. Subtle design characteristics typically also differ even when researchers seek to identically replicate a prior study. More important, it is desirable that replications differ, because the differences provide information about the generalizability of findings as noted.

This last observation may suggest that the more variability between the original study and a replication, the better. For example, why not conduct a replication on counselors that are both less sophisticated and are paid using a different compensation system? One obtains evidence that the results generalize over both potential moderator variables if the results of the replication and the original results are similar. This strategy is often acceptable as long as the results from the replication mirror the results in the original study. However, when they do not, the replication provides little information about whether the difference is due to differences in counselor sophistication, differences in pay systems, or both.

As a consequence, researchers must seek a balance when designing replications. On the one hand, it is desirable to generalize as broadly as possible. This encourages varying replications along values of several potential moderators. On the other hand, it is also important to link replications to previous research. Cumulative knowledge is only possible when research studies share important characteristics, when they are similar enough so that results obtained in one study provide useful information when interpreting results from another.

RESEARCH HIGHLIGHT 14.1

Triangulation As Replication

There are many challenges for studies investigating causal conceptual relationships as emphasized throughout this book. Seldom does a single study lead to great confidence that construct or internal validity is established, much less both. These reservations are raised in part because each research method has shortcomings. To illustrate, experiments potentially address certain threats to internal validity but may be problematic in other respects. For example, one may question whether a research manipulation of an independent variable properly captures the construct of interest in an experiment that is otherwise exemplary.

Researchers are encouraged to address this type of challenge by *triangulation,* by investigating a research question using other methods of measurement, design, and even analysis. In triangulation, the concern is not so much substantive as it is methodological. Replications are designed to see if results hold up across different research methods for obtaining them.

How close replications should mirror prior research depends largely on the strength of the conceptualization underlying the research and the "maturity" of the finding(s). Replications should closely approximate the design of original research when a research result is novel and has little conceptual support. Researchers conducting replications involving relationships that are supported in several prior studies, or by strong conceptual models, may be justified in testing the limits of generalization.

Replications serve as the best method for addressing external generalization. As more replications are conducted, more potential moderator variables can be drawn inside the ellipse shown in Exhibit 14.1. Replication is even desirable for external statistical validation because of the probabilistic, and hence potentially erroneous, conclusions that emerge from statistical inference procedures.

However, drawing valid external generalizations from replications is a challenging exercise. Challenges arise because results obtained on studies of the same conceptual relationship(s) are seldom identical. Two studies of the same relationship often obtain different results even though they use the same measures, are conducted at about the same time, and study cases that appear to be similar. The water is muddied further when another replication obtains results that are similar to one of the first two but differs from it on some important characteristic. Now, multiply these ambiguous outcomes across many more replications, and you begin to appreciate the difficulties confronting external generalization.

Narrative Reviews of Replications

Until about 25 years ago, most generalization of replications was performed through *narrative research reviews.* A narrative research review reports a researcher's judgmental summary and evaluation of a body of research on some topic. The quality of the review depends on the reviewer's knowledge of the topic and research methods.

For example, a reviewer may wish to know what research says about the effectiveness of investment derivative training for improving investment performance. Such reviews begin with a search for studies of investment derivative training that have already been conducted and summarized in research reports. The studies found serve in the same role as cases in an empirical study; each study contains information that is analogous to information provided by research cases more generally.

Typically, reviewers next evaluate the studies and make decisions about which "cases" to include for analysis. Should all studies found be included, regardless of design characteristics? Or, should some studies be excluded because they do not meet standards for design (e.g., evidence of internal validity), sampling (e.g., sample size), or other characteristics? For example, should training studies only be included if they are true experiments, in which counselors are randomly assigned to training or control conditions? Or should quasi-experiments also be included? Reviewers using different evaluation standards often reach different conclusions about a body of research because they impose different standards in this stage.

Reviewers then analyze the studies; they make judgments about the findings obtained in each study reviewed. An assessment is made about whether, and to what degree, each study finds support for the investigated relationship(s) of interest. For example, to what degree does each study find evidence that investment derivative training improves subsequent investment performance?

Evaluations of specific studies, often combined with a description of noteworthy design characteristics, are followed by conclusions regarding the findings overall. For example, what can be concluded about the direction and strength of relationship between investment derivative training and investment performance, and under what conditions does this relationship likely hold? In narrative reviews, judgments about findings, and the probable conditions over which these findings generalize, are made qualitatively by the reviewer.

Reviews of the type described can make valuable contributions. They are especially useful when combined with thoughtful suggestions for additional research and conceptual development.

But such reviews also face difficulties. As with discussions of generalization found in single studies, they depend heavily on the expertise and good judgment of the reviewer. Though these may be substantial, they cannot be articulated for public examination. Such reviews become increasingly problematic as the number of studies to review becomes large. As the number of studies increases, so do burdens on reviewers; it is an increasing challenge to apply consistent standards for the many decisions that must be made about each study.

META-ANALYSIS

Meta-analysis is a more recent procedure used to evaluate and generalize from research replications. It is designed to overcome some of the problems of traditional narrative reviews. It does so by using quantitative procedures developed for conducting original research. Meta-analysis is especially useful as the number of studies to review becomes large.

Unlike many research methods, meta-analysis methods are still in the process of development. Controversy still clouds a number of basic issues; advocates of different methods compete for support in the marketplace of ideas. These points are raised to signal caution. Ideas expressed in this section are not accepted by all those interested in meta-analysis. However, an effort is made to emphasize points of view that are generally accepted and to alert you to issues that are still contentious.

It is generally agreed that meta-analysis techniques sprang up independently in several different academic disciplines. Researchers started to conduct reviews using meta-analysis techniques before a methodology was codified and named; the techniques have been used in the social sciences beginning at least as early as the 1930s (Bangert-Drowns, 1986). Codification of meta-analysis procedures were reported beginning in the 1970s.

Meta-analysis is distinguished from narrative reviews by its use of additional empirical research methods. Indeed, a good way to understand meta-analysis is to think of it as a special form of field study research, as described in Chapter 7. Exhibit 14.2 summarizes characteristics that differentiate meta-analysis from a typical original survey or field study.

EXHIBIT 14.2. Special characteristics of meta-analysis

Research Elements	Elements in Meta-Analysis
Cases to study	Research studies, or results of research studies
Dependent variable	Direction and strength of relationships observed in the studies reviewed
Independent variables	Substantive and methodological characteristics of the studies reviewed

As Exhibit 14.2 shows, "cases" in meta-analysis are studies, or results from studies, just as in narrative literature reviews. A feature that distinguishes meta-analysis techniques from both narrative reviews and conventional empirical research involves the dependent variable. In meta-analysis, the dependent variable is a statistic that describes the results of the studies reviewed. Preferred dependent variables describe the size and direction of a relationship(s) found in the studies reviewed. For example, a meta-analysis of investment derivative training studies might take the mean difference in client investment performance between groups receiving training versus control groups. This difference is standardized for each study so that comparisons can be made across studies.

Another characteristic that distinguishes meta-analysis from conventional empirical research involves independent variables. In meta-analysis, independent variables are study characteristics that may account for differences in the relationship (difference) that represents the dependent variable. For example, market conditions prevailing when the training was conducted

RESEARCH HIGHLIGHT 14.2

An Inappropriate Dependent Variable for Meta-Analysis

Sometimes reviewers use statistical significance values reported in the studies reviewed as the dependent variable. For example, a review of investment derivative studies may calculate and then report the percentage of studies that found investment derivative groups to obtain statistically significantly greater client investment performance ($p < 0.05$) than control groups.

This **box-score method** has three related limitations and is generally to be avoided. First, what is statistically significant, at any level, depends only partly on the strength of the relationship between the variables. It also depends on sample size. Small sample sizes require larger relationships (differences) to be statistically significant. Thus, the statistical significance between two studies can differ, even though the strength of the relationship does not, because the studies employed different sized samples. Second, the box-score method ignores valuable information about the strength of the relationships (differences). Studies with large samples may have statistically significant results even though the relationships, or differences, are small. Finally, the studies reviewed may not have used statistical significance appropriately. Statistical significance testing is often used when the sampling or participant assignment procedures do not warrant it. In such cases, statistical significance testing was used improperly in the original studies and would thus also be used improperly as a criterion for review.

may serve as an independent variable if a meta-analyst believes that market conditions influence the effectiveness of training.

Independent variables may be either substantive or methodological. Substantive characteristics are specific to the conceptual issue researched (e.g., market conditions, in the investment training illustration). Methodological characteristics refer to design issues. For example, a meta-analysis of derivative training may differentiate between studies that used a control group to contrast with a training group (between-cases design) and studies that compared investment performance before and after a group of counselors have been trained (within-cases design). Methodological variables are investigated to see whether results depend on the methods used to study the substantive issue.

These substantive and methodological variables are thus investigated as potential moderator variables that may influence the generalizability of results. Meta-analysis evaluates these variables quantitatively. This represents an advantage of meta-analysis compared to narrative reviews that only provide judgmental evaluations of potential moderating conditions.

Example

Statistical analyses are carried out once the dependent variable and potential independent variables have been identified and coded. To some extent, the type of analyses recommended vary across different meta-analysis procedures. A hypothetical data set using the investment derivative training example is used here to illustrate major similarities and differences among different meta-analysis procedures.

Illustrative Data. Characteristics of 10 original studies investigating the relationship between investment derivative training and client investment performance have been created and are summarized in Exhibit 14.3. (An actual meta-analysis generally would not be conducted with so few studies.) These 10 studies involved a total of 510 counselors who were either trained or served as controls.

The dependent variable used by the meta-analyst is the simple correlation coefficient (see Chapter 10) between client investment performance measured after training and whether or not counselors experienced training. Training (versus control) is coded so that a positive coefficient indicates clients of trained counselors obtained greater returns than clients of untrained counselors. In Exhibit 14.3, the correlation coefficient of 0.28 in Study 1 signals that clients of trained counselors obtained a higher rate of investment return than the clients of untrained counselors. Exhibit 14.3 shows that investment performance of clients with trained counselors are greater in 8 of the 10 studies.

The results shown in Exhibit 14.3 oversimplify a meta-analyst's coding task. Studies often report results using a variety of statistics. For example, some might report mean investment performance differences between trained and untrained counselors. Others might report results in correlation

---

EXHIBIT 14.3. Summary characteristics from 10 studies on investment training

Study	Number of Counselors	Study Results*	Market Conditions	Study Design
01	12	0.28	<.15	Between
02	30	0.40	<.15	Between
03	20	0.36	>.20	Within
04	18	0.22	<.15	Between
05	22	−0.03	<.15	Between
06	30	0.32	>.20	Between
07	18	0.42	>.20	Between
08	24	0.44	>.20	Within
09	16	0.26	<.15	Within
10	20	−0.12	<.15	Between

*Correlation coefficient between investment derivative training
(trained = 1; not trained = 0) and client investment performance.

coefficients and yet others may report results in still other ways. A meta-analyst must report results from all studies using a common statistic, so that results can be summarized across the studies quantitatively. Fortunately, results reported using one statistic can often be converted into others.[1]

Exhibit 14.3 shows that the meta-analyst has also coded two independent variables, one substantive and one methodological. The substantive independent variable is the market conditions prevailing at the time of the study. The meta-analyst finds that studies were conducted during time periods when average market returns were less than 15 percent or more than 20 percent. The researcher hypothesizes that the benefits of investment derivative training are greater when market conditions are more favorable. Method-

---

[1]For example, a simple transformation of Formula 10.6 could be performed to convert a simple regression coefficient into a simple correlation coefficient. A variety of conversion formulas are provided in Glass, McGaw, & Smith (1981, Ch. 5) and Hunter & Schmidt (1990, Ch. 7).

ologically, the meta-analyst records whether the studies compared client investment performance with trained counselors or controls (between-cases studies) or compared performance before and after training (within-cases studies). The researcher believes that within-cases studies often obtain more favorable results than between-cases studies.

Meta-Analysis Interpretations. Steps recommended for data collection and coding are generally not controversial among meta-analysts. Moreover, researchers agree that an important outcome from meta-analysis is an average value to characterize the dependent variable. In the illustration from Exhibit 14.3, the average correlation coefficient is calculated ($r_{yx} = 0.26$).[2] This signals that whether or not counselors were trained accounts for about 7 percent of the variance in average investor returns across the studies conducted ($r^2_{yx} = 0.07$). Meta-analysis is attractive relative to traditional narrative reviews, because it provides this type of quantitative summary of the results of previous research.

Controversy arises regarding the interpretation of such averages and recommendations for additional analyses. This controversy centers on appropriate statistical inferences to be drawn from meta-analysis. There are differences in viewpoints regarding both external statistical inference and internal statistical inference.

External Statistical Inference. Some meta-analysts take the studies reviewed as a population.[3] From this perspective, meta-analysis is a way to describe the studies in statistical terms, not to generalize to some broader population. Proponents of this perspective question whether meta-analysis is more useful than traditional narrative reviews for external generalization, statistical or otherwise.

Alternatively, other researchers argue that the studies reviewed represent a sample that can be generalized to a broader population.[4] Although this broader population is not well defined, advocates of this approach use external statistical inference procedures to test statistical hypotheses or to create

---

[2] A technical disagreement involves whether summary statistics should be weighted (e.g., by sample size) when averaging. In the example, the weighted and unweighted correlation coefficients are the same. There is also disagreement over whether the coefficients from each study should be transformed to a distribution that is more normal than a distribution of correlation coefficients before averaging (see Appendix 13A). Details of these disagreements go beyond purposes here.

[3] This approach is represented by Glass, McGaw, and Smith (1981).

[4] Hunter and Schmidt's (1990) approach to meta-analysis represents this perspective.

confidence intervals about these broader population parameters (see Chapter 13). This perspective thus claims more for meta-analysis than is claimed for traditional narrative reviews.

Internal Statistical Inference. There are also different perspectives regarding appropriate procedures to address internal statistical inference. These differences are related to differences in views regarding external generalization.

Some researchers who see meta-analysis as a way of describing a population of studies emphasize assignment error over sampling error. To illustrate, advocates of this perspective might correlate the dependent variable in Exhibit 14.3 with the two independent variables, market conditions and design type. Exhibit 14.4 shows the results of this procedure when market conditions ($> .20 = 1$) and design type (within-cases $= 1$) are dummy coded. Exhibit 14.4 shows that both independent variables are positively correlated with investment return; market conditions are statistically significantly correlated with investment return ($p < 0.05$; one-tailed). A meta-analyst using this perspective would conclude that market conditions moderate the relationship between training and investment performance in the population of studies performed. In the studies reviewed, investment derivative training results in higher client performance when market conditions are more favorable.

EXHIBIT 14.4. Correlation coefficients between the training dependent variable and the substantive and methodological independent variables

	Correlation Coefficients		
Variable	*1*	*2*	*3*
1. Study results	1.00		
2. Market conditions	.59*	1.00	
3. Study design	.36	.36	1.00

*$p < .05$ (one-tailed).

Alternatively, those meta-analysts who view results from the studies as a sample to be generalized to a population emphasize sampling error. One widely used procedure recommends that variability in the study results first be adjusted for an estimate of sampling error (Hunter & Schmidt, 1990). Possible moderator variables should only be investigated if substantial variability between results of studies remain after the estimated variability due to sampling error is removed. This procedure applied to the results summarized in Exhibit 14.3 leads to the conclusion that sampling error is responsible for most of the variation between the studies.[5] A researcher using this procedure concludes that the results all come from a single population; the results are not influenced by market conditions or by any other moderator variable.

Evaluation

One of the most serious shortcomings of empirical research has been a lack of trustworthy procedures to evaluate and make appropriate external generalizations from research once conducted. Traditionally, evaluations of and generalizations from previous research have been made after researchers conduct narrative reviews. These reviews depend primarily on the quality of judgments and decisions made by a reviewer. Conclusions reached by one reviewer are often challenged by another, even after examining the same body of literature.

Disagreements between narrative reviews often increase as the body of replications increases. More research findings, paradoxically, can lead to greater confusion about the internal and external validity of relationships. Standard narrative review procedures are increasingly vulnerable to errors as the number of studies reviewed becomes large.

Contributions of Meta-Analysis.   Given the problems associated with narrative reviews, it is not surprising that meta-analysis has been embraced with great enthusiasm. Meta-analysis introduces quantitative and publicly replicable research methods to research literature reviews.

Some meta-analysis procedures are as applicable to narrative as to quantitative reviews. In particular, meta-analysis calls for systematic coding not

---

[5]Calculations using procedures from Hunter and Schmidt (1990) are not shown here.

only of a quantitative dependent variable, but of independent variables as well. This practice can be emulated to improve narrative reviews.

For example, a narrative reviewer may focus on the sample size of one study in the review. The reviewer may conclude it is attractively large, or too small. The point: If sample size is a salient characteristic of one study, it is potentially salient for all. A good narrative review will systematically code sample size for all studies, just as in a meta-analysis.

Meta-analysis also extends contributions made by narrative reviews. Quantifying study results and converting them to a common statistic (e.g., a correlation coefficient) allows reviewers to generate an average result across studies. This is useful summary information, even if you conclude that meta-analysis is best used only to describe prior research. If you conclude further that meta-analysis can be used for inference, the average may be extended more broadly.

The analysis of relationships between study results and coded independent variables is an especially attractive feature of meta-analysis. Relationships between the dependent variable and either substantive or methodological independent variables provide information about potential moderator variables. This feature of meta-analysis provides researchers with quantitative estimates about the external generalizability of research findings. As noted, however, there is still disagreement among meta-analysts about how best to address these potential moderator variables.

Meta-Analysis Reservations. Despite its promise, meta-analysis is not a panacea. In the first place, although meta-analysis may reduce controversy about findings from prior research, it does not eliminate it. The use of meta-analysis requires researcher skill and judgment, just as with any other empirical technique. Different meta-analysts will reach different conclusions about the most appropriate ways to carry out a meta-analysis. As a consequence, two researchers using the same meta-analysis procedure will likely arrive at somewhat different conclusions regarding a body of research.[6]

Furthermore, there is still disagreement about how best to think about and understand the variation between results of different studies. It is now generally agreed that variation between studies is due at least in part to sampling error and other sources of differences between studies (e.g., the reliability of

---

[6]For example, compare the conclusions of Scott and Taylor (1985) with Hackett and Guion (1985) regarding the relationship between satisfaction and absenteeism.

measurement). The perspective that this variation can be viewed solely as a result of potential moderator variables and assignment error has fallen out of favor among most meta-analysts. However, the currently popular view that sampling error is likely responsible for all or most of the variation between studies is also increasingly challenged. Advances in meta-analysis require better methods for differentiating between sampling error within a single population and variation that is due to differences between populations.[7]

Closing Observations.   Meta-analysis is a method in process. However, the still-emerging character of the methodology should not discourage your use of meta-analysis. Meta-analysts have written books describing procedures they recommend. These should be understandable to those who understand the topics covered in this book.

SUMMARY

Many times researchers and research consumers are more interested in the generalization of research findings than they are in the original findings themselves. For example, do the findings that have been observed in one population apply in another? Will findings obtained in the past still apply in the future? These questions illustrate challenges for external generalization. They go beyond external statistical generalization, which only speaks to the likelihood that statistics observed on a probability sample of cases apply to the population from which the sample was drawn.

Moderator variables serve as limits to external generalization. A relationship(s) observed in one context generalizes to another context as long as characteristics that differ between the two contexts do not act as moderator variables. Researchers who have studied a relationship in only one context can only speculate on whether their results generalize. They do not have empirical evidence on variation in the moderator variables.

Evidence on external generalization must be obtained by ***replication.*** Replications are studies of the same research relationship(s) in another context. Replications that differ on values of potential moderator variables provide evidence on the generalizability of results across these potential moderators.

---

[7]Promising work in this direction is reported by Erez, Bloom, and Wells (1996).

Until recently, interpretation of replications were confined to traditional *narrative research reviews.* A narrative review consists of a researcher's judgmental summary and evaluation of a body of research on a topic. Narrative reviews draw heavily on nonquantifiable skills and knowledge of the reviewer and hence are often subject to challenge.

Meta-analysis is a developing method for evaluating and generalizing research replications. Meta-analysts apply standard quantitative procedures to review and evaluate previous research. These include standardized measures to represent the results from previous results. Standard measures of characteristics that may influence the results are also created. Results of previous studies are then analyzed statistically. Meta-analysis is especially attractive when the number of studies on a particular topic is large because results are coded and evaluated more systematically than is true of most narrative reviews.

There are still a number of contentious issues in meta-analysis. These issues hinge on how best to evaluate the differences in results found in the studies reviewed.

FOR REVIEW

Terms to Know

Replication. A research study that addresses the same research issue(s) as an earlier study.

Triangulation. In research, a form of replication that seeks to discover whether research findings generalize across different research methods.

Narrative research review. A review of prior research studies that depends largely on a reviewer's knowledge of the topic and research methods. The review typically includes a summary and evaluation of the previous research.

Meta-analysis. Procedures to review and evaluate prior research studies that depend on quantitative research methods.

Box-score method. In meta-analysis, the use of statistical significance values as the dependent variable. Its use is not recommended.

Questions for Review

1. How do potential moderator variables limit external generalization?
2. What major meta-analysis procedures are also desirable in narrative research reviews?
3. How do replications contribute to external generalization?
4. What are advantages of meta-analysis compared to traditional narrative reviews?
5. What are major characteristics of meta-analysis that are still contentious among meta-analysts?

Issues to Discuss

1. Suppose it is established that Scholastic Achievement Tests (SAT) predict grade-point average among freshmen enrolled in large public universities. What potential moderator variables would concern you regarding the likely predictive value of SAT scores in exclusive private universities?
2. Evaluate the following statement:

"Researchers and research consumers are always interested in generalizing findings obtained in the past to findings expected in the future. For example, research evidence of a successful advertising campaign suggests that the advertising should continue only if you are willing to assume that what applied in the past will apply in the future. As a result, external generalization over time is always essential to research. Furthermore, since the future is never known, research findings can never be confidently generalized."

PART VI: SUGGESTED READING

A number of books describing meta-analysis procedures are available. These include Hedges and Olkin (1985), Hunter and Schmidt (1990), Glass, McGaw, and Smith (1981), and Rosenthal (1991). Although now somewhat dated, Bangert-Drowns (1986) provides a readable summary of meta-analysis and explains differences in viewpoints. Rosenthal (1995) offers suggestions for summarizing meta-analysis studies in research reports.

Meta-analysis is now the standard way of reviewing and generalizing research in many social science disciplines. A few examples from substantive areas of interest to me include reviews of relationships between satisfaction and absenteeism (Hackett & Guion, 1985; Scott & Taylor, 1985, as mentioned in this chapter), satisfaction and job performance (Petty, McGee, & Cavender, 1984), motivation and job performance (Schwab, Gottleib-Olian, & Heneman, 1979; Van Eerde & Thierry, 1996), perceived employment opportunity and turnover (Steel & Griffeth, 1989), job performance and turnover (McEvoy & Cascio, 1987), strategic planning and firm performance (Miller & Cardinal, 1994), applicant characteristics and interviewer evaluations (Olian, Schwab, & Haberfeld, 1988), and college grade point average and subsequent employment success (Bretz, 1989; Roth, BeVier, Switzer, & Schippmann, 1996).

There are a very large number of studies on relationships between tests of mental ability and job performance. Many meta-analyses have been conducted on these studies. An article by Schmidt, Law, Hunter, Rothstein, Pearlman, and McDaniel (1993) has references to many of these meta-analyses.

VII

RESEARCH REPORTS

15

Research Report Writing

Chapter Outline

- *Research Report Format*
  - *Introduction*
  - *Methods*
  - *Results*
  - *Discussion*
- *Alternative Research Report Formats*
- *Additional Suggestions*
  - *Begin by Organizing*
  - *Rewrite, Then Rewrite*
  - *Draft a Critic*
  - *Take a Scout's Oath*
- *Summary*
- *Appendix 15A: On Table Construction*

Chapter 1 argues that empirical research, when appropriately carried out, has two important advantages over other methods for understanding observable events. First, research is systematic. Measurement, design, and data analysis are all carried out in a methodical way. Previous parts of this book emphasize these systematic procedures to conduct research.

Second, it argues that good research is a public process. Research methods, as well as results, are made available by researchers so that others may critically evaluate the research. This second characteristic of research is important for research reports. It means that researchers must do more than simply summarize research findings. They must also describe the methods that produced the results so that critical evaluation is possible.

This chapter is designed to help you write clear research reports. It describes a format that is suitable for most research reports. This format corresponds closely to one recommended in the *Publication Manual of the American Psychological Association* (1994). The chapter also identifies an alternative research report format and concludes with additional recommendations for successful report writing. An appendix at the end of the chapter provides suggestions for using tables in research reports.

RESEARCH REPORT FORMAT

Introduction

Your introduction provides the best opportunity to grab the readers' interest in the study. Make it address three issues about the problem investigated. First, state the research problem clearly and succinctly. Place this statement early in the paper so readers understand what to expect. From a research perspective, the trick here is to state the problem in a way that can be solved by the study conducted.

Second, link the research problem to prior conceptualization and research. Knowledge obtained from research is cumulative; no one study alone is very persuasive. In context, however, with conceptual models and findings from other research, results of a study can often be quite convincing. Make the introduction provide that context. Think of your study as one piece of a puzzle. Where does this piece fit in that puzzle?

Finally, state why the research problem is important. For example, will its solution advance understanding of a conceptual model? Will it answer a specific organizational question? Will the study speak to an important policy question? Stating why a research problem is important can help motivate reader interest.

Methods

The methods section differentiates research report writing most clearly from other types of writing. It is thus often a difficult section for fledgling researchers.

The methods section describes the overall plan of the study and the steps taken to obtain and analyze scores. It reports on cases studied, measures, administrative procedures used to obtain scores, and the methods used to analyze scores. The order of these topics may vary within the section.

A good method section is the key to providing the information needed for critical evaluation and potential replication. As a consequence, your objective should be to describe the methods so that another researcher could repeat (replicate) your study.

Cases. Research cases are the objects whose characteristics are measured in a research study. Identify the number and type of cases and report how they were chosen. For example, all employees in an organization may serve as cases. Or, a sample of those employees may be studied. If the latter, also describe the sampling procedure used to obtain participants.

Here is an idea for deciding what participant information to report: Include information about cases that can be used to decide how the research results may generalize to other cases. In addition, describe the population if your study involves statistical generalization.

Report the size of the sample drawn and the sampling procedure used. Also report any attrition between sample cases chosen and those that actually participate (i.e., provide information about nonrespondents).

Measures. Provide several types of information about each measured variable used. Unless the study is very simple, remind the reader how each measure serves in the model investigated. Is it a dependent, independent, or control variable?

Always report whether a measure was constructed especially for the study or whether it came from another source. In either case, it is usually appropriate to include the item(s) that make up the measure in the report. If there are only one or two of these, you may place them in the body of the report. Or, you may choose to put them in an appendix.

Regardless of source, tell how each item(s) is scaled (i.e., how numerical values are assigned to responses). This is especially important when variables have no intuitively sensible numerical order. For example, a measure of gender is often scaled 0 and 1. To understand relationships between gender and any other variable it is essential to know whether female = 0 and male = 1, or female = 1 and male = 0.

Cite the source for measures that are borrowed. In addition, include information about the measure from prior research that speaks to its quality. For example, report evidence on characteristics of the measures that address construct validity.

Procedure.   The procedure describes how measurement information was obtained from the cases studied. This should include a description of the methods and inducements used to obtain participation in the study.

Many organizational studies use designs that obtain scores using questionnaires or interviews. In such cases, questions to be answered in the procedures section include: How did participants obtain questionnaires (e.g., through the mail, at a meeting)? Where did they complete the questionnaire or interview (e.g., at home, at work)? When did participants complete them (e.g., during regular work hours)?

Experimental and quasi-experimental designs place cases in different circumstances representing different levels of the independent variable. For example, customers may be placed in one of two groups, each exposed to a different type of advertisement. Subsequent purchasing behavior may serve as the dependent variable. In such studies, describe the procedures used to assign participants to different levels of the independent variable. For example, were participants assigned to different levels of the independent variable using a random procedure? Or, were intact groups assigned different levels (e.g., groups located in different geographical regions)?

Research procedures used to obtain scores have important implications for most types of research validity. The way measures are administered to participants can influence construct validity. The way participants are assigned to levels of independent variables can influence internal validity. Procedures also influence conditions under which external validity can be expected. It is essential, therefore, that the research procedures employed be thoroughly described for a reader's understanding.

Analyses.   The *Publication Manual of the American Psychological Association* (1994) does not include a description of the analyses conducted in the methods section. I nevertheless recommend you provide such a description. When included, the methods section contains a description of the entire research plan. If written well, another researcher can replicate a study by working from just your methods section.

Provide information about two types of analyses. First, describe methods used for any initial analyses performed to investigate, and perhaps to prepare, the data for the main analyses. These initial analyses include investigating the data set for missing values. They also include the calculation of descriptive statistics, such as means and standard deviations, on each of the variables measured. Assessments of reliability are usually also examples of preliminary analyses to describe.

Second, describe analysis methods used to investigate the main research question(s). These are usually statistics that address relationships between variables. Examples include correlation, regression, and analysis of variance.

Results

Your results section may be brief, especially if the methods section includes a description of the procedures used to perform analyses as recommended.

Begin with a description of the results from initial analyses. Report descriptive statistics on independent and dependent variables. Include any evidence addressing the quality of the measures. Follow results of these preliminary analyses with a summary of results from analyses investigating the main research issue(s).

Tables often help communicate results of both initial and main analyses. There are several tricks and conventions to successful table construction (see the appendix). Make the results section descriptive and concise. Just the facts, but all the facts! Save interpretation and editorializing for the discussion.

Discussion

The discussion is the capstone of a research report. It is the place to summarize and interpret results, to speculate on generalizations to other contexts, and to identify limitations. In short, it is the section that pulls all parts of a study together, makes sense of them, and makes them interesting.

Although the organization of the discussion section may vary, it is often good to summarize findings first. Which of the hypothesized relationships obtained support? Was internal validity established? Do the measures employed suggest that causal conceptual relationships are tenable among the cases studied? If sampling procedures warrant, you can also discuss external statistical validity at this point.

A discussion of the study's implications logically follows the summary of basic findings. If a conceptual model was tested, was support obtained? Do the findings suggest the model be modified? How?

If an applied issue was investigated, the summary can be followed by policy recommendations. For example, was the program tested (e.g., training, advertising) successful enough to recommend for implementation?

The discussion may then become more speculative. External validity, for example, may be discussed. For example, to what other contexts or populations are your findings likely to apply? Why do you think so?

Another issue to discuss involves implications of findings from the current study for additional research. During the course of a study, limitations in the methods used will likely surface. Some findings will be ambiguous. New questions will occur as the study is in process. These can serve to formulate useful recommendations not only for additional research but for methods to effectively address them.

Finally, perhaps as part of other topics identified, include candid recognition of the study's limitations. Research studies inevitably require compromises with "ideal" methods. Difficulties confronting any researcher may include cost constraints, difficulty in obtaining access to cases, and suboptimal measurement. Some research decisions thought to be ideal when made will inevitably turn out to be less than satisfactory.

Communicate such limitations. The purpose of research is to learn about relationships between variables. The object of a research report is to communicate what was learned. Sometimes the primary knowledge obtained from a study may be that little was learned.

It is ethical to report these research shortcomings in the discussion. Moreover, sophisticated readers will likely identify a study's shortcomings whether articulated in the discussion or not. Explicit identification of limitations signals that you are knowledgeable about research methods.

ALTERNATIVE RESEARCH REPORT FORMATS

The outline described here follows closely one recommended in the *Publication Manual of the American Psychological Association* (1994). All original research journals sponsored by the American Psychological Association follow this format, as do many independent journals covering related topics (e.g., *Personnel Psychology*). This outline is also followed by the academic journals of the Academy of Management.

Many other journals that publish original social science research follow similar, although not identical, outlines. The main difference between the outline described and outlines used by journals in related fields, such as economics, sociology and industrial relations, involves the results and discussion sections. These latter journals are more likely to include much of the discussion with the explanation of results. The last section in such journals usually contains a short summary and conclusions.

The advantage of combining results and discussion material is that it can make for more succinct presentation of the material. The disadvantage is that it does not clearly distinguish the objective results material from the more subjective discussion material.

When given a choice, I prefer to separate results from discussion. It helps me distinguish between what is supported by evidence generated from the study and how I interpret that evidence.

ADDITIONAL SUGGESTIONS

Novices often experience difficulty writing research reports. In part, this is because research writing is different from most other writing experiences. However, research report writing is simply difficult. A research study is a complicated enterprise involving measurement, design, and analysis. Communication of these complicated activities presents a challenge for anyone.

It is helpful for both writer and reader to keep the explanation as simple and straightforward as possible.

Begin by Organizing

The outline presented in this chapter can serve as a start. Fill in details by arranging your story around the variables in the study. Start the variables off properly with conceptual definitions in the introduction. Report on how you believe they are connected (the conceptual model). In the methods section, describe how these variables are operationalized. Tell how the scores on the measured variables relate in the results section. Provide meaning to relationships between these variables in the discussion.

Daft (1985) offered an interesting analogy. He recommended that variables in a research report be treated as characters in a novel. Don't bring vari-

RESEARCH HIGHLIGHT 15.1

Reporting and Discussing Statistical Significance

Here are four conventions for reporting on statistical significance levels (see Part V):

1. Establish a significance level a priori, state it explicitly, then use it faithfully. Do not report results that miss your stated level as "nearly significant," or the like. A sample statistic provides a correct estimate of the population parameter, or it does not. Use of terms such as *nearly significant* implies you do not understand what statistical significance means.

2. Always use the entire term: *statistical significance* when you mean to refer to results of an inferential test; *significance* by itself can refer to many things. Something can be statistically significant and yet not be significant in any practical sense.

3. Provide information on the magnitude of relationships, or differences, as well as whether or not a result is statistically significant. Information on variance explained by an independent variable is almost always helpful to the reader.

4. Do not use failure to reach statistical significance as evidence that there is no relationship, or difference, unless you also provide evidence on the statistical power of your inferential test.

ables into a study without a proper introduction. And don't let variables disappear from a study without a suitable burial. Exhibit 15.1 provides a summary of information to report on each variable in various sections of the research report.

Rewrite, Then Rewrite

Even the best authors rewrite drafts to obtain satisfactory results. Three or more major drafts of a report are typical. Schedule time so that a week or more can elapse between rewrites. Problems that aren't visible as you work on a report may become visible when you pick it up at a later time.

EXHIBIT 15.1. A tale for each variable

Report Section	Information to Provide
Introduction	1. Define each variable at a construct level.
	2. Describe where each variable fits in the research model (e.g., dependent variable).
Methods	1. Describe how each variable is measured.
	2. Describe how scores are obtained on the measures.
	3. Describe how scores on the measure are analyzed.
Results	1. Describe results of scores on measures.
	2. Describe relationships between scores across measures.
Discussion	1. Summarize findings regarding measures.
	2. Discuss how measures address constructs (including shortcomings)

Draft a Critic

Motivate someone to read and make comments on your draft(s). A colleague, particularly if critical, can provide invaluable assistance in ferreting out inconsistencies, illogic, omissions, and other sins that invariably creep into writing projects.

Take a Scout's Oath

Your study will probably not be the greatest scientific achievement of the century. It will not be flawlessly conducted, nor will it generalize to all cases or to all time. Write your research report accordingly. Be honest, be descriptive, be modest.

SUMMARY

Research reporting holds a special place in the research process; it provides essential information for making research public. Research reports must include a detailed description of the method employed as well as research findings. Exhibit 15.2 summarizes information that is important to include in research reports.

EXHIBIT 15.2. Research report outline and checklist of topics to include

Section	*Topics to Include*
Introduction	Statement of the problem; relationships to other research; importance of problem.
Methods	
Cases	Number; characteristics relevant for generalization; sampling procedure; population.
Measures	Constructed (how?) or borrowed (source?)? Items; scaling formats; construct validity evidence.
Procedure	Methods to obtain participation; steps for administering measures; types of manipulations; methods to assign cases to levels of independent variables.
Analyses	Describe procedures to conduct preliminary analyses, analyses of measures, and tests of research hypotheses.
Results	Summary of results from descriptive and substantive analyses.
Discussion	Summary of findings; generalizability findings and/or policy recommendations; implications for future research; research limitations.

APPENDIX 15A:
ON TABLE CONSTRUCTION[1]

Decisions about when to use tables and how to construct them are important for effective communication of research findings. Tables can help readers understand and can help you communicate statistical findings efficiently.

When to Use Tables

Use tables to summarize quantitative information about results obtained on the measures used in a study. The more variables in a study, the more helpful are tables for summarizing results. Two types are often appropriate:

1. Table(s) to summarize descriptive information about the participants studied and the measures used.
2. Table(s) to summarize the results from the main statistical analyses performed to test the research expectations or to address the research questions.

Table Characteristics

Tables vary because table content varies. However, it is good practice to see that all tables have the following characteristics:

1. *Table numbers.* Number each table consecutively so that reference can easily be made to it in the body of the paper.
2. *Descriptive title.* A title should accurately, but briefly, describe the content reported in the body of the table.
3. *Table headings.* Title each column in the table.
4. *Abbreviations.* Avoid abbreviations except for common statistical symbols, such as M (for mean), SD (for standard deviation), and N (for number). Explain necessary abbreviations in a footnote in the table.

---

[1]For details on table construction see *Publication Manual of the American Psychological Association* (4th ed., pp. 120–141), (1994). Washington, DC: American Psychological Association.

Integrate Tables and Text

Design each table so it is understandable without reference to the text. However, do not assume readers will understand a table. Thus, explain the content and summarize important information from the table in the text. This is very important and often overlooked by beginning research report writers. Also, identify every table by number when referring to it in the body of the report.

An Example

Suppose you are interested in explaining variation in yearly income (Y) as a function of age (X_1), years of work experience (X_2), and years of education (X_3). The population consists of working adults in a metropolitan area, and you draw a random sample of participants from this population. Scores on measures of the four variables are obtained and analyses performed. The following tables and descriptive information are appropriate.

Descriptive Results.   One type of table, illustrated in Exhibit 15A.1, includes descriptive statistics that are generally useful in a research report. The mean shows central tendency, the standard deviation shows the average variability, and the simple correlation coefficients among the variables show how scores on the measures are related. Reporting the number of cases for each variable is useful when there are missing data. Otherwise, the sample size can be reported in a note at the end of the table. For ease of reading, place the dependent variable either at the head or end of the list of variables.

In describing the contents of Exhibit 15A.1, call attention to any of the statistics that are unusual for samples of this sort. For example, correlation coefficients that are unusually high (or low) might be identified. Not all statistics should be discussed in the body of the report; to do so would make the table unnecessary.

Substantive Results.   A second type of table(s) should ordinarily summarize the substantive results. For example, suppose you use multiple regression to test your hypotheses. Y is regressed on the X variables. A summary of results as reported in Exhibit 15A.2 is appropriate.

In describing the contents of Exhibit 15A.2, point out independent variables that are related to income as expected and which, if any, are not. The

---

EXHIBIT 15A.1. Table of variable means, standard deviations, and intercorrelations among income, age, years work experience, and education

| Variables | N | M | SD | *Correlation Coefficients* | | | |
				1	2	3	4
1. Yearly income	281	34,631.21	7,211.40	1.00			
2. Age in years	283	41.68	13.12	.58*	1.00		
3. Years work experience	284	19.79	8.91	.58*	.68*	1.00	
4. Years education	282	13.13	2.78	.41*	−.15*	.19*	1.00

Note: The number for each variable is smaller than the 285 participants sampled due to missing data. Correlation coefficients calculated using listwise deletion.

$*p < .05$ (two-tailed).

statistical significance of findings is appropriate for both the table and for discussion in the text, since you are interested in generalizing results from the probability sample of participants studied to the population they came from.

An explanation could also be given for one relationship to help readers interpret the results of the entire table. Given the results reported in Exhibit 15A.2, for example, you could say that a 1-year increase in age results in an expected yearly income increase of $320, holding years work experience and education constant.

Notice that the tables in both exhibits have several desirable characteristics:

1. Titles are descriptive.
2. Decimals are to the same number of places (two are almost always enough).
3. Asterisks are used to indicate statistically significant results (a common convention). The level of significance signified by the asterisk is reported in a footnote.
4. Notes are added to the end of each table to explain material that might otherwise leave readers with questions.

EXHIBIT 15A.2. Summary of multiple regression predicting yearly income for age, years work experience, and education

Variable	Regression Coefficient	Standard Error
Age in years	320.17*	31.64
Years work experience	79.39	46.06
Years education	1,143.39*	102.80
Constant	4,732.29*	1,753.19

Note: Adjusted R^2 = .48, p < .05. Missing data eliminated listwise, N = 278.

*p < .05 (one-tailed).

VIII

EXTENSIONS

16

On Incomplete Data

Chapter Outline

- *Avoid Incomplete Data*
- *Evaluate Nonresponse*
- *Address Missing Data*
  - *Dependent Variables*
  - *Independent Variables*
- *Summary*
- *For Review*
- *Suggested Reading*

A study is conducted on a random sample of 14 individuals. Scores are obtained on one dependent and two independent variables. These scores are recorded in a matrix where rows represent individuals and columns represent variables, as shown in Exhibit 16.1.

The researcher is eager to perform statistical analyses. But, wait! Not all cells in the matrix have values.

Entire rows are without values. Individuals 8 and 9 did not respond to the study—they are **nonrespondents.** They may be individuals who fail to return questionnaires. Or, they may be individuals chosen for an experiment who fail to participate.

Exhibit 16.1 also shows that Individuals 3, 5, 7, and 14 are **missing data** for Y or $X1$. They participated, but incompletely. Survey participants may fill out only a portion of a questionnaire; experimental participants may participate for a time, but drop out before the study is complete.

EXHIBIT 16.1. Matrix with missing data

Individual	Y	X1	X2	Missing
1	28,054	31	3	0
2	37,555	28	2	0
3	37,643	.	3	1
4	24,264	20	5	0
5	.	25	4	.
6	44,521	29	1	0
7	27,878	.	5	1
8	.	.	.	.
9	.	.	.	.
10	37,318	32	4	0
11	37,798	29	1	0
12	28,071	25	3	0
13	43,104	35	2	0
14	39,374	.	1	1
Mean	35,052.82	28.63	2.73	.27
Std Dev	6,814.56	4.57	1.49	
n	11	8	11	11

Note: Individual 5 removed from all analysis because of a missing datum on Y.

Nonresponse and missing data present two problems for research. First, lost cases result in loss of statistical power when internal or external statistical validity is an issue. The more cases lost, the more power lost.

More seriously, nonresponse and missing data can lead to a misinterpretation of relationships that exist among the group of cases the researcher seeks to study. For example, suppose a researcher is interested in the relationship between education level and income. A group of individuals from some population is sampled. However, suppose that sample members at the high (or low) end of the income distribution are less likely to respond to a question about income. The range of income values obtained by the researcher is restricted compared to the range that exists in the entire sample. Consequently, the relationship between income and education observed will differ from the relationship that exists in the entire sample.

AVOID INCOMPLETE DATA

The best way to address nonresponse and missing data is to prevent them. A plan to elicit high levels of participation should be carefully developed as a part of the research design.

Whether participants respond or not depends on both their ability and their motivation. Ability issues include the opportunity (e.g., time) to participate. Another issue is participants' ability to respond to the requirements of the study. For example, missing data and nonresponses are certain if participants are asked for information they do not understand.

Participants may be motivated to participate for various reasons. Monetary incentives are often used when the time and location demands of a study are extensive, as is frequently true of experiments. Other motivators are the stated purpose(s) of the research and the research sponsor.

Participant groups differ in ability and motivation. Thus, decisions about participants studied should be made early in the design process. Reading levels of questionnaires constructed and motivational incentives used are examples of design issues that depend on the intended participants.

Great effort should be made to minimize nonresponses and missing data. However, it is unlikely that either will be eliminated. The next two sections describe procedures to be used when nonresponses and missing data are present.

EVALUATE NONRESPONSE

Sometimes it is possible to get information on the consequences of nonresponse by comparing respondents with nonrespondents on variables known for all intended participants. For example, suppose a charitable organization solicits contributions in December, just before the end of the tax year. A study is initiated to learn whether donors are willing to make contributions throughout the year. A questionnaire is developed and sent to a random sample drawn from the organization's data base of recent donors. This data base contains donor names, addresses, and contributions. A 25 percent response rate is obtained.

The organization can compare the 25 percent who responded with the 75 percent who did not on information in its data base: amount of contribution, location (from addresses), and sex (estimated from names). Differences between respondents and nonrespondents on any of these variables suggest that the questionnaire responses obtained may not apply to all contributors. Regrettably, the charitable organization cannot know that respondents and nonrespondents would provide similar answers even if the two groups are similar on all characteristics compared.

Consequently, comparing respondents and nonrespondents on variables available for both provides only limited information. Research information obtained from respondents may apply to nonrespondents if the groups are similar on the comparison variables; but it may not. However, it is likely that information provided by respondents does not generalize to nonrespondents when the two groups differ on comparison variables. Despite this frequently gloomy outcome, a comparison is recommended, if possible, to inform the researcher (and research consumers) of potential research limitations.

ADDRESS MISSING DATA

Researchers have several options when confronted with missing data. These options depend on whether the missing data represents the dependent or independent variables.

Dependent Variables

Some participants may provide partial information but fail to provide information on the dependent variable(s). Individual 5 is an example in Exhibit 16.1. Such cases are best dropped from a study since research is aimed at explaining or predicting the dependent variable. Researchers cannot explain what they have no information on; participants with missing Y scores are effectively nonrespondents.

It is possible to see if participants who provide or do not provide Y scores differ on the independent variables. Relationships observed among Y score providers may apply to cases with missing Y scores in the unlikely event that scores do not differ between the two groups across independent variables. However, it is likely that independent variables will differ between those who provide and those who do not provide Y scores. Generalization of research results to participants with missing Y scores is then problematic.

Independent Variables

Exhibit 16.2 summarizes methods to deal with missing values on independent variables; each may be appropriate in certain circumstances. More than one method can be used in a single investigation when there are several independent variables.

EXHIBIT 16.2. Methods to account for missing independent variable values

---

Delete Variables

Delete Cases

  Listwise

  Pairwise

Estimate Scores

  Mean substitution

  Other

Identify "Missingness"

Delete Variables. The amount of missing data may vary greatly from variable to variable. Variables may have missing data because some participants do not reveal certain information about themselves (e.g., age, income). In such situations, and if the variable is important to the conceptual model investigated, it may be useful to estimate missing values and identify "missingness" (more on this later).

Alternatively, a researcher may conclude the problem rests with the measure of the variable. For example, it may be a poorly worded item on a questionnaire. In such situations, it is probably best to drop the variable from the study. Responses from those answering are suspect (e.g., unreliable) if the wording kept other participants from answering.

Delete Cases. Cases can be dropped two ways when there are two or more independent variables; neither method is typically attractive. *Listwise deletion* drops an entire case if responses to any independent variable are missing. A participant with any missing data is treated like a nonrespondent.

Listwise deletion can result in a large loss of cases even though the total amount of missing information is small. This happens if the missing data is spread more or less evenly across cases. Listwise deletion is not recommended in such circumstances. Only if missing data are concentrated among a small proportion of cases is listwise deletion potentially attractive. (However, if concentrated, the missing data signals that these cases probably differ systematically from cases with complete data. Generalization of findings to all cases again becomes suspect.)

Pairwise deletion uses all data available for each statistic calculated. For example, the mean of $X2$ is calculated using scores of Individuals 3, 7, and 14 in Exhibit 16.1 even though their values for $X1$ are missing. Pairwise deletion is thus attractive because all data that can be used is used.

However, there are problems that make the procedure generally unattractive as a research practice. First, different sample statistics are not generalizable to the same population unless missing data are randomly distributed among participants and variables.

Second, there is another generalization problem when relationships between more than two variables are examined in the same statistical model. For example, multiple correlation and regression account for relationships between two or more pairs of simple relationships. Each pair may have a different sample size when pairwise deletion is used. The appropriate sample size for multiple correlation and regression is thus ambiguous. To illustrate, Exhibit 16.1 shows that the pairwise sample size for r_{YX1} is 8, but for r_{YX2}, it is 11.

Estimate Missing Scores.   Occasionally, researchers estimate missing independent variable scores from scores available on respondents. *Mean substitution* is most common; it replaces missing independent variable values with the mean score obtained from responding cases. For example, the mean of $X1$ would be substituted for the missing values of Individuals 3, 7, and 14 in Exhibit 16.1.

Replacing missing values with the mean has two predictable statistical consequences for simple correlation and regression. First, the simple regression coefficient Y on X is the same whether missing X scores are replaced with the mean or whether cases with missing values are dropped from the analysis. Second, the simple correlation coefficient between Y and X is generally attenuated (made smaller) by the substitution of means for missing data.

Exhibit 16.3 illustrates these outcomes using Y and $X1$ scores from Exhibit 16.1. Model 1 shows regression and correlation output when individuals with missing values on $X1$ are deleted; Model 2 shows results when missing $X1$ are replaced with the mean of $X1$.

EXHIBIT 16.3. Correlation and regression output from data in Exhibit 16.1 given alternative ways to handle missing data

Variable	Model 1	Model 2	Model 3	Model 4	Model 5	Model 6
Regression Coefficient X1	1,122.38	1,122.38*	1,122.38*	714.23	716.66	710.81
X2				-2,818.45	-2,801.63*	-2,842.07*
"Missing" dummy			-120.63			945.15
Intercept	2,957.36	2,924.46	2,957.36	22,039.29	22,179.03	22,199.18
$\hat{\rho}(\hat{\rho}2)$	.39	.33*	.24	.57	.65*	.60*
n	8	11	11	8	11	11

Note: Individuals 5, 8, and 9 deleted from all analyses.

*$p < .05$.

The regression coefficient for $X1$ is the same in Models 1 and 2. This illustrates that replacing missing $X1$ values with the mean does not increase or decrease the error that may be present in the regression coefficient due to missing data.

Alternatively, the estimated population variance in Y explained by $X1$ decreases in Model 2. In this example, the decrease in the variance explained is more than offset by the increase in power. The coefficient for $X1$ (and $\hat{\rho}^2$) is statistically significant ($p < .05$) in Model 2, but not in Model 1.

Some researchers recommend replacing missing independent variables with the mean. They argue that it is a "conservative" technique, since it tends to attenuate the relationship observed, yet power is increased. Others argue that the increase in power is spurious, since the researcher does not actually have scores for the missing values. There is no definitively correct answer.

The only thing certain is the need to report to the research consumer how missing data were handled and why.

Statistical outcomes are not as predictable when more than two variables are involved. Models 4 (listwise deletion) and 5 (mean replacement) in Exhibit 16.3 illustrate this point. Y scores are regressed on $X1$ and $X2$ scores from Exhibit 16.1. The regression coefficients on $X1$ are no longer the same in the two equations. This result is typical. It occurs because the multicollinearity between $X1$ and $X2$ differs between the entire sample (missing $X1$ values replaced with means—Model 5) and the subsample (without mean replacement—Model 4).

Alternative methods for replacing missing independent variables are sometimes suggested. For example, cases with missing values on a variable may be matched on other independent variables with responding cases. Scores of the matched responding cases are then used to replace missing values of nonresponding cases. To illustrate, Individuals 4 and 7 have the same value on $X2$ in Exhibit 16.1. The $X1$ value for Individual 4 (20), can be assigned to nonrespondent Individual 7.

Little is known about the consequences of using alternative methods for replacing missing values. For example, it is generally not known whether they increase or decrease bias in sample estimates of population parameters. (Substituting scores from one case to another does result in dependence among the correlation and regression errors if the model is misspecified. This may introduce bias. But, it is generally not known whether this bias is greater or smaller than the potential bias resulting from missing values when addressed by deleting cases.)

Identify "Missingness."   Cohen and Cohen (1983) have championed a procedure to accompany replacing missing values with the mean; it involves creating a dummy coded variable for "missingness." Participants who provide scores on the independent variable are coded 0; participants who do not provide scores are coded 1.

Models 3 and 6 in Exhibit 16.3 show statistical outcomes of this procedure for simple and multiple correlation and regression, respectively. Results of Model 3 suggest the procedure is attractive for simple correlation and regression problems. Adding the "missing" variable to the equation in Model 2 does not change the regression coefficient of $X1$. This results because the correlation coefficient of $X1$ and "missing" is necessarily 0.00. The mean of $X1$ is the same for both values of "missing."

RESEARCH HIGHLIGHT 16.1

Another Type of Mean Replacement

Sometimes researchers seek to measure constructs with multiple items. A questionnaire may contain five items designed to measure satisfaction with some service. The sum of the five items is used to measure satisfaction more reliably than would be true of only one item.

In such cases, it is not generally useful to replace a missing value on one of the items with the mean score across participants. However, it may be sensible to replace missing values with mean scores obtained within participants. For example, the mean of a participant's scores on four items responded to could be substituted for one item missing a value.

Judgment must be exercised regarding the number of missing items replaced. In the example, it is probably unwise to replace four missing items with the score obtained on one item. Nevertheless, the procedure is recommended if the amount of missing data is small.

The coefficient for "missing" shows the predicted difference in Y scores between those individuals who provide scores on $X1$ and those who do not. In the example, respondents on $X1$ are predicted to score 121 points higher on Y than nonrespondents (although this difference is not statistically significant, $p < .05$). The addition of the "missing" dummy variable thus provides additional information about cases without influencing the regression coefficient of $X1$. The issue is more complicated when there is another independent variable(s) in the equation. This is shown by Models 5 and 6 in Exhibit 16.3. The partial regression coefficients for $X1$ and $X2$ differ between Model 5 and 6. This occurs because there is multicollinearity between $X2$ and "missing."

Replacing missing values with the mean and use of a dummy variable coded for "missingness" thus adds complexity when there are two or more independent variables. This is shown by a comparison of Models 4, 5, and 6 in Exhibit 16.3. Since there is no unambiguous way to address the situation, it is important to explain whatever model was employed to the reader. The problem is more complex if there are missing data in more than one independent variable. It is technically feasible to create a "missingness" variable for every independent variable, sample size permitting. But, this can make interpretation unduly difficult. "Missingness" variables should be created sparingly. Probably only one such variable should be created for the independent variable most central to the objective of the study.

SUMMARY

An incomplete research data set may result because participants do not respond to a researcher's request for participation (**nonresponse**). Or, participants may respond, but only partially (**missing data**).

Incomplete data results in loss of statistical power. It can also result in statistical output that erroneously describes relations in the entire sample and can provide biased estimates of population parameters.

The most effective method for addressing incomplete data is to prevent it. The research design must be planned and executed to minimize the amount of incomplete data.

When present, incomplete data should be investigated for possible implications on the generalizability of results. It may be possible to compare respondents and nonrespondents on variables available to the researcher. This is a desirable research practice even though it is likely to suggest generalization problems.

For practical purposes, cases with missing data on dependent variables are treated as nonrespondents. Only comparisons with respondents are possible to determine if generalization problems are likely.

A broader array of procedures is available for missing independent variables. These include dropping variables, dropping cases, either **listwise** or **pairwise,** and/or replacing missing variables in one of several ways. There generally are not unambiguously correct or incorrect ways to address missing data among independent variables. Each of the procedures may be warranted in certain circumstances. Since there is no single missing data standard, it is important to report their frequency and to describe the procedures used to handle them.

FOR REVIEW

Terms to Know

Nonrespondents. Cases that provided no data for a research study.

Missing data. Data that is absent from a case.

Listwise deletion. When an entire case with missing data is removed from a research study.

Pairwise deletion. When a case is deleted only if there is missing data on variables from the specific analyses conducted. The case is retained for any other analyses in which data is present.

Mean substitution. Missing data on a variable is replaced with the mean of the responding cases on that variable.

Questions for Review

1. What problems do nonresponse and missing data present to researchers?
2. Suppose you are able to compare research respondents from nonrespondents on several variables that are not part of your research study. In what way(s) is such a comparison useful?
3. Deleting cases and deleting variables are two ways to address missing data on independent variables. Under what circumstances would you choose one over the other?
4. Listwise and pairwise are two methods for deleting cases. Under what circumstances would you choose one over the other?
5. What are the consequences for simple correlation and regression if the mean for an independent variable is used to replace missing data?
6. A regression of Y is performed on $X1$ and $X2$; $X1$ has missing data. What can you say about the partial regression coefficient on $X1$ if cases with missing data are deleted rather than if missing data are replaced by the mean? Are there any circumstances in which the partial regression coefficients will be the same using the two procedures?
7. Under what circumstances would the creation of a dummy variable(s) to differentiate between cases with data and cases with missing data be most attractive? Why?

SUGGESTED READING

A detailed description of creating dummy variables to account for missing data in multiple correlation and regression is provided by Cohen and Cohen (1983, Chap. 7). Donner (1982) and Donner and Rosner (1982) also discuss methods to address missing data in multiple correlation and regression. Roth (1994) is a good place to start for a general review of missing data and alternative methods for addressing them. Roth concludes that listwise deletion is often the least satisfactory way to address missing data.

17

On Reliability

Chapter Outline

- *Reliability Defined*
- *Estimating Reliability*
  - *Coefficient Alpha*
  - *Interpreting Coefficient Alpha*
- *Consequences of Unreliability*
  - *Consequences for Simple Correlation and Regression*
  - *Demonstrations*
- *Summary*
- *For Review*
- *Suggested Reading*

This chapter extends the discussion of measurement reliability introduced in Part II. Two points introduced in that part are summarized here. First, scores from measures of constructs invariably contain random (unsystematic) error. **Reliability,** the opposite of random error, refers to the systematic or consistent portion of scores. Reliable measurement is thus necessary for construct valid measurement.

Second, there are three contexts in which reliability is often of interest to researchers. These three differ regarding the type of reliability addressed. *Internal consistency* applies to multiple items in a measure, *interrater reliability* applies to multiple observers or raters, and *stability* applies to multiple time periods. In each case, reliability means that scores obtained across repetitions of measurement (item-to-item, observer-to-observer, time-to-time) are consistent.

This chapter provides a more formal description of reliability. Although more formal, the description nevertheless does not address many subtleties of reliability theory or techniques to estimate it; these theories and techniques are many and often elegant. Rather, this chapter introduces one commonly articulated way of thinking about reliability and one widely used and useful way of estimating it. The chapter also describes consequences of unreliability for simple correlation and regression output.

RELIABILITY DEFINED

Several formal theories of reliability are available; these differ in assumptions made about the nature of variability in scores. A simple formulation is presented here. Think of scores obtained on a measure as consisting of a systematic component and a random error component. These components cannot be observed directly, but an observed score can be *thought* of as:

$$x_{oi} = x_{ti} + x_{ei}$$

where x_{oi} = an observed score on the ith case

x_{ti} = systematic score component of the ith case

x_{ei} = random error score component of the ith case

The error score, x_{ei} is typically assumed to have two properties. First, it is assumed that the random error is as likely to inflate as deflate scores. Thus, it is expected that $\Sigma x_e = 0$. As a consequence:

$$\mu_{Xo} \approx \mu_{Xt}$$

where μ_{Xo} and μ_{Xt} are the means of the observed and systematic scores, respectively

Second, it is also assumed that the error score is unrelated to the systematic score component of the observed score:

$$\rho_{XtXe} = 0$$

where ρ_{XtXe} = the correlation coefficient between the systematic and random error components

When components are uncorrelated, the variance (σ^2) of the sum of these components is equal to the sum of the variances of each component. Thus:

$$\sigma^2_{Xo} = \sigma^2_{Xt} + \sigma^2_{Xe}$$

where σ^2_{Xo} = variance of observed scores

σ^2_{Xt} = variance of systematic scores

σ^2_{Xe} = variance in random errors

In words, the variance in observed scores is equal to the sum of the variances of the systematic and random error components of the observed scores. Unreliability increases variance in observed scores relative to systematic scores:

$$\sigma^2_{Xo} > \sigma^2_{Xt}$$

Given this perspective, reliability is formally defined as:

$$\rho_{XX} = \frac{\sigma^2_{Xt}}{\sigma^2_{Xo}} \qquad (17.1)$$

where ρ_{XX} = reliability of scores on a measure X

Formula 17.1 defines reliability as the proportion of observed score variance that is systematic. (Although characterized as a correlation coefficient, an accident of history, ρ_{XX} is really a coefficient of determination, it reports the proportion of observed score variance that is explained by true score variation.)

$$\rho_{XX} = \rho^2_{XoXt} = \text{Systematic Variance / Total Variance}$$

Reliability can range from 0.00 (all the observed score variance is random) to 1.00 (all the observed score variance is systematic).

ESTIMATING RELIABILITY

Regardless of whether internal consistency, interrater or stability reliability is of interest, rows and columns of a data matrix will be set up as shown in Exhibit 17.1. Columns (variables) represent repetitions of measurement and rows represent cases. Columns refer to items for internal consistency, observers for interrater reliability, and time periods for stability.

EXHIBIT 17.1. Data matrix for reliability analysis

Cases	*Measurement Repetitions*					
	1	*2*	.	*j*	.	*k*
1						
2						
.						
i						
.						
N						

Coefficient Alpha

Since the data matrix is the same regardless of reliability interest, a common method to estimate reliability can be used in all these cases. A widely used method is **coefficient alpha.** One formula estimates coefficient alpha by:

$$\hat{\rho}_{XX} = \frac{k * \rho_{(Ave)ij}}{1 + (k-1) * \rho_{(Ave)ij}} \tag{17.2}$$

where $\hat{\rho}_{XX}$ = **coefficient alpha estimated from observed scores**

k = **number of repetitions (items, observers, or time periods)**

$\rho_{(Ave)ij}$ = **the average correlation among scores of repetitions (items, judges, time periods, etc.)**

Technically, Formula 17.2 is appropriate only when the variability in all of the repetitions is equal. It is used here instead of a less restrictive formula because it clearly shows that reliability, as estimated, is a positive function of the average intercorrelation among repetitions, and the number of repetitions. Formula 17.2 shows that alpha increases as the number of repetitions increase, holding the average intercorrelation constant. It also shows that alpha increases as the average intercorrelation increases, holding the number of repetitions constant.

EXHIBIT 17.2. Factors that influence coefficient alpha: Measurement repetitions and average intercorrelations

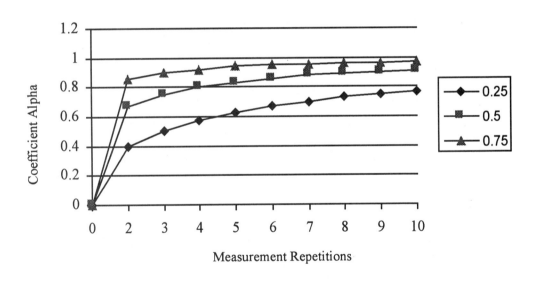

Exhibit 17.2 illustrates how the number of repetitions influences coefficient alpha estimates for three different average intercorrelations among repetitions ($\rho_{(Ave)ij}$ = .25, .50 and .75). The estimates approach asymptotes as the number of repetitions grow larger. For example, with an average intercorrelation of .75, there is little improvement in reliability beyond about 10 repetitions.

RESEARCH HIGHLIGHT 17.1

Other Estimation Procedures

Coefficient alpha is one of many methods to estimate reliability. Methods similar (or in some cases identical) to coefficient alpha go by names such as the Kudar-Richardson, Spearman-Brown, and Hoyt formulas. These are used in special situations. Coefficient alpha is probably the most frequently used and reported of these methods.

Interpreting Coefficient Alpha

There are several ways to interpret coefficient alpha. One useful way is to understand that it provides an estimate of the correlation coefficient that is expected between a summary score from a measure studied (e.g., average score of the repetitions studied) and another (hypothetical) measure of the same thing using the same number of repetitions. For example, suppose coefficient alpha is computed on a sample of ice skater scores provided by a group of international judges. In this case, alpha estimates the correlation coefficient between average scores from this group of judges and the averages that would be generated by another similar group of the same number of judges.

This is an important estimate to obtain. The performance of ice skaters should be evaluated similarly regardless of what specific group of judges provide the evaluations. In general, we want measurement that provides comparable scores beyond the immediate items, observers, or times that are studied.

Nevertheless, understand that high reliability, as estimated by coefficient alpha, does not insure construct validity. Reliability does not address systematic errors that may contaminate scores or leave them deficient. Contamination may include systematic variance associated with another construct. Coefficient alpha does not directly address whether the scores are getting at only a single (unidimensional) construct. For example, the ice skating judges may provide reliable scores as estimated by coefficient alpha even though they evaluate skaters on two or more constructs, as long as they do so consistently.

RESEARCH HIGHLIGHT 17.2

Generalizing Reliability

Standard reliability estimates do not distinguish between different sources of unsystematic error. For example, suppose a researcher estimates the reliability of two intentionally similar measures of a construct (called parallel forms) administered to a group of individuals two weeks apart. A typical measure of reliability does not distinguish between random error generated by differences due to the forms and differences due to time.

Generalizability theory provides a rationale and methods designed to differentiate between sources of unreliability. These sources may be time, items, individuals providing the scores (observers or research participants), as well as others. The generalizability model thus provides multiple reliability estimates depending on what source(s) of unreliability is of interest to a researcher. Although the objectives of the generalizability model are accessible and desirable, the design and analysis of generalizability studies are typically complex. It is probably for these reasons that the model has not been widely used.

CONSEQUENCES OF UNRELIABILITY

Statistical procedures generally provide misleading information when variables are measured unreliably. Unreliability also leads to errors when statistical inferences are drawn. This section identifies consequences of unreliability for simple correlation and regression output. Problems of unreliability for statistical inference are discussed in Chapter 19.

Consequences for Simple Correlation and Regression

Consequences of unreliability for simple correlation and regression are well known. Specifically:

1. Unreliability in either X or Y attenuates (reduces) the expected correlation coefficient relative to the correlation coefficient that is obtained if X and Y are measured with perfect reliability.

2.   Unreliability in X attenuates the expected regression coefficient, and increases the intercept, relative to the regression coefficient that is obtained if X is measured with perfect reliability.
3.   Unreliability in Y has no expected effect on the regression coefficient and hence no expected effect on the intercept.

Demonstrations

These outcomes are understood by reviewing formulas for simple correlation and regression or by recalling that unreliability has no expected effect on the mean of a variable but that it increases the variance.

$$\mu_{Xo} \cong \mu_{Xt}, \text{ and}$$

$$\sigma^2_{Xo} > \sigma^2_{Xt}$$

where o and t refer to observed scores and systematic scores, respectively

Correlation Coefficients.   One formula for the correlation coefficient from Chapter 10 using covariance is:

$$\rho_{YX} = \frac{CoVar_{YX}}{\sigma_Y * \sigma_x} \qquad (10.2a)$$

where ρ_{YX} = **correlation coefficient between Y and X**

σ_Y and σ_X = **standard deviations of Y and X, respectively**

CoVar$_{YX}$ = covariance of Y and X

Covariance, in turn, is defined as:

$$CoVar_{YX} = \frac{\Sigma(Y_i - \mu_Y) * (X_i - \mu_x)}{N} \qquad (10.1)$$

where **CoVar$_{YX}$ = the average cross-product of the deviations about their respective means of Y and X**

Unreliability increases the denominator of Formula 10.2b but leaves the numerator unchanged. Begin with the denominator. Unreliability in either Y or X will increase their variances and hence standard deviations relative to perfectly reliable measurement.

$$\sigma_{Xo} > \sigma_{Xt} \text{ and } \sigma_{Yo} > \sigma_{Yt}$$

where σ_{Xo} and σ_{Yo} = observed standard deviations of X and Y, respectively

σ_{Xt} and σ_{Yt} = true score standard deviations of X and Y, respectively

Alternatively, unreliability does not effect covariance, the numerator in Formula 10.2a. Unreliability serves to inflate some scores and deflate others; these are expected to be offsetting:

$$\text{CoVar}_{YoXo} \approx \text{CoVar}_{YtXt}$$

where CoVar_{YoXo} = covariance of observed (unreliable) scores

CoVar_{YtXt} = covariance of true scores

Thus, unreliability in either Y and/or X is expected to leave the numerator of Formula 10.2b the same but increase the denominator. As a consequence, *unreliability attenuates* a correlation coefficient relative to what it would be if there was no unreliability. This attenuation occurs whether the unreliability is in the independent and/or dependent variable. The amount of attenuation is shown by:

$$\rho_{YoXo} = \rho_{YtXt} \sqrt{\rho_{YY}} \sqrt{\rho_{XX}} \qquad (17.3)$$

where ρ_{YoXo} = correlation coefficient on observed scores

ρ_{YtXt} = **true score correlation coefficient**

Formula 17.3 can be rearranged to provide an estimated *correction for attenuation* due to unreliability.

$$\rho_{YtXt} = \frac{\rho_{YoXo}}{\sqrt{\rho_{YY}} \sqrt{\rho_{XX}}} \qquad (17.4)$$

If the reliability of the Y and X measures are known, Formula 17.4 can be used to estimate the correlation coefficient if Y and X were measured with perfect reliability. However, this estimate can be in substantial error if ρ_{Ye} or ρ_{Xe} is not equal to zero, assumptions of reliability analysis.

Regression Coefficients and Intercepts.   The effect of unreliability in regression depends on whether it is in the X or Y variable. From Chapter 10:

$$B_{YX} = \frac{\rho_{YX} * \sigma_Y}{\sigma_X} \qquad (10.6)$$

where B_{YX} = regression coefficient of Y on X

$$\alpha = \mu_Y - \mu_X * B_{YX} \qquad (10.7)$$

where α = regression intercept, the predicted value of Y when $X = 0$

Unreliability in X.   Given unreliability in X, $\sigma_{Xo} > \sigma_{Xt}$ and $\rho_{YXo} < \rho_{YXt}$ (from Formula 17.3). The former increases the denominator in Formula 10.4 (relative to reliable measurement of X) and the latter decreases the numerator. Both these consequences of unreliability in X serve to decrease the regression coefficient in Formula 10.4.

$$B_{YXo} < B_{YXt}$$

where B_{YXo} = the regression coefficient when X is measured unreliably

B_{YXt} = the regression coefficient when X is measured with perfect reliability

The decrease in the regression coefficient of Formula 10.4 will serve in Formula 10.5 to increase the intercept.

Unreliability in Y.   When there is unreliability in Y, then $\sigma_{Yo} > \sigma_{Yt}$ and $\rho_{YoX} < \rho_{YtX}$ (from Formula 17.3). Both of these are components of the numerator in Formula 10.4 and they move in opposite directions. Indeed, it can be shown that the effects in the numerator of Formula 10.4 are offsetting.

$$B_{YoX} \approx B_{YtX}$$

where B_{YoX} = the regression coefficient when Y is measured unreliably

B_{YtX} = the regression coefficient when Y is measured with perfect reliability

Because unreliability in Y has no expected effect on the regression coefficient it also has no expected effect on the intercept. (However, unreliability in Y does have implications for statistical inference. Specifically, other things equal, unreliability makes it less likely that an observed regression coefficient will lead to a conclusion to reject the null hypothesis.)

SUMMARY

Reliability refers to consistency of measurement. It is formally defined as the proportion of observed score variance that is systematic.

The reliability of measures can be estimated in a number of ways. *Coefficient alpha* provides an estimate that is useful in many situations. Coefficient alpha generally increases as the correlation between items (time periods, observers) increases and as the number of items (time periods, observers) increases. Coefficient alpha is interpreted as the correlation coefficient to be expected between two similar measures of the same phenomena.

An observed correlation coefficient is attenuated by unreliability in the independent and/or dependent variable. If the reliability of the measures is known, the *correction for attenuation* estimates the relationship to be expected if both measures had perfect reliability. Unreliability in the dependent variable has no effect on the regression coefficient, although unreliability in the independent variable attenuates it.

FOR REVIEW

Terms to Know

Reliability. The consistency of measurement. Formally, it is the ratio of systematic score variance to total variance.

Coefficient alpha. An estimate of reliability; it provides an estimate of the correlation coefficient that is expected between a summary score

RESEARCH HIGHLIGHT 17.3

Unreliability in Multiple Correlation and Regression

Consequences of unreliability for simple correlation and regression are straightforward, as described. Unfortunately, the same cannot be said for the consequences of unreliability on partial coefficients in multiple correlation and regression. Unreliability may attenuate partial coefficients, but it may also leave them unchanged; inflate them; or worse, change their sign. Identifying consequences of unreliability in multiple correlation and regression is difficult, especially as the number of independent variables becomes large. The problem is best confronted by the development and use of measures with high reliability.

RESEARCH HIGHLIGHT 17.4

Reliability Guidelines

Okay, you're convinced; reliability is important. It is important for construct validity and it is important for statistical output. How reliable must measures be?

That's a good question, but it doesn't have a simple answer. First, there are many different kinds of reliability. A reliability value that is acceptable in one situation may not be acceptable in another. For example, the reliability of a measure administered twice, two weeks apart, will generally have greater reliability than if it is administered twice, one year apart. Second, what is acceptable or unacceptable reliability also depends on how the measure is used. To illustrate, higher reliability is needed to make accurate predictions about individual cases than is needed to draw conclusions about whether two or more groups differ on some measure.

It is often possible to improve reliability in the course of constructing measures. Because of its importance for construct validity, high reliability should be a top measurement priority.

from a measure studied and another hypothetical measure of the same thing using the same number of repetitions.

Attenuation due to unreliability. Formula that estimates the degree to which unreliability in either or both variables reduces a correlation coefficient relative to perfectly reliable measurement of the variables.

Correction for attenuation. Formula that estimates the correlation between two variables if they are measured with perfect reliability; it requires knowledge of the reliability of each variable.

Formulas to Use

Reliability

$$\rho_{XX} = \frac{\sigma^2_{Xt}}{\sigma^2_{Xo}} \qquad (17.1)$$

Coefficient alpha

$$\hat{\rho}_{XX} = \frac{k * \rho_{(Ave)ij}}{1 + (k-1) * \rho_{(Ave)ij}} \qquad (17.2)$$

where $\rho_{(Ave)ij}$ = average correlation among scores of repetitions

Attenuation due to unreliability

$$\rho_{YoXo} = \rho_{YtXt} \sqrt{\rho_{YY}} \sqrt{\rho_{XX}} \qquad (17.3)$$

where ρ_{YoXo} = correlation coefficient on observed scores

ρ_{YtXt} = true score correlation coefficient

Correction for attenuation

$$\rho_{YtXt} = \frac{\rho_{YoXo}}{\sqrt{\rho_{YY}} \sqrt{\rho_{XX}}} \qquad (17.4)$$

Questions for Review

1. How does unreliability in an independent variable influence the simple correlation coefficient, regression coefficient, and regression intercept? How do these conclusions change if the unreliability was in the dependent rather than the independent variable?

2. Simple correlation coefficients among four items designed to measure opinions about the nutritional value of herbal tea are shown.

   Simple Correlation Coefficients

	X1	X2	X3	X4
X1	1.00	.55	.35	.45
X2		1.00	.65	.50
X3			1.00	.45

   a. Calculate coefficient alpha for the four items.
   b. What three items would form the most reliable scale if only three items were used?
   c. What is coefficient alpha for these three items?
   d. Given your alpha value from Question c, what correlation would you expect between the sum of these three items and the sum of another three items measuring the same thing?

3. You observe that $\rho_{YX} = .35$ and $\rho_{YZ} = .45$. Reliabilities are $\rho_{YY} = .90$, $\rho_{XX} = .80$, and $\rho_{ZZ} = .70$. What has the higher true score relationship, ρ_{YX} or ρ_{YZ}?

4. If you have covered the material in Chapter 10: Be able to describe how the random error term (ε_i) is different in the regression model than in the reliability model? How is it the same?

Exercise

The following data set shows reliable Y and X scores and Y and X scores with unreliability.[1] (The eight values in parentheses are only included to show

---

[1]The random appearing errors in this data set are really not random at all. With such a small sample of observations, unreliability can have *unexpected* results. This data set is constructed to have *expected* unreliability consequences for correlation and regression.

how the variables are influenced by unreliability. Do not include them in your analysis.)

Reliable Y	Unreliable Y	Reliable X	Unreliable X
2	2	1	1
2	3 (up 1)	2	1 (down 1)
2	1 (down 1)	3	4 (up 1)
2	2	4	4
4	4	3	3
4	3 (down 1)	4	5 (up 1)
4	5 (up 1)	5	4 (down 1)
4	4	6	6

Use the data set to calculate the following statistics:

1. Descriptive statistics that provide means and standard deviations for each variable. What is noteworthy about these statistics in terms of your knowledge of reliability?
2. Simple correlation coefficients between all the variables. What is noteworthy about these statistics in terms of your knowledge of reliability?
3. Regress reliable Y on reliable X. Then, regress unreliable Y on reliable X. Finally, regress reliable Y on unreliable X. What is noteworthy about these statistics in terms of your knowledge of reliability?

SUGGESTED READING

Reliability has received a great deal of attention by researchers, probably because it can be addressed with mathematics more rigorously than many other construct validity topics. Two good general discussions of reliability that go beyond the level of presentation here but are nevertheless accessible are provided by Ghiselli, Campbell, and Zedeck (1981) and Nunnally (1978). I also like Campbell's (1976) chapter on reliability.

There are also many writings on specific topics discussed in the chapter. Cortina (1993) presents a readable discussion of the use and limitations of coefficient alpha. Cohen and Cohen (1983) have a short but readily understandable discussion of problems presented by unreliability for multiple correlation and regression. Problems created by unreliability are discussed by Schmidt and Hunter (1996). Finally, Shavelson, Webb and Rowley (1989) provide an introduction to Cronbach, Rajaratnam, and Gleser's (1963) complex generalizability theory.

18

On Multicollinearity

Chapter Outline

Multicollinearity is a big word to describe a simple concept; it means that in-dependent variables are correlated (e.g., $r_{X1X2} < > 0$) in multiple correlation–regression. Chapter 11 explained that the multiple coefficient of determination (P^2_{YX1X2}) is not equal to the sum of the simple coefficients of determination ($\rho^2_{YX1} + \rho^2_{YX2}$) when there is multicollinearity in a two-independent variable case. Typical consequences of multicollinearity are shown in Exhibit 18.1 where multicollinearity between $X1$ and $X2$ is shown by the area $d + d'$. Some variance that each explains in Y is redundant (the area d). Consequently, the total variance explained in Y is less than the simple sum of the variance that each Xi explains. This two- independ-ent-variable case generalizes to three or more independent variables.

This chapter addresses additional multicollinearity issues. A major issue involves problems created by multicollinearity for statistical inference.

EXHIBIT 18.1. Multicollinearity with two independent variables

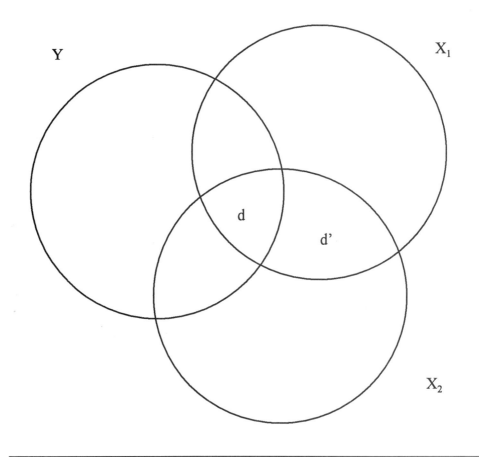

Next, several multicollinearity effects are demonstrated through simulation. A common multicollinearity misconception is then identified. Finally, suggestions for addressing multicollinearity are offered.

Problems for Statistical Inference: Bouncing Betas

The standard error of any partial coefficient for Xi (regression or correlation) increases as multicollinearity in Xi increases. [A standard error is a standard deviation of a sampling distribution (see Chapter 12). The larger the standard error, the greater the variability in sample estimates of a parameter.] As a consequence, the partial coefficients (e.g., $B_{YXi \cdot Xi}$) from one sample may not be similar to coefficients calculated on another sample drawn from the same population. Because of this, standardized regression coefficients calculated when independent variables are collinear are sometimes called *bouncing betas.*

A DEMONSTRATION

Data for two populations are simulated to illustrate several multicollinearity outcomes. Both populations have 6,000 cases. Both have a standardized ($\mu = 0$; $\sigma = 1$) dependent variable (Y) and three standardized independent variables ($X1$, $X2$, and $X3$). Each Xi was specified to correlate with its respective Y, $r_{YXi} = .30$. However, Population 1 was created to have no multicollinearity (simple correlation coefficients among the Xs equal zero). Population 2 was created to have multicollinearity of $\rho_{xixj} = .50$ for all three pairs of relationships. Descriptive statistics in Exhibits 18.2 and 18.3 show that the populations created conform closely to specification.

EXHIBIT 18.2. Population 1: Descriptive statistics

Variables			Correlation Coefficients			
	μ	σ	Y	$X1$	$X2$	$X3$
Y	0.00	1.00	1.00			
X1	0.00	1.00	.28	1.00		
X2	0.00	1.00	.32	.00	1.00	
X3	0.00	1.00	.30	−.01	−.00	1.00

EXHIBIT 18.3. Population 2: Descriptive statistics

Variables			Correlation Coefficients			
	μ	σ	Y	$X1$	$X2$	$X3$
Y	0.00	1.00	1.00			
X1	0.00	1.00	.30	1.00		
X2	0.00	1.00	.30	.51	1.00	
X3	0.00	1.00	.31	.51	.50	1.00

Population Parameters

Exhibits 18.4 and 18.5 show results of a regression of Y on all Xi in Populations 1 and 2, respectively. Standardized partial regression coefficients (betas) and P^2, the multiple coefficient of determination, are shown in each. No inferential statistical values (e.g., t or F statistics) are shown, because the coefficients shown are population parameters.

EXHIBIT 18.4. Population 1: Regression output

Variable	Beta
X1	.28
X2	.32
X3	.30
P^2	.28

$N = 6,000.$

EXHIBIT 18.5. Population 2: Regression output

Variable	Beta
X1	.14
X2	.15
X3	.17
P^2	.14

$N = 6,000.$

Beta coefficients in Exhibit 18.4 correspond closely to the simple correlation coefficients in Exhibit 18.2. This result occurs because there is nearly zero correlation among the independent variables. Also observe that $P^2_{YX1X2X3}$ ($=.28$) is about equal to the sum of the simple coefficients of determination ($\Sigma[p^2_{YXi}] = .28^2 + .32^2 + .30^2 = .27$). Again, this result obtains because the independent variables have nearly zero multicollinearity.

Contrast the population results in Exhibit 18.4 with Exhibit 18.5. The standardized regression coefficients in Exhibit 18.5 are all smaller than their counterparts in Exhibit 18.4. And, they are all smaller than the zero-order correlation coefficients of Xi with Y. These outcomes result from multicollinearity among the independent variables; some of the variance explained in Y by each variable is redundant with variance explained by others. Thus, Y variance explained in Population 2 ($P^2_{YX1X2X3} = .14$) is smaller than in Population 1, and smaller than the sum of the simple coefficients of determination ($\Sigma[p^2_{YXi}] = .30^2 + .30^2 + .31^2 = .28$).

Sample Statistics

Twenty-five random samples of 25 cases each were drawn from each population. Exhibits 18.6 (Population 1) and 18.7 (Population 2) summarize statistics calculated on these samples. The exhibits show standardized regression coefficients, standard errors, and the corrected coefficient of determination, $\hat{P}^2_{YX1X2X3}$.

The corrected coefficient of determination $\hat{P}^2$, called **adjusted R^2**, is a better estimate of the population coefficient of determination than unadjusted R^2. $\hat{P}^2$ is found by:

$$\hat{P}^2 = R^2 - \frac{k(1-R^2)}{n-k-1} \tag{18.1}$$

where $\hat{P}^2$ = corrected coefficient of determination
R^2 = sample coefficient of determination
n = sample size
k = number of independent variables

Average $\hat{P}^2$ and beta values obtained in the 25 samples from the two populations are shown near the bottom of Exhibits 18.6 and 18.7. These averages illustrate the unbiasedness of population estimates obtained from random

EXHIBIT 18.6. **Population 1: Sample regression output from 25 samples ($n = 25$)**

Sample	$\hat{R}^2$	X1	SE X1	X2	SE X2	X3	SE X3
1	.44**	.43*	.13	.37*	.21	.48*	.12
2	.31*	.29	.15	.38	.17	.34	.11
3	.04	.19	.22	.40	.19	.01	.26
4	.54**	.64**	.17	.30*	.17	.58**	.17
5	.27*	.08	.25	.29	.21	.43*	.23
6	.33*	.25	.22	.39*	.16	.40*	.12
7	.24*	.57**	.14	−.04	.15	.05	.18
8	.27*	.38	.17	.51*	.16	.16	.16
9	.26*	.26	.13	.34	.11	.40*	.19
10	.57**	.36*	.13	.56**	.10	.52*	.14
11	.58**	.60**	.18	.35*	.13	.44*	.17
12	.24*	.57	.16	.21	.16	.06	.21
13	.10	.18	.15	.11	.16	.44*	.17
14	.47**	−.04	.23	.69**	.17	.13	.17
15	.11	.34	.26	.26	.24	.32	.21
16	.00	.09	.22	.11	.19	.03	.20
17	.23*	.45	.21	.44*	.20	.50*	.22
18	.48**	.43*	.16	.38*	.17	.52**	.16
19	.37**	.36	.22	.14	.25	.44*	.18
20	.22*	.32	.16	.40*	.18	.27	.20
21	.04	−.10	.19	.05	.16	.39	.17
22	.44**	.48*	.14	.56**	.15	−.12	.17
23	.33*	.26	.16	.57**	.19	.27	.20
24	.30*	.37	.22	.27	.18	.29	.18
25	.00	.06	.23	.22	.16	.23	.19
Mean	.29	.31	.18	.33	.17	.30	.18
Std. Dev.	.17	.20	.04	.18	.03	.19	.03

$*p < .05.$

$**p < .01.$

EXHIBIT 18.7. Population 2: Sample regression output from 25 samples ($n = 25$)

Sample	$\hat{R}^2$	X1	SE X1	X2	SE X2	X3	SE X3
1	.08	−.13	.23	.18	.17	.39	.23
2	.03	−.44	.28	.36	.27	.06	.29
3	.00	−.32	.27	.40	.27	−.09	.26
4	.14	.06	.30	.38	.26	.13	.33
5	.26*	.03	.14	−.17	.16	.63*	.18
6	.30*	.13	.23	.48	.30	.08	.25
7	.00	.23	.28	.11	.38	−.15	.29
8	.03	−.42	.30	.18	.30	.41	.33
9	.06	−.12	.25	.56	.29	−.19	.29
10	.32*	.73**	.25	−.08	.23	−.16	.20
11	.14	.14	.20	−.15	.18	.47*	.15
12	.08	.27	.22	.34	.24	−.48	.17
13	.26	.27	.17	.45	.21	−.04	.21
14	.06	.14	.32	.07	.39	.30	.28
15	.14	−.51	.22	.06	.18	.61*	.20
16	.14	.39	.20	.23	.20	−.11	.21
17	.02	.14	.24	.07	.28	.26	.23
18	.23*	.26	.23	−.35	.21	.58*	.18
19	.16	.20	.29	.27	.31	.19	.25
20	.50	.10	.14	−.02	.27	.70**	.15
21	.53	.76	.20	.07	.15	−.05	.19
22	.08	−.13	.23	.18	.17	.39	.23
23	.03	−.44	.28	.36	.27	.06	.29
24	.00	−.32	.27	.40	.27	−.09	.26
25	.14	.06	.30	.38	.26	.13	.33
Mean	.15	.04	.24	.19	.25	.16	.23
Std. Dev.	.14	.33	.05	.23	.06	.31	.06

*$p < .05$.

**$p < .01$.

365

samples. Average $\hat{P}^2$ from samples of both population are close to the population parameters. Further, with one exception ($beta_{YX1 \cdot X2X3}$, Population 2), average betas are also close to their respective population parameters.

The mean standard errors associated with the betas are informative about multicollinearity. On average, these errors are all larger in Population 2 with multicollinearity. This signals that statistical power is reduced by multicollinearity.

Exhibits 18.6 and 18.7 reveal results of multicollinearity in three additional ways. All are consistent with the standard error results, and all are associated with loss of power due to multicollinearity.

1. Beta estimates for all three independent variables have larger standard deviations in samples drawn from the population with multicollinearity (Population 2).
2. An examination of the signs of the beta coefficients is also revealing. Though the population betas are all positive, 23 of the sample beta coefficients are negative in Population 2. Only four of the betas are negative in Population 1.
3. Power is low in statistical tests from both populations (the sample sizes are only 25 in each case), but it is lower in the population with multicollinearity. Thirty of the 75 partial coefficients are statistically significant ($p < .05$) in samples from Population 1 (Exhibit 18.6); only six are statistically significant in samples from Population 2 (Exhibit 18.7). Keep in mind, all Xi are related in the populations (see, Exhibits 18.4 and 18.5). Thus, only Type II error is possible (failing to conclude H_1 when H_1 is true).

MULTICOLLINEARITY MISCONCEIVED

If discussed, multicollinearity is almost always described as problematic by statistics and research methods books. Indeed it is; as shown, multicollinearity attenuates multiple correlation and regression coefficients, and makes any sample estimates less reliable predictors of population parameters (i.e., reduces power).

However, absence of multicollinearity is not an assumption of multiple correlation and regression as is sometimes suggested. Standard errors remain correct even with multicollinearity (although larger than they would otherwise be). Hypothesis tests and confidence intervals thus remain correct.

Think of it another way: With zero multicollinearity, we could obtain R^2 simply by summing the simple r^2_{YXi} (see Formula 11.1). Furthermore, any simple regression coefficient would be the same as its corresponding partial coefficient. If multicollinearity were not present, multiple correlation and regression would provide no information beyond what we can learn from simple correlation and regression.

But multicollinearity is no virtue. Although multicollinearity does not invalidate multiple correlation and regression, it nevertheless has the undesirable consequences identified. Researchers prefer less to more.

ADDRESSING MULTICOLLINEARITY

The best way to address multicollinearity is to view it in conceptual terms before data are collected and analyses performed. Design, measurement, and data analysis responses to multicollinearity should be driven by the conceptual model of interest. For example, suppose an interest in some work attitude and a conceptual model suggests that employee age and work experience impact on this attitude, but for different reasons. That being the case, both variables should be included in the model, even though they are typically related (collinear).

Alternatively, a conceptual model may not distinguish between the roles of age and experience. They may only represent approximations (proxies) for longevity in some sense. If so, one might include only one of the two variables in a statistical model, or the two could be combined in a single index representing longevity.

SUMMARY

Multicollinearity refers to the correlation among independent variables. It presents two problems for multivariate data analysis procedures. First, it reduces the dependent variable variance explained relative to what would be the case if the independent variables have the same simple relationships with the dependent variable but less multicollinearity. Second, multicollinearity results in sample statistics that are less stable estimates of population parameters. A simulation demonstrated both effects.

Your approach to multicollinearity should be guided by the conceptual model explaining relationships among the variables. Independent variables may be collinear. However, if they are important to the conceptual model they should be retained in the analysis.

It is wise to aim for a large sample when there is multicollinearity. The increase in standard errors of the partial coefficients associated with the collinear independent variables reduces power.

FOR REVIEW

Term to Know

Adjusted R^2. Multiple coefficient of determination adjusted for sample size and number of independent variables. It is a better estimate of the parameter than is the unadjusted sample multiple coefficient of determination.

Formula to Use

Corrected coefficient of determination

$$\hat{P}^2 = R^2 - \frac{k(1-R^2)}{n-k-1} \tag{18.1}$$

where $\hat{P}^2$ = corrected coefficient of determination

R^2 = sample coefficient of determination

n = sample size

k = number of independent variables

Questions for Review

1. Multicollinearity leads to an increase in the standard error of partial correlation and regression coefficients. What are the implications of this increase for statistical inference?
2. Two studies are performed by drawing random samples from two populations. Selected characteristics of the studies are summarized below.

	Study 1	*Study 2*
	$R^2 = .35$	$R^2 = .45$
	$n = 1500$	$n = 150$
	$k = 4$	$k = 6$

where n = sample size; k = number of independent variables

At a population level, how much of the variance in the dependent variable do you estimate is accounted for in each study?

19

On Multiple Correlation and Regression Modeling

Chapter Outline

- *Causal Models*
  - *Evaluating Causal Models*
  - *Four Causal Models*
  - *Importance of Specification*
- *Empirical Models*
  - *Stepwise Regression*
  - *Evaluation of Stepwise Regression*
- *A Closing Caution*
- *Summary*
- *For Review*
- *Suggested Reading*
- *Appendix 19A: Additional Assumptions for Inference*

This chapter serves as a capstone. It shows how researchers address causal challenges raised in Chapter 3 using multiple correlation and regression (Chapter 11) and statistical inference (Chapter 13). Researchers frequently employ statistical models involving correlation or regression to address causal models. A *causal model* refers to variables that operate in a causal system and to their true relationships. A *statistical model* consists of the variables that a researcher uses to investigate a causal model. Statistical procedures can sometimes help identify whether certain causal models are plausible, given the empirical relationships obtained. They may also help decide when certain statistical models are causally implausible.

This chapter introduces statistical modeling using multiple correlation and regression and describes how statistical inference is used in the process. A major distinction is drawn between two quite different ways for doing this. In one, a researcher seeks to evaluate a specific causal model linking independent variables with the dependent variable. The causal model is specified first and then evaluated using the statistical model and statistical inference. In the other, a researcher lets statistical inference play a prominent role in model identification.

Procedures for both methods are illustrated using a hypothetical data set. These data represent information on a random sample of 100 low- to middle-level managers from a simulated population of 4,861 managers in a large organization.

Statistics on the variables are summarized in Exhibit 19.1. Yearly salary serves as the dependent variable in all models. Depending on the model evaluated, independent variables include:

- Years of experience at the organization.
- Job level numerically scaled from 1 (first-level supervisor) to 4 (highest-level middle manager).[1]
- Performance rating provided by each manager's supervisor ranging from 1 (marginal performance) to 7 (highest performance).
- Gender, dummy coded, male = 1; female = 0.
- Set of occupations: finance/accounting, dummy coded, finance/accounting = 1, all other occupations = 0. Similar dummy variables are created for the other occupations: human resources, manufacturing, and sales/marketing.
- A moderator variable formed by multiplying gender times years of experience.

Different examples use different sets of these independent variables to illustrate major methods for conceptual and empirical modeling.

---

[1]The relationship between salary and this variable, treated as a numerical scale, is linear. If it were not linear, three dummy variables could be created to account for the four job levels.

EXHIBIT 19.1. Summary statistics on hypothetical managerial data set

Simple Correlation Coefficients

	μ	σ	Y	X1	X2	X3	X4	X5	X6	X7	X8	X9
Y Yearly salary	63,800.00	9,000.70	1.00									
X1 Years experience	9.20	3.02	.44*	1.00								
X2 Job level	2.36	1.07	.58*	.66*	1.00							
X3 Performance	4.62	1.81	.13	.12	.17	1.00						
X4 Gender	.70	.46	.20*	.15	.06	.03	1.00					
X5 Finance/Accounting	.24	.43	.17	-.08	-.04	-.02	-.14	1.00				
X6 Human Resources	.24	.43	-.03	.04	-.15	-.09	.16	-.32*	1.00			
X7 Manufacturing	.28	.45	-.33*	.07	.02	.08	-.13	-.35*	-.35*	1.00		
X8 Sales/Marketing	.24	.43	.21*	-.04	.16	.03	.11	-.32*	-.32	-.35*	1.00	
X9 Gender * Years exp	6.65	5.04	.40*	.54*	.35*	.10	.87*	-.10	.13	-.11	.09	1.00

Note. * $p < .05$ (two-tailed).

Job level ranges from 1 (first level supervisor) to 4 (top middle manager).

Performance ranges from 1 (marginal performance) to 7 (highest performance).

Gender dummy coded (male = 1; female = 0).

Financial Accounting dummy coded (Finance/Accounting = 1; other = 0); likewise for the other occupational areas.

Gender * Years experience is an interaction (moderator) term formed by multiplying gender times years of experience.

371

CAUSAL MODELS

Causal models can take a variety of forms. Four simple but frequently investigated models are described. These four are all **recursive models** meaning that causal influence is assumed to go in only one direction. Further, only a simple version of each recursive model is described. In practice, each model can include many variables.

Two terms are commonly used to describe variables in causal models. **Endogenous variables** are explained by the causal model. Thus, dependent variables are always endogenous. Independent variables are also endogenous if they depend on some other independent variable(s) in the model. Alternatively, independent variables are *exogenous* when their cause(s) are not included in the model.

Evaluating Causal Models

Statistical hypothesis testing is typically used to evaluate relationships between exogenous and endogenous variables and between linked endogenous variables. Support for a causal link is claimed if a relationship under investigation is statistically significant at some specified level (e.g., $p < .05$).

For example, a model might hypothesize that years experience influences salary. Support for this expectation from a research study is claimed if the observed relationship (e.g., simple regression coefficient from salary regressed on years experience) is statistically significant (e.g., $p < .05$). Support is said to be lacking if the relationship is not statistically significant at the specified level.

Four Causal Models

Direct Effects Models. A direct effect refers to a causal relationship between an independent and a dependent variable that is not mediated by some other variable(s). Exhibit 19.2 shows an example of a direct effects model involving two independent variables. The model belongs to Researcher A who believes that employee salary levels depend on years of work experience and level in the job hierarchy of an organization. The independent variables are exogenous because the model offers no explanation of their causes.

The arrows represent the researcher's causal model. Years of work experience and job level are both expected to have positive causal influences on

---

EXHIBIT 19.2. Direct causal effects model

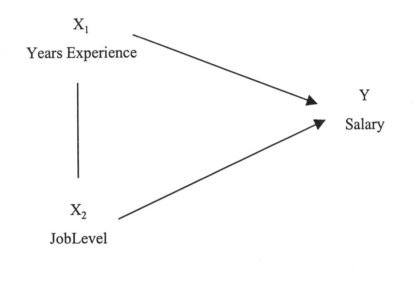

---

salary level. The line between years of experience and job level acknowledges there may be a relationship between these two variables. However, A's causal interest does not go beyond explaining salary as a joint function of the two independent variables.

Statistical information on direct effects can be obtained from partial regression or partial or semipartial correlation coefficients. Exhibit 19.3 shows three regression models involving salary and the two independent variables obtained from the data set described. Model 3 shows statistical output addressing A's model. For comparison, Models 1 and 2 show results from simple regressions of salary on years work experience and job level, respectively.

The first partial regression coefficient in Model 3 estimates the direct effect of years experience, holding job level constant, as $324.19. This coefficient is smaller than the coefficient in the simple regression of salary on years experience (Model 1), because years experience and job level are collinear ($r_{X1X2} = .66$, see Exhibit 19.1). Furthermore, although the simple regression coefficient for years of experience is statistically significant, $p <$ .05 in Model 1, its partial regression coefficient is not statistically significant in Model 3.

EXHIBIT 19.3. **Three statistical models of salary as a function of years experience and job level**

Variable	Model 1 b_{YXi}	Model 2 b_{YXi}	Model 3 $b_{YXi \cdot Xj}$
X1 Years experience	1,320.99*		324.19
X2 Job level		4,850.96*	4,242.48*
Intercept (a)	51,646.92*	52,351.74*	50,805.17*
r^2 (R^2)	.20	.33	.34
$\hat{\rho}^2$ ($\hat{P}^2$)	.19*	.32*	.32*

Notes. *$p < .05$ (two-tailed).

Job level ranges from 1, first level supervisor, to 4, top middle manager.

Exhibit 19.3 also shows that the direct effect of job level is $4,242.48, holding years of experience constant. This coefficient is statistically significant, $p < .05$. Researcher A concludes that support is obtained for job level but not years experience using the statistical inference criterion identified previously.

Finally, Exhibit 19.3 shows that Model 3 explains 34 percent of the salary variance in the sample (R^2). It estimates that 32 percent of salary variance is jointly explained by years of experience and job level in the population of employees ($\hat{P}^2$). (See Formula 18.1 for an explanation of $\hat{P}^2$.)

Mediated Models. Researcher B posits an alternative model as shown in Exhibit 19.4. It includes the same three variables as A's model but with a different hypothesized causal model. Job level has a direct effect on salary as in A's model. However, years experience is expected to influence both salary and job level. Researcher B reasons that increases in years of experience has a direct effect on salary, but that it also has an ***indirect effect*** on salary through its positive influence on job level. An indirect effect is present when some or all of the influence of an independent variable operates through a mediator variable. Job level is expected to serve as a mediator variable in this example; more senior employees are more likely to obtain promotions to

EXHIBIT 19.4. Mediated effects model

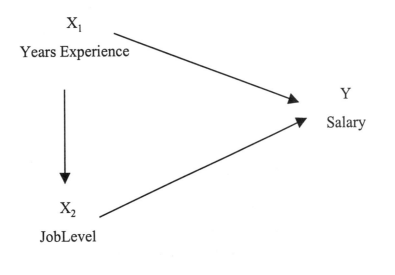

higher job levels, other things equal. In this model, salary and job level are endogenous; both are consequences of another independent variable in the model. Only years experience is exogenous.

The combined direct effects of years experience and job level on salary are estimated just as for Researcher A (Model 3—Exhibit 19.3). Each partial regression coefficient shows the direct effect of its variable on salary.

However, in B's conceptual model (Exhibit 19.4), years experience also has an indirect effect. Direct and indirect (through job level) effects of years experience on salary can be estimated as follows:

1. Take the partial regression for years experience from Model 3 as its direct effect, $324.19, as before.
2. Estimate the influence of years experience on job level. To do this, regress job level on years experience. The equation is:

$$^\wedge \text{job level} = .20 + .23 * (\text{years experience})$$

3. Estimate the indirect effect of years experience on salary by multiplying its direct effect on job level times the direct effect of job level on salary (.23 * $4,242.48 =$975.77). A unit change in years experience

is expected to increase job level by .23. In turn, a .23 increase in job level is expected to increase salary by $975.77.

4. Calculate the total effect of years of experience on salary by summing the direct and indirect effects ($975.77 + $324.19 = $1,299.96). Except for rounding error, this total effect equals the simple regression coefficient in Model 1 (Exhibit 19.3) when salary is regressed just on years experience. The sum of the direct and indirect effects equals the coefficient from the simple regression of salary on years experience.

A more general procedure for identifying direct and indirect effects capitalizes on this relationship between total, direct, and indirect effects. The simple regression coefficient of an exogenous independent variable represents its total effect. Its partial regression coefficient represents its direct effect when all other appropriately specified endogenous independent variables are in the equation. The difference between the total and direct effects represents the indirect effects of this exogenous variable through the endogenous independent variables in the model.

Moderated Models.   Researcher C models salary determination from a different perspective. Years of experience is expected to increase salary level as in the models of Researchers A and B. However, C does not see a causal role for job level. Instead, employee gender is expected to influence salary. C assumes men obtain higher salaries than women, other things equal.

Further, C expects that gender moderates the relationship between years experience and salary. Specifically, C believes the relationship between years experience and salary is larger for men than for women; men benefit more from an additional year of experience in the salary setting process.

The model is diagrammed in Exhibit 19.5. Arrows pointing from gender and years experience to salary signal direct effects as before. The arrow from gender to the line connecting years experience and salary indicates that gender is expected to moderate this relationship. The line linking gender and years experience indicates C believes the two variables may be related but has no reason to believe a causal relationship exists.

Direct effects of years experience and gender can be addressed statistically, as already seen with years experience and job level. Model 3 in Exhibit 19.6 shows these results on all sample members. In this model, the direct effect of years experience on salary is $1,257.20, gender held constant. This effect is statistically significant, $p < .05$. The direct effect of gender is $2,742.80. Given the dummy coding of gender (male = 1), the results indi-

EXHIBIT 19.5. Moderated effects model

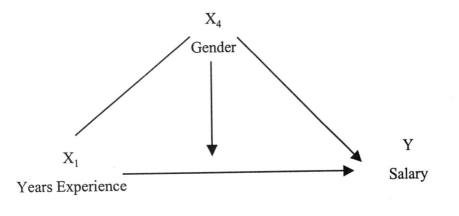

EXHIBIT 19.6. Four statistical models of salary as a function of years experience and gender

Model #	Model 1	Model 2	Model 3	Model 4
	Male Participants	*Female Participants*	*All*	
Variable	b_{YmXm}	b_{YfXf}	$b_{YXi \cdot Xj}$	$b_{YXi \cdot Xj}$
X1 Years experience	1,626.79*	377.84	1,257.20*	377.84
X4 Gender			2,742.80	-8,,242.78
X9 Gender * Years experience				1,248.94*
Intercept (a)	49,545.54*	57,788.32*	50,313.79*	57,788.32*
r^2 (R^2)	.29	.02	.22	.25
$\hat{\rho}^2$ ($\hat{P}^2$)	.28*	.00	.20*	.23*

Note. *$p < .05$ (two-tailed).

cate a $2,742.80 salary advantage for men, controlling for years experience. This effect is not statistically significant.

However, Model 3 does not address the expectation that gender moderates the relation between years experience and salary. Researcher C can perform two types of analysis to address this issue.

When the moderator is a nominal variable, the sample can be subgrouped. Here the sample can be subgrouped into male and female subsets. Salary is then regressed on years experience in each. Exhibit 19.6 shows results from a simple regression of salary on years experience among men (Model 1) and women (Model 2). The relationship between years experience is stronger among men than women, as expected by C. A statistical test, whether the relationship between years experience and salary observed among men is greater than the relationship observed among women, is statistically significant, $p < .05$.[2]

Moderated regression is a second, more general, method to address potential moderator variables. Think of a moderated relationship as nonlinear in multiple correlation and regression. In combination, gender and years experience are expected to produce different salary results than their direct (linear) effects alone.

The nonlinear component is captured by a new variable that is the product of the two variables (gender * years experience). Given the scaling, this variable has values of 0.0 for all female participants in the sample; and it has values equal to years experience for all males. As a consequence, the variable allows for different salary returns for experience to be estimated for men and women using a linear regression model.

Results of a regression of salary on all three variables is shown in Model 4 of Exhibit 19.6; it can be used to reproduce results from subgrouping on gender. Specifically, Model 4 predicts salaries for males:

$$\hat{Y}_m = 57,788.32 + 377.84(X1) - 8,242.78(X4) + 1,248.94(X9)$$

However, since for males, $X9 = X1$ and $X4 = 1$ (see text),

---

[2]The test is described in the appendix to Chapter 13. Researchers often perform an incorrect test of moderation when subgrouping. Specifically, they conclude there is a moderated relationship if the coefficient is statistically significant in one group but not the other, as is the case here (the coefficient is statistically significant in the male subsample, but not the female subsample). However, a moderator expectation is that the relationships *differ* from each other, not whether the difference is greater than zero in only one population.

$$\hat{Y}_m = 57{,}788.32 + 377.84(X1) - 8{,}242.78(1) + 1{,}248.94(X1) =$$
$$49{,}545.54 + 1{,}626.78(X1)$$

This result is identical (except for rounding error) to the simple regression equation of salary on years experience in the male subsample (Model 1, Exhibit 19.6).

For females:

$$\hat{Y}_f = 57{,}788.32 + 377.84(X1) - 8{,}242.78(X4) + 1{,}248.94(X9)$$

In this case $X4 = X9 = 0$ for females (see text),

$$\hat{Y}_f = 57{,}788.32 + 377.84(X1) - 8{,}242.78(0) + 1{,}248.94(0) =$$
$$57{,}788.32 + 377.84(X1)$$

As in the male subsample, results reproduce simple regression results in the female subsample.

Thus, moderated regression reproduces results obtained from subgrouping on nominal variables. In addition, the statistical significance of the partial regression coefficient on the interaction term provides a direct test of the moderator expectation. Finally, the coefficient on gender provides evidence of its direct effect.

Multiple regression and correlation tests of moderated relationships must include the components of the product variable as well as the product variable in the statistical model. In the example, the regression equation must include gender, $X4$, and years experience, $X1$, along with their product, $X9$. If $X4$ and $X1$ are not included, the product variable will reflect any linear influence of the variable(s) not included, as well as the nonlinear influence. It will thus be a biased estimate of the nonlinear influence.[3]

Moderated regression is an attractive method for assessing moderated models because of the information provided. The method is also quite general. In the example shown, the moderator is a discrete and dichotomous variable. However, moderated regression can also be used when the moderator variable has more than two discrete values and when it is continuous.

---

[3]This point has been controversial. Some researchers have not recognized the need to account for linear influences before evaluating nonlinear influences in multiple correlation and regression. Rosnow and Rosenthal (1991) elaborate on the need to account for the linear influences before addressing nonlinear influences.

On the problematical side, it is often the case that the product term in moderated regression is collinear with one or both of the components that form the product. Exhibit 19.1 shows that the moderator variable in C's model has a correlation with years of work experience, $r_{X1X9} = .87$. Although the moderator term is statistically significant in the example ($p < 0.05$), multicollinearity generally reduces statistical power as noted in Chapter 18.

Hierarchical Models. The class of models just described represents one way to address causal models. Regression equations are developed for each endogenous variable in the model. Direct and indirect effects are then estimated as described. Modeling of this sort describes results in units of dependent variables and is common in fields such as economics, marketing, political science, and sociology.

Hierarchical modeling is an alternative method for addressing causal models of this type. A *hierarchical model* links a set or sets of independent variables in a causal chain rather than individual independent variables. Hierarchical modeling focuses on explaining proportions of variance in the ultimate dependent variable (i.e., on coefficients of determination). Researchers frequently use this approach in management and psychology.

The procedure involves entering independent variables in a series of equations based on a causal model. The first equation regresses the dependent variable on the exogenous independent variable(s). To illustrate using Researcher B's model (Exhibit 19.3), this is a regression of salary on years experience (Model 1). Endogenous independent variables are then entered sequentially, beginning with those directly influenced by the exogenous variable(s). Again, using B's model, salary is regressed on both years experience and job level (Model 3).

Explanations of hierarchical models focus on dependent variable variance explained and changes in variance explained from model to model. Years experience alone explains 20 percent of the variance in salary (Model 1). Adding job level in Model 3 increases salary variance explained from 20 percent to 34 percent. This increment is a squared semipartial correlation coefficient, (Formula 11.6b), $sr^2_{YX2 \cdot X1} = R^2_{YX2 \cdot X1} - r^2_{YX1} = .34 - .20 = .14$. This increment is statistically significant ($p < .05$) providing support for the hierarchical model.[4]

---

[4]An incremental F test is used for this situation, see the appendix to Chapter 13 (Formula 13A.14).

Hierarchical analysis is especially attractive when a researcher can specify sets of variables in causal order but not necessarily variables within sets. For example, Researcher D believes three sets of independent variables influence salary as shown in Exhibit 19.7.

EXHIBIT 19.7. Hierarchial model

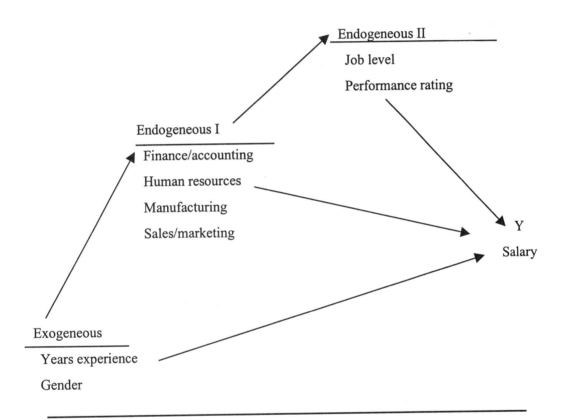

Years experience and gender are believed to be exogenous direct determinants of salary. In addition, these two independent variables are expected to indirectly influence salary through their effects on the occupation that participants enter. Occupations, in turn, are expected to have direct and indirect effects on salary through job level and participant performance ratings.

Three equations can be created to evaluate this model, as shown in Exhibit 19.8. Model 1 includes just the exogenous variables. Their total effects are estimated as $1,257.20 and $2,742.80 for years experience and gender, respectively. They explain 22 percent of the salary variance in the sample, and they are estimated to explain 20 percent of the salary variance in the population.

EXHIBIT 19.8. Hierarchical models with sets of independent variables

Variable	Model 1 $b_{YXi \cdot Xj}$	Model 2 $b_{YXi \cdot Xj}$	Model 3 $b_{YXi \cdot Xj}$
X1 Years experience	1,257.20*	1,388.23*	430.81
X4 Gender	2,742.80	2,296.26	2,666.79
X5 Finance/Accounting		8,633.72*	8,375.51*
X6 Human resources		3,884.11	4,999.62*
X8 Sales/Marketing		8,350.39*	6,728.62*
X2 Job level			3,871.48*
X3 Performance rating			292.33
Intercept (a)	50,313.79*	44,412.49*	42,657.62*
R^2	.22	.38	.49
$\hat{P}^2$	.20*	.34*	.45*
R^2 Change		.14*	.11*

Note. *$p < .05$ (two-tailed).
Job level ranges from 1 (first level supervisor) to 4 (top middle manager).
Performance ranges from 1 (marginal performance) to 7 (highest performance).
Gender dummy coded (male = 1; female = 0).
Finance/Accounting dummy coded (Finance/Accounting = 1; other = 0); likewise for the other.

Model 2 adds occupation dummy variables (manufacturing is omitted) and Model 3 adds job level and performance rating. The change in R^2 is .16 between Models 1 and 2, and .11 between 2 and 3. These changes are statistically significant, $p < .05$. The addition of each set of independent variables adds to the salary variance explained at a statistically significant level.

Results obtained using the hierarchical method are sensitive to the order in which independent variables are entered whenever there is

EXHIBIT 19.9. Variance explained in "A's" model

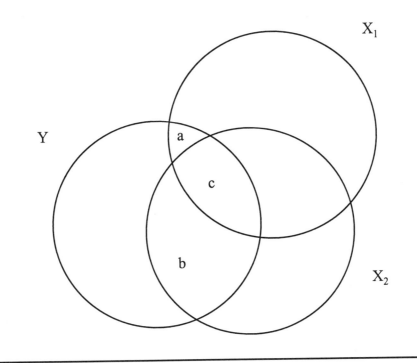

multicollinearity. This is illustrated with Researcher A's models in Exhibit 19.3. Years experience is credited with explaining 20 percent of salary variance if it is entered first (Model 1). Job level, entered second, is credited with adding 14 percent to explain salary variance in Model 3. Alternatively, if job level is entered first using Model 2, it is credited with explaining 33 percent of salary variance. Years experience is now credited with explaining only one additional percent of salary variance.

The reason for these order sensitive results is seen by examining the representation of these three variables using variance explained circles in Exhibit 19.9. The area c represents the collinear variance in years experience and job level that overlaps with salary. When years experience is entered first, it gets credit for areas a and c; when years experience is entered second, it gets credit only for area a.

Importance of Specification

Proper specification of a conceptual model is essential if multiple correlation and regression and tests of statistical inference are to provide useful information about causal relationships between variables. The statistical models and inferential tests provide little causal information by themselves.

For example, consider two models in Exhibit 19.3. A conclusion that age and salary are related in the population would be reached if a researcher hypothesized Model 1. Alternatively, results from a test of Model 3 (shown in Exhibit 19.2) leads to a conclusion that age and salary may not be related in the population. Thus, one must assume that a statistical model is properly specified if the parameter estimates and significance levels are to be meaningful. The appendix to this chapter describes two additional assumptions required for statistical inference when using correlation and regression.

EMPIRICAL MODELS

The models described so far all depend on a researcher's specification of a causal model. Statistical tests help researchers evaluate whether the model specified is plausible given the data obtained on a group of cases. The causal model dominates; statistical tests only help the researcher decide if the data do or do not provide support for the model.

Alternatively, in *empirical models* independent variables are chosen using statistical criteria. Researchers identify the dependent variable and a set of independent variables that may account for variance in it. However, results from statistical tests are used to decide which specific independent variables are retained for further consideration. Several such modeling procedures are available.

Stepwise Regression

Stepwise regression procedures choose independent variables sequentially in a series of models using variance explained and statistical significance as criteria. This section describes *forward loading stepwise regression,* the most widely used empirical modeling procedure. It uses variance explained to enter independent variables sequentially. Statistical significance is used to decide how many independent variables are included.

Data from the continuing example, salary as the dependent variable, and the independent variables listed in Exhibit 19.10, are used to illustrate the forward loading stepwise procedure. A statistical significance level of $p <$ .05 (two-tailed) is used in this example.

EXHIBIT 19.10. Forward loading stepwise models

Variable	Model 1 b_{YX2}	Model 2 $b_{YXi \cdot Xj}$
X1 Years experience		
X2 Job level	4,850.96*	4,906.14*
X3 Performance rating		
X4 Gender		
X5 Finance/Accounting		
X6 Human resources		
X7 Manufacturing		−6,780.08*
X8 Sales/Marketing		
Intercept (a)	52,351.74*	54,119.93*
R^2	.33	.45
$\hat{P}^2$	.32*	.44*
R^2 Change		.12*

Note. *$p < .05$ (two-tailed).
Job level ranges from 1 (first level supervisor) to 4 (top middle manager).
Gender dummy coded (male = 1; female = 0).
Finance/Accounting dummy coded (Finance/Accounting = 1; other = 0); likewise for the
Human Resources and Sales/Marketing.

The procedure begins by identifying the independent variable that explains the most variance in the dependent variable. Exhibit 19.1 shows that
this variable is job level ($X2$). Job level is statistically significant ($p < .05$);
Exhibit 19.10 shows the regression results as Model 1.

The procedure then searches for the independent variable that explains the
most variance that is left unexplained by the previous model. In effect, the
dependent variable becomes $Y - \hat{Y}$. In the example, manufacturing ($X7$) accounts for the most variance remaining after $X2$ is entered. Manufacturing is
statistically significant ($p < .05$); Exhibit 19.10 shows the regression results

as Model 2.[5] No other independent variable is statistically significantly ($p <$ .05) related to the variance left unexplained by job level and manufacturing. Consequently, the forward loading stepwise procedure stops at this point.

Other stepwise regression procedures are available. For example, ***backward unloading stepwise regression*** begins with all independent variables in an equation and then deletes variables that explain the least variance in the dependent variable. However, in all cases, the independent variables that end up in the final model are chosen based on statistical criteria.

Evaluation of Stepwise Regression

Procedures that rely on statistical criteria to identify independent variables are not recommended for most research situations. They are definitely inappropriate for testing causal models. Statistical significance, even when appropriately used, and variance explained are not substitutes for conceptual model building.

Variance explained and statistical inference procedures are most suitable when research is focused on predicting a dependent variable in some applied context. For example, a study may focus on identifying credit risk (Y) among loan applicants. A lending organization has a large number of biographical (e.g., age) and other personal history (e.g., income level) variables from past and current borrowers. The organization has no particularly good reason to suppose some independent variables may predict credit risk better than others.

In this situation, the independent variables may be assessed using stepwise procedures to identify a subset that explains a statistically significant amount of variance in Y. However, care must be taken using statistical criteria even in this context. Results are likely to be unstable if either small sample size and/or multicollinearity leads to low statistical power. Replication of the study on another sample is recommended.

A CLOSING CAUTION

Statistical inference plays a central role in both the development and evaluation of the empirical models just described. It also plays a prominent role in statistical tests of causal models. Direct, mediated, and moderated modeling

---

[5]Manufacturing does not have the second highest relationship with salary; years experience does. However, some of the salary variance explained by years experience is redundant with job level. Manufacturing explains more salary variance left unexplained by job level.

all use statistical inference as the main criterion for judging whether a conceptual independent variable obtains support from the statistical model tested.

Caution is in order. The research model presented in this book shows that statistical inference is only one of several criteria needed to conclude a causal conceptual relationship is tenable. Statistical significance is never sufficient.

SUMMARY

Statistical models using multiple correlation and regression are often used to help researchers evaluate *causal models.* Variables explained by a causal model are *endogenous. Exogenous* variables help explain endogenous variables but are not themselves explained by the model.

Conceptual models can take several forms when there are three or more exogenous or endogenous variables involved. Two or more independent variables are believed to influence a dependent variable without mediation in *direct effects* models. Such models are often assessed using multiple regression; the partial regression coefficients provide evidence on the direct effects.

A mediated model involves an endogenous independent variable(s). Exogenous variables may influence the dependent variable two ways. They may influence it directly as mentioned, and they may influence it *indirectly* through their influence on endogenous independent variables. Such models can be evaluated statistically by allowing each endogenous variable to serve as a dependent variable in a series of regression equations.

Models involving moderator variables can be assessed two ways. One method involves subgrouping on the moderator; relationships between other variables in the model are investigated within each subgroup. The other method involves creating a new variable that accounts for the interaction between the moderator variable and the independent variable it moderates. This interaction variable is then included with the other variables in the model.

Hierarchical models include a set or sets of variables that are believed to form a causal chain. Statistical tests of hierarchical models involve a series of equations in which the dependent variable is regressed sequentially on the independent variables in causal order. Changes in the variance explained in the dependent variable, as independent variables are added to the model, typically serve as the criterion for judging the adequacy of the model.

All of the models described are causal in the sense that a researcher specifies them before they are tested on a set of observations. *Empirical models* use statistical criteria, typically variance explained and statistical significance, to decide which independent variables are to be retained. Several *stepwise regression* procedures are available to carry out empirical modeling. *Forward loading stepwise regression* enters independent variables based on their contribution to the explanation of dependent variable variance explained. *Backward unloading stepwise regression* deletes independent variables that do not contribute to variance explained. Both methods use statistical significance as a criterion to include or exclude variables.

Causal model testing is generally preferred to empirical model building. Research is ordinarily concerned with the validity of causal models. Only causal model testing can contribute to that objective.

FOR REVIEW

Terms to Know

Causal Model. Refers to variables that operate in a causal system and to their true relationships.

Statistical model. The variables that a researcher uses to investigate a causal model.

Recursive model. Model in which causal influence is assumed to go in only one direction.

Endogenous variable. Variable explained by a causal model.

Exogenous variable. Independent variable in a causal model that is not explained by the model.

Direct effect. In a causal model, relationship between an independent and a dependent variable that is not mediated by some other variable(s).

Indirect effect. In a causal model, the influence of an independent variable that operates through a mediator variable.

Moderated regression. Regression procedure in which an independent variable is created to capture the nonlinear effects of a moderator variable.

Hierarchical model. A model in which a set or sets of variables are believed to form a causal chain. Evidence of causal effects is assessed by an examination of variance explained in the dependent variable.

Empirical model. A model in which independent variables are chosen by statistical criteria.

Stepwise regression. Statistical procedures that use variance explained and statistical significance to choose independent variables sequentially.

Forward loading stepwise regression. Stepwise regression method that enters independent variables in a statistical model based on their contribution to variance explained and statistical significance.

Backward unloading stepwise regression. Stepwise regression method that deletes independent variables in a statistical model based on their contribution to variance explained and statistical significance.

Misspecification. When a statistical model does not include all variables in the underlying causal model (see Appendix 19A).

Homoskedasticity. In regression and correlation, equal variability in the error distribution of Y at each value of X (see Appendix 19A).

Heteroskedasticity. In regression and correlation, unequal variability in the error distribution of Y at different values of X (see Appendix 19A).

Questions for Review

1. In what way is an endogenous independent variable a dependent variable?
2. Compare and contrast moderated causal models with mediated causal models.
3. You read an article in the *New Yorker* that states: "Smoking increases lung cancer among smokers and among persons in close proximity to smokers." Diagram a causal model that accounts for this statement using the variables smoker (v. not smoker), person in proximity (v. not in proximity), and lung cancer.
   a. What type of causal model is this?
   b. What variable(s) is endogenous in this model? What is exogenous?
   c. If data on these three variables are available, how would you assess this model using correlation and regression?

4. You overhear the following at a party with friends: "Whether you make the basketball team in high school depends on whether the coach likes you. In college it depends on whether you have athletic ability." Diagram this statement with a causal model that has variables for athletic ability, participation on a basketball team (v. no participation), and school level.

   a. What type of causal model is this?

   b. What variable(s) is endogenous in this model? What is exogenous?

   c. If data on these three variables are available, how would you assess this model using correlation/regression? How else could you assess this model?

5. Simple correlation coefficients among a dependent variable and three independent variables are shown below. A researcher conducts a forward loading stepwise regression on the data that produced these correlation coefficients. Why might no variables enter the statistical model? If any enter, which variable will enter first? What can you say about which variable might enter second?

Y	1.00		
X1	.30	1.00	
X2	.40	.60	1.00
X3	.20	.10	.30

6. Under what circumstances, if any, would you recommend using empirical modeling rather than causal modeling to investigate relationships between variables?

7. From Appendix 19A, how does homoskedasticity differ from normality of error distributions of Y at each value of X?

8. From Appendix 19A, what are the consequences of heteroskedasticity for statistical inference? What are the consequences if the errors are not normally distributed at each value of X?

Issues to Discuss

A causal model consists of direct positive effects of $X1$ and $X2$ on Y. However, a researcher tests the model by regressing Y only on $X1$.

1. Suppose $X1$ and $X2$ are positively related. Discuss the implications of the researcher's misspecification for the regression coefficient on $X1$ and for the variance explained by the model overall. What are the implications for the statistical significance level of the coefficient on $X1$ and for the statistical significance level of the variance explained overall?

2. Suppose now that $X1$ and $X2$ are not related. Discuss the implications of the researcher's misspecification for the regression coefficient on $X1$ and for the variance explained by the model overall. What are the implications for the statistical significance level of the coefficient on $X1$ and for the statistical significance level of the variance explained overall?

SUGGESTED READING

Cohen and Cohen (1983) and Frees (1996), two books recommended in Part IV, have extensive discussions of statistical modeling using multiple correlation and regression. Good articles on regression modeling are also provided by Alwin and Hauser (1975) and Baron and Kenny (1986).

The power of moderated regression has received substantial attention by researchers. *Centering* is a method that sometimes reduces the multicollinearity between the moderator variable and its components. Frees (1996, p. 275) and Cronbach (1987) describe the method. A recent simulation study on power determinants in moderated regression and references to other studies is provided by Aquinis and Stone-Romero (1997).

APPENDIX 19A:
ADDITIONAL ASSUMPTIONS FOR INFERENCE

Material covered in this chapter shows the centrality of proper statistical specification. A statistical model is *misspecified* if it does not contain all variables in the causal model. Misspecification results in biased estimates of parameters and erroneous statistical inference values. For example, suppose salary is a function of both years of experience and job level as hypothesized in Researcher A's model (Exhibit 19.2). A statistical model that includes only years of experience leads to an inflated parameter estimate for years of experience and an overestimate of its statistical significance (compare Models 1 and 3 in Exhibit 19.3). Proper specification is an important assumption for the correct use and interpretation of parameter estimates and statistical significance levels.

This appendix describes two additional assumptions when one is interested in using correlation and regression statistics to make inferences about parameters. One has to do with the distribution of errors resulting from a correlation and regression model. The other has to do with relationships between errors.

Characteristics of the Error Term

F tests of overall correlation and regression models and t tests of partial coefficients require that the error terms are normally distributed at each level of a X variable. Exhibit 19A.1 illustrates how this assumption is satisfied in the case of a single independent variable.

Violation of this assumption does not bias correlation or regression statistics. However, it does introduce error in the standard errors and therefore results in problematic significance levels and confidence intervals. Fortunately, the Central Limit Theorem applies here; as sample size increases, error terms become more normally distributed.

It is also assumed that error terms are *homoskedastic,* meaning that the variances of error terms are equal at each X level. Exhibit 19.4 shows the error terms to be homoskedastic as well as normal.

Consequences of *heteroskedasticity* (unequal variances) are the same as if errors are not normally distributed. Correlation and regression statistics are not biased. However, heteroskedasticity introduces error in standard errors with attendant problems for statistical significance levels and confidence intervals.

EXHIBIT 19A.1. Relationship between *Y* and *X* with normal and homoskedastic error terms

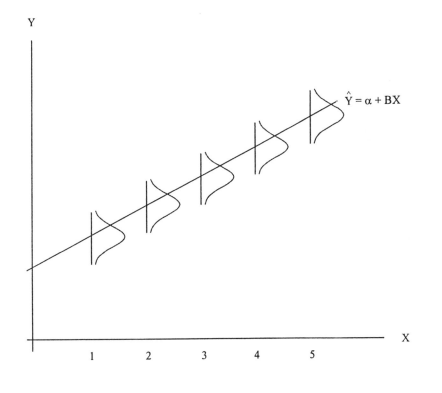

Independence Among the Errors

Statistical significance tests involving correlation and regression also assume that errors in any model are uncorrelated. The error from the correlation or regression model (e_i) of any one case is not related to the error of any other (e_j).

Statistical textbooks often describe correlated error terms as a separate problem for correlation and regression (hence its separate heading here). However, correlated errors result from misspecification of the underlying causal model. An independent variable(s) is omitted from the model. If this variable(s) is included, the correlation among the errors goes away.

Omitted variables that lead to correlated errors are frequently present in two situations. One involves time series; for example, *Y* and *X* scores obtained on one case over a series of time periods, as described in Chapter 7. In such situations, it is likely that the residual error in one period is related to the residual error in adjacent time periods.

A second situation occurs in cross-sectional designs (in which Y and X are measured only once) when cases in the overall sample are also members of different subgroups. For example, an organization might conduct a study by sampling from all of its employees. However, these employees may be grouped in plants at different locations. If the correlation or regression model does not include plant location as an independent variable, errors may be correlated. Location differences may result in positive or negative error values for all employees in a plant.

Consequences of omitted variables that lead to correlated errors are the same as for omitted variables. Standard errors (hence statistical significance levels and confidence intervals) are in error in all cases.

If the omitted variable(s) responsible for the correlated error is correlated with independent variables in the model, partial coefficients will be biased. If the omitted variable is not correlated with independent variables in the model (as often assumed in time series), partial coefficients are unbiased.

Glossary

Adjusted R₂ Multiple coefficient of determination adjusted for sample size and number of independent variables. It is a better estimate of the parameter than is the unadjusted sample multiple coefficient of determination.

Analyses Used to describe scores on single measures and to identify relationships that may exist between scores across different measures; typically involve the use of statistics.

Assignment error Results because the random allocation of cases to levels of an independent variable typically does not exactly equalize scores on the dependent variable across groups.

Attenuation due to unreliability Formula that estimates the degree to which unreliability in either or both variables reduces a correlation coefficient relative to perfectly reliable measurement of the variables.

Backward unloading stepwise regression Stepwise regression method that deletes independent variables in a statistical model based on their contribution to variance explained and statistical significance.

Bar chart Reports the values of a discrete variable on one axis and the frequency (number and/or percentage) of cases with scores at each value on the other.

Beta coefficient A standardized (mean = 0.0, standard deviation = 1.0 of all variables in the model) regression coefficient. In simple regression the beta coefficient is identical to the simple correlation coefficient.

Between-cases design Design that uses two or more cases or groups of cases in which each case or group experiences different levels of an independent variable. Effect of an independent variable is assessed by

395

comparing dependent variable scores across the cases or groups of cases.

Biased relationship An observed relationship between an independent and dependent variable that under or overstates the causal relationship. Occurs if a nuisance variable is causally related to the dependent variable and is related to the independent variable(s).

Binomial probability distribution Discrete probability distribution that results from a set of trials where the values of each trial is independent, the probability remains constant from trial to trial, and each trial can lead to one of two values.

Boundary condition Synonym for *moderator variable*. A relationship between an independent and dependent variable depends on the value (boundary) of another independent variable.

Box-score method In meta-analysis, the use of statistical significance values as the dependent variable. Its use is not recommended.

Cases Entities (e.g., individuals, groups, organizations, transactions) investigated in research.

Causal conceptual relationship A relationship where variation in the independent construct is responsible for variation in the dependent construct.

Causal model Refers to variables that operate in a causal system and to their true relationships.

Causal relationship When variation in one factor is responsible for variation in another.

Central Limit Theorem States that as sample sizes randomly obtained become larger, the sampling distribution becomes less variable and more normally distributed. Applies to several, but not all, sampling distributions.

Central tendency The middle of a distribution of scores.

Central tendency error Present when an observer clusters responses in the middle of a scale when more variable responses should be recorded.

Close-ended response formats Questionnaire scaling in which the researcher provides participants with fixed response categories.

Coefficient alpha An estimate of reliability; it provides an estimate of the correlation coefficient that is expected between a summary score from a measure studied and another hypothetical measure of the same thing using the same number of repetitions.

Coefficient of determination The square of the correlation coefficient. A statistic that reports the proportion of linear variance in one variable that is explained or associated with variance in another variable.

Comparison groups Groups of research cases thought to be comparable on levels of potential nuisance variables.

Conceptual variable; also a *construct* A mental definition of a characteristic of some object that can vary.

Confidence intervals A range of statistical values that likely include the population parameter.

Confidence level The likelihood that a confidence interval includes the population parameter.

Construct validation Methods used to estimate a measure's construct validity.

Construct validity Present when there is a high correspondence between cases' scores on a measure and the mental definition of the construct it is designed to represent.

Contamination In measurement, the portion of scores that measure something other than the defined construct.

Content validation Procedures employed to obtain content validity.

Content validity When a measure is judged to be construct valid, usually are individuals who are thought to be subject matter experts.

Continuous probability distribution Probability distribution where probabilities are assigned to regions of the continuous random variable.

Continuous variable Variable that is infinitely divisible between any two values.

Convenience sampling (also **judgment sampling**) The selection of cases (usually an intact group) to study using nonprobability methods.

Convergent validity Is present when there is a high correspondence between scores from two different measures of the same construct.

Correction for attenuation Formula that estimates the correlation between two variables if they are measured with perfect reliability; it requires knowledge of the reliability of each variable.

Correlation coefficient A statistic that describes the degree of linear relationship between two variables in a standardized form ranging from ± 1.00.

Covariance A statistic that provides information about how values of two variables go together. It is the average cross-product of the deviations of the values of each variable about its respective mean.

Covariate A synonym for an independent variable that is not manipulated by a researcher in experiments and quasi-experiments.

Cross-sectional design Design in which the independent and dependent variables are measured only once. The relationship between the variables is taken as evidence of the influence of X on Y.

Data Scores characterizing cases obtained on measures. *Datum* refers to one score.

Data matrix A rectangular array of scores with cases in the rows and variables in the columns.

Deficiency In measurement, the portion of the defined construct that is not captured by scores on a measure of the construct.

Degrees of freedom (d.f.) The amount of information available to estimate population parameters from sample statistics. Are used to identify the appropriate sampling distribution for statistical hypothesis tests and confidence intervals.

Demand characteristics Characteristics of a research study that motivate participants' expectations about what is investigated; a threat to internal validity.

Dependent variable Research outcome; the consequence in a causal relationship.

Direct effect In a causal model, relationship between an independent and dependent variable that is not mediated by some other variable(s).

Discrete probability distribution Probability distribution has a probability associated with each value of the discrete random variable.

Discrete variable Variable with a countable number of values.

Discriminant validity Is present when measures of constructs that are supposed to be independent are found to have a low correspondence.

Distribution shape Degree to which a distribution is symmetrical/asymmetrical and the degree to which it is peaked or flat. These characteristics are defined by *skew* and *kurtosis*.

Dummy variable A nominal variable with two values coded 0 and 1.

Empirical model A model where independent variables are chosen by statistical criteria.

Empirical relationship The correspondence between scores obtained from cases on measures.

Empirical research Systematic study of relationships between scores obtained from cases on measures.

Endogenous variable Variable explained by a causal model.

Exhaustive values When one of the values on a variable must result.

Exogenous variable Independent variable in a causal model that is not explained by the model.

Expectancy effects A nuisance variable that influences the dependent variable because a researcher treats some cases differently from others based on assumptions made about expected research results; a threat to internal validity.

Experiments A research design in which cases are randomly assigned to levels of an independent variable(s).

External validation Methods used to estimate external validity.

External validity Present when findings obtained in a research study, other than statistical generalization, are correctly generalized.

F distributions A set of asymmetrical sampling distributions with positive skew. F distributions are designed to test the equality of variances from two populations.

Face validity When a measure appears to be construct valid by individuals who use it including participants.

Factorial design Studies with two or more independent variables. Factor is a synonym for independent variable, which is under the control of a researcher.

Field study A research design in which values of the independent variable(s) are characteristics of the cases studied and where cases are not randomly selected from some larger population.

Forced choice scales Scales in which response categories are equated on favorability or other characteristics to control for response styles.

Forward loading stepwise regression Stepwise regression method that enters independent variables in a statistical model based on their contribution to variance explained and statistical significance.

Frequency table Provides a summary of cases' scores from a data matrix by reporting the number (and/or percentage) of cases at each level of a discrete variable, or within each interval of a continuous variable.

Full mediation The relationship between an independent and dependent variable operates only through a mediator variable. The independent variable has no direct effect on the dependent variable.

Halo error Present when an observer evaluates an object in an undifferentiated manner.

Heteroskedasticity In regression and correlation, unequal variability in the error distribution of Y at different values of X.

Hierarchical model A model in which a set or sets of variables are believed to form a causal chain. Evidence of causal effects is assessed by an examination of variance explained in the dependent variable.

Histogram Reports values of a continuous variable placed in intervals.

History An exogenous event that occurs between measurements of the dependent variable; a threat to internal validity in longitudinal designs.

Homoskedasticity In regression and correlation, equal variability in the error distribution of Y at each value of X.

Hypothesis An expected relationship between an independent and dependent variable.

Independence Two variables are independent when information about the value on one variable provides no information about the probability of values on the other variable.

Independent variable Helps explain or predict a dependent variable; cause in a causal relationship.

Indirect effect In a causal model, the influence of an independent variable that operates through a mediator variable.

Instantaneous model Time series model in which changes in the independent and dependent variables are assumed to occur without an intervening time interval.

Instrumentation A threat to internal validity in longitudinal designs when the measure of the dependent variable changes over time.

Interaction variable Synonym for *moderator variable*. A relationship between an independent and dependent variable depends on the value of another independent variable.

Internal consistency A form of reliability that addresses the consistency of scores from a set of items in a measure.

Internal statistical validity Present when an empirical relationship is not due to chance.

Internal validation Methods used to determine whether internal validity is likely.

Internal validity Present when variation in scores on a measure of an independent variable is responsible for variation in scores on a measure of a dependent variable.

Interrater reliability A form of reliability that addresses the consistency of scores from a set of observers.

Interval variable Variable with ordinal properties, and the distance between values is meaningful.

Interviews Measuring instruments in which another individual (the interviewer) asks the questions verbally and is responsible for recording responses.

Intragoup history An exogenous event(s) that has impact on a group of cases that experience one level of an independent variable differently than the event influences groups experiencing other levels of the independent variable; a threat to internal validity.

Kurtosis Describes the flatness or peakedness of a distribution relative to a normal distribution. Kurtosis > 0.0 when a distribution is more peaked than a normal distribution. Kurtosis < 0.0 when a distribution is less peaked than a normal distribution.

Lagged model Time series model in which changes in the independent variable are assumed to take some time to influence the dependent variable.

Least Squares Criterion A rule that establishes the regression line so that the sum of the squared deviations between the actual dependent variable values and the values predicted are minimized.

Leniency error Present when an observer systematically inflates ratings of a group of objects.

Levels of measurement Refers to the amount of information provided by scores.

Listwise deletion When an entire case with missing data is removed from a research study.

Longitudinal design Design in which the dependent (and perhaps, independent) variable is measured more than once.

Matching Cases are selected for research so that those who experience different levels of an independent variable(s) are equated on levels of nuisance variables.

Maturation Changes in cases between measurements of the dependent variable; a threat to internal validity in longitudinal designs.

Mean A statistic describing central tendency; the sum of the values of each score divided by the number of scores.

Mean substitution Missing data on a variable is replaced with the mean of the responding cases on that variable.

Measurement Activities associated with measuring cases.

Measures Instruments used to obtain scores from participants.

Median A statistic describing central tendency; the middle score in a distribution (or if there are an even number of scores, the sum of the two middlemost scores divided by 2).

Mediator variable Also ***intervening variable,*** comes between an independent and dependent variable in a causal chain.

Meta-analysis Procedures to review and evaluate prior research studies that depend on quantitative research methods.

Missing data Data that is absent from a case.

Misspecification When a statistical model does not include all variables in the underlying causal model.

Mode A statistic describing central tendency; the most frequent score in a distribution of discrete values.

Moderated regression Regression procedure where an independent variable is created to capture the nonlinear effects of a moderator variable.

Moderator variable A variable whose values are associated with different relationships between an independent and dependent variable. May or may not be an independent variable.

Mortality Occurs when some cases terminate between measurements of the dependent variable; a threat to internal validity in longitudinal designs.

Multicollinearity Nonzero correlation coefficient among independent variables in a multiple correlation or regression context.

Multiple coefficient of determination Describes the proportion of linear variance in one ordered dependent variable that is accounted for jointly by two or more independent variables. It ranges from 0.0 to 1.0.

Multiple correlation coefficient Describes the degree of linear relationship between one ordered dependent variable and two or more independent variables. It describes the relationship in standardized form and ranges from 0.0 to 1.0.

Multiple regression Describes relationships between a dependent and two or more independent variables in units of the dependent variable.

Multiple regression intercept The predicted value of Y when all independent variables = 0.0.

Mutually exclusive values When the presence of one value precludes the presence of another value, and vice versa.

Narrative research review A review of prior research studies that depends largely on a reviewer's knowledge of the topic and research methods. The review typically includes a summary and evaluation of the previous research.

Noisy relationship Occurs when a nuisance variable is related to the dependent variable, but not to the independent variable(s).

Nominal (categorical) variable Variable in which similar values signal the same thing, different values signal different things.

Nomological network Relationships between a construct under measurement consideration and other constructs. It is the measurement analog to a conceptual model of interest to causal research.

Nonrespondents Cases that provided no data for a research study.

Normal distribution A distribution of continuous variable that is unimodal, symmetrical around its middle, and has 68.3 percent of scores falling within ± one standard deviation of the mean, 95.5 percent of scores falling within ± two standard deviations and 99.7 percent of scores falling within ± three standard deviations.

Normal probability distribution Continuous probability distribution where probabilities assigned to regions conform to a normal distribution.

Nuisance variable A variable in the causal model that is not controlled in a research study.

Null hypothesis (H_0) The hypothesis of no relationship (or no difference) in the population.

Omitted category The value of a nominal variable assigned zeros to all dummy variables established to account for the nominal variable in multiple correlation and regression.

Omitted variable An independent variable that operates in the causal system studied but is not included in the model studied. Serves as a threat to internal validity in the same way as selection is a threat.

One-tailed hypothesis A research hypothesis that is directional; the researcher believes a relationship is positive or negative.

Open-ended response format Questionnaire scaling that has participants respond in their own words.

Operational variable Variable with a measure to obtain scores from cases.

Ordinal variable Variable with nominal properties, and values signal order from highest to lowest (or lowest to highest).

Pairwise deletion When a case is deleted only if there is missing data on variables from the specific analyses conducted. The case is retained for any other analyses where data is present.

Panel studies Independent and dependent variables are measured two or more times on a group of cases; design to measure changes in the dependent variable as a function of changes in an independent variable(s).

Parameter Statistic that describes a statistical inference drawn by a researcher.

Partial mediation The relationship between an independent and dependent variable operates partially through a mediator variable. The independent variable has a direct effect on the dependent variable and an indirect effect through the mediator.

Partial regression coefficient The predicted value of Y for a unit change in one independent variable when all other independent variables in the equation are held constant.

Phi coefficient A correlation coefficient, sometimes calculated when both variables are dichotomous.

Point-biserial correlation coefficient A correlation coefficient, sometimes calculated when one variable is ordered and one has two values.

Probability (P_r) Specifies the likelihood that a particular value of a variable will be obtained. It can range from 0.0 to 1.0.

Probability distribution A distribution that summarizes probabilities associated with values of a random variable.

Probability sample Obtained when the likelihood of each case chosen for the sample is known.

Probability sampling The selection of a subset of cases obtained from a larger population of cases using rules of probability.

Quasi-experiments A research design in which cases do not control the levels of the independent variable(s) they experience; cases are not randomly assigned to levels of the independent variable(s).

Questionnaires Measuring instruments that ask individuals to respond to a set of questions in verbal or written form.

Random assignment Allocation of cases to levels of an independent variable(s) without order; a procedure designed to match cases on levels of nuisance variables.

Random errors In measurement, also called *unreliability,* errors in scores on a measure that are unsystematic. Random errors are uncorrelated with *true (systematic)* scores.

Random variable A variable whose values are not known exactly but are described by probability.

Randomization test Used to develop a null probability distribution by generating all possible ways that cases may be assigned to levels of the independent variable.

Ratio variable Variable with interval properties, and there is a true zero point.

Recursive model Model in which causal influence is assumed to go in only one direction.

Regression As a statistic, describes relationships between a dependent and independent variable in the scale values of the variables.

Regression A threat to internal validity in longitudinal designs when (a) groups are chosen for levels of the independent variable based on dependent variable performance on a first measurement and (b) there is unreliability in the dependent variable measure.

Regression coefficient A statistic that reports the predicted change in the value of the dependent variable for a unit change (change of 1.0) in the independent variable.

Regression intercept A statistic that reports the predicted value of the dependent variable when the independent variable is equal to 0.0.

Reliability The consistency of measurement. Formally, it is the ratio of systematic score variance to total variance.

Replication A research study that addresses the same research issue(s) as an earlier study.

Research Confederate A member of the research team who interacts with participants but is not known by participants to be a member of the research team.

Research design Overall plan of a study. Establishes procedures to obtain cases for study and to determine how scores are obtained on measures of cases.

Research hypothesis (H_1) Represents a researcher's expectation about what is true of the population parameter.

Response acquiescence (also *yea-saying*) A self-report response style in which the respondent tends to agree with a questionnaire item regardless of its content.

Restriction of range A reduction in the variance of a variable through selection of cases.

Rho coefficient A correlation coefficient, sometimes calculated when the variables represent only rank order.

Sampling distribution A probability distribution of a sample statistic obtained on all possible probability samples of a given sample size.

Sampling distribution of the mean A sampling distribution created by calculating means for all possible probability samples of a given size.

Sampling error The difference between a sample statistic and population parameter brought about because the sample size is smaller than the population. The size of this error can be estimated when probability sampling is used.

Scores (also, *data*) Numerical information about cases obtained on measures.

Secondary data Information collected for other purposes that is used for research.

Selection A threat to internal validity when there are preexisting differences between groups experiencing different levels of an independent variable. These differences may account for differences observed on the dependent variable.

Self-report questionnaires Questionnaires that ask respondents to provide information about themselves.

Severity error Present when an observer systematically deflates ratings of a group of objects.

Simple random sample A probability sample where every unique sample of a given size from a population has an equal chance of being selected.

Simultaneity When causal influence goes from the independent to the dependent variable and vice versa.

Skew Describes the symmetry or asymmetry of a distribution relative to a normal distribution. When a distribution is symmetrical, skew = 0.0. When the distribution is asymmetrical and the tail is toward the right, skew > 0.0; when the tail is to the left, skew < 0.0.

Social desirability A self-report response style designed to present the respondent in a publicly favorable light.

Spurious relationship An observed relationship between an independent and dependent variable but no causal relationship. Occurs when a nuisance variable accounts for all of the observed relationship between a dependent and independent variable(s).

Squared partial correlation coefficient Represents the proportion of Y variance explained by an independent variable that is not otherwise explained.

Squared semipartial (or part) correlation coefficient Represents the proportion of the total variance in Y that is uniquely (non-redundantly) explained by an independent variable.

Stability reliability A form of reliability that addresses the consistency of scores across time periods.

Standard deviation The average variability of scores around the mean.

Standard error Standard deviation of a sampling distribution.

Standard error of the correlation coefficient Standard deviation of a sampling distribution of the correlation coefficient.

Standard error of the mean Standard deviation of a sampling distribution of the mean.

Standard normal distribution A normal distribution with a mean = 0.0 and a standard deviation = 1.0.

Standard score A score that results by subtracting its distribution mean and dividing the result by the distribution standard deviation.

Standard score distribution A distribution of scores on a variable that have been transformed to a mean = 0.0 and standard deviation = 1.0.

Statistical generalization validity Present when an empirical relationship observed on a sample of cases provides a correct estimate of the relationship in the population of cases from which the sample was drawn.

Statistical hypothesis test Estimates whether or not a relationship (or difference) observed on a sample of cases suggests there is a relationship (difference) in the population from which the sample was drawn.

Statistical inference Use of statistics and probability theory to draw conclusions about population parameters or the likelihood that observed relationships (differences) are due to chance.

Statistical model The variables that a researcher uses to investigate a causal model.

Statistical power The likelihood that a statistical hypothesis test will lead to the rejection of the null hypothesis when the research hypothesis is true in the population.

Statistical significance level Level of risk researcher takes when rejecting the null hypothesis.

Statistical validation The use of probability theory to investigate internal statistical validity or statistical generalization validity.

Statistics Refers to a field of study, procedures to analyze data, or a term to describe outcomes of statistical procedures. It also refers to a summary characteristic of scores.

Stepwise regression Statistical procedures that use variance explained and statistical significance to choose independent variables sequentially.

Student's t-distributions A set of symmetrical sampling distributions that are shaped as a standard normal distribution but more variable. Student's t-distributions become more like a standard normal distribution as the sample size gets larger.

Suppressor variable A nuisance variable that biases an observed relationship between an independent variable downward; usually occurs when a nuisance variable has a positive relationship with the independent variable and a small negative relationship with the dependent variable.

Survey study A research design in which values of the independent variable(s) are characteristics of the cases studied and where cases are randomly selected from some larger population.

Systematic errors In measurement, when scores from a measure consistently vary from construct validity because of contamination and/or deficiency.

Testing A threat to internal validity in longitudinal designs when the initial measurement of a dependent variable influences participants' responses to the dependent variable on a subsequent measurement of it.

Threats to internal validity Characteristics of research studies that make a causal claim that an independent variable leads to a dependent variable vulnerable to alternative explanations.

Time series Design to investigate longitudinal changes in a dependent variable; independent and dependent variables are measured more than once over time.

Treatment contamination Occurs when a level of an independent variable assigned to one group of participants is communicated to another; a threat to internal validity.

Triangulation In research, a form of replication that seeks to discover whether research findings generalize across different research methods.

True scores Also called *systematic,* the consistent (repeatable) portion of scores obtained from participants on a measure.

Two-tailed hypothesis A research hypothesis that is not directional; the researcher believes there is a relationship, but does not speculate on whether it is positive or negative.

Type I error, also α *error* In hypothesis testing, the error of concluding a relationship exists in the population when it does not.

Type II error, also β *error* In hypothesis testing, the error of failing to conclude a relationship exists in the population when it does.

Validity In research, when a conclusion or inference is true.

Variability The spread in a distribution of scores.

Variables Characteristics of objects that can take on two or more values.

Variance The standard deviation squared.

Verisimilitude Having the appearance of truth. In research validity is best thought of as verisimilitude.

Within-cases design Design that uses one case or one group of cases. Effect of an independent variable is assessed by measuring the dependent variable before and after a change in the level of the independent variable.

References

Abelson, R. P. (1995). *Statistics as principled argument.* Hillsdale, NJ: Lawrence Erlbaum Associates.

Aguinis, H., & Stone-Romero, E. F. (1997). Methodological artifacts in moderated multiple regression and their effects on statistical power. *Journal of Applied Psychology, 82,* 192–205.

Alwin, D. F., & Hauser, R. M. (1975). The decomposition of effects in path analysis. *American Sociological Review, 40,* 37–47.

American Psychological Association. (1994). *Publication manual of the American Psychological Association* (4th ed.). Washington, DC.

Asher, H. A. (1976). *Causal modeling.* Newbury, CA: Sage.

Bangert-Drowns, R. L. (1986). Review of developments in meta-analytic method. *Psychological Bulletin, 99*(3), 388–399.

Baron, R. M., & Kenny, D. A. (1986). The moderator–mediator variable distinction in social psychological research: Conceptual, strategic, and statistical considerations. *Journal of Personality and Social Psychology, 51,* 1173–1182.

Barrett, G. V. (1992). Clarifying construct validity: Definitions, processes and models. *Human Performance, 5,* 13–58.

Berry, W. D. (1984). *Nonrecursive causal models.* Newbury Park, CA: Sage.

Blalock, H. M., Jr. (1968). The measurement problem: A gap between the languages of theory and research. In H. M. Blalock, Jr., & A. B. Blalock (Eds.), *Methodology in social research* (pp. 5–27). New York: McGraw-Hill.

Bobko, P. (1995). *Correlation and regression: Principles and applications for industrial/organizational psychology and management.* New York: McGraw-Hill.

Bretz, R. D., Jr. (1989). College grade point average as a predictor of adult success: A meta-analytic review and some additional evidence. *Public Personnel Management, 18,* 11–21.

Campbell, D. T., & Fiske, D. W. (1959). Convergent and discriminant validation by the multitrait-multimethod matrix. *Psychological Bulletin, 56,* 81–105.

Campbell, D. T., & Stanley, J. C. (1963). *Experimental and quasi-experimental designs for research.* Chicago: Rand-McNally.

Campbell, J. P. (1976). Psychometric theory. In M. D. Dunnette, (Ed.), *Handbook of industrial and organizational psychology* (pp. 185-222).

Cochran, W. G. (1982). *Planning and analysis of observational studies.* New York: Wiley.

Cohen, J. (1988). *Statistical power analysis for the behavioral sciences* (2nd. ed.). Hillsdale, NJ: Lawrence Erlbaum Associates.

Cohen, J. (1994). Things I have learned (so far). *American Psychologist, 45,* 1304–1312.

Cohen, J., & Cohen, P. (1983). *Applied multiple regression/correlation analysis for the behavioral sciences.* Mahwah, NJ: Lawrence Erlbaum Associates.

Cook, T., & Campbell, D. T. (1979). *Quasi-experimentation: Design and analysis issues for field settings.* Boston: Houghton Mifflin.

Cook, T. D., & Shadish, W. R. (1994). Social experiments: Some developments over the past fifteen years. *Annual Review of Psychology, 45,* 545–580.

Cortina, J. M. (1993). What is coefficient alpha? An examination of theory and application. *Journal of Applied Psychology, 78*(1), 98–104.

Cronbach, L. J. (1987). Statistical tests for moderator variables: Flaws in analyses recently proposed. *Psychological Bulletin, 102*(3), 414–417.

Cronbach, L. J., & Meehl, P. E. (1955). Construct validity in psychological tests. *Psychological Bulletin, 52*(4), 281–302.

Cronbach, L. J., Rajaratnam, N., & Gleser, G. C. (1963). Theory of generalizability: A liberalization of reliability theory. *The British Journal of Statistical Psychology, 16*(2), 137–163.

Cryer, J. D., & Miller, R. B. (1993). *Statistics for business: Data analysis and modeling* (2nd ed.). Belmont, CA: Duxbury.

Donner, A. (1982). The relative effectiveness of procedures commonly used in multiple regression analysis for dealing with missing values. *The American Statistician, 36,* 378–381.

Donner, A., & Rosner, B. (1982). Missing value problems in multiple linear regression with two independent variables. *Communications in Statistics, 11,* 127–140.

Erez, A., Bloom, M. C., & Wells, M. T. (1996). Using random rather than fixed effects models in meta-analysis: Implications for situational specificity and validity generalization. *Personnel Psychology, 49,* 275–306.

Frees, E. W. (1996). *Data analysis using regression models: The business perspective.* Upper Saddle River, NJ: Prentice-Hall.

Ghiselli, E. E., Campbell, J. P., & Zedeck, S. (1981). *Measurement theory for the behavioral sciences.* San Francisco: Freeman.

Glass, G. V., McGaw, B., & Smith, M. L. (1981). *Meta-analysis in social research.* Newbury Park, CA: Sage.

Hackett, R. D., & Guion, R. M. (1985). A reevaluation of the absenteeism-job satisfaction relationship. *Organizational Behavior and Human Decision Processes, 35,* 340–381.

Hagen, R. L. (1997). In praise of the null hypothesis statistical test. *American Psychologist, 52,* 15–24.

Hays, W. L. (1988). *Statistics* (4th. ed.). New York: Holt, Rinehart & Winston.

Hedges, L. V., & Olkin, I. (1985). *Statistical methods of meta-analysis.* Orlando, FL: Academic Press.

Hunter, J. E., & Schmidt, F. L. (1990). *Methods of meta-analysis.* Newbury Park, CA: Sage.

Keppel, G., (1982). *Design & analysis: A researcher's handbook* (2nd ed.). Englewood Cliffs, NJ: Prentice Hall.

Kish, L. (1987). *Statistical design for research.* New York: Wiley.

Lowin, A., & Craig, J. R. (1968). The influence of level of performance on managerial style: An experimental object-lesson in the ambiguity of correlational data. *Organizational Behavior and Human Performance, 3,* 440–458.

McEvoy, G. M., & Cascio, W. F. (1987). Do good or poor performers leave: A meta-analysis of the relationship between performance and turnover. *Academy of Management Journal, 30,* 744–762.

Miller, C. C., & Cardinal, L. B. (1994). Strategic planning and firm performance: A synthesis of more than two decades of research. *Academy of Management Journal, 37,* 649–665.

Morrison, D. E., & Henkel, R. E. (Eds.). (1970). *The significance test controversy.* Chicago: Aldine.

Nunnally, J. C. (1967). *Psychometric theory.* New York: McGraw-Hill.

Nunnally, J. C. (1978). *Psychometric theory* (2nd ed.). New York: McGraw-Hill.

Nunnally, J. C., & Bernstein, I. H. (1994). *Psychometric theory* (3rd ed.). New York: McGraw-Hill.

Oakes, M. (1986). *Statistical inference: A commentary for the social and behavioural sciences.* Chichester, UK: Wiley

Olian, J. D., Schwab, D. P., & Haberfeld, Y. (1988). The impact of applicant gender compared to qualifications on hiring recommendations: A meta-analysis of experimental studies. *Organizational Behavior and Human Decision Processes, 41,* 180–195.

Payne, S. L. (1951). *The art of asking questions.* Princeton, NJ: Princeton University Press.

Pedhazur, E. J. (1982). *Multiple regression in behavioral research: Explanation and prediction* (2nd ed.). New York: Holt, Rinehart & Winston.

Petty, M. M., McGee, G. W., & Cavender, J. W. (1984). A meta-analysis of the relationships between individual job satisfaction and individual performance. *Academy of Management Journal, 9,* 712–721.

Price, J. L., & Mueller, C. W. (1986). *Handbook of organizational measurement.* Marshfield, MA: Pitman.

Rosenthal, R. (1991). *Meta-analytic procedures for social research* (Rev. ed.). Beverly Hills, CA: Sage.

Rosenthal, R. (1995). Writing meta-analytic reviews. *Psychological Bulletin, 118,* 183–192.

Rosnow, R. L., & Rosenthal. R. (1989). Statistical procedures and the justification of knowledge in psychological science. *American Psychologist,* 44, 1276–1284.

Rosnow, R. L., & Rosenthal, R. (1991). If you're looking at the cell means, you're not looking at only the interaction (unless all main effects are zero). *Psychological Bulletin, 110,* 574–576.

Roth, P. L. (1994). Missing data: A conceptual review for applied psychologists. *Personnel Psychology, 47,* 537–560.

Roth, P. L., BeVier, C. A., Switzer, F. S., III, & Schippmann, J. S. (1996). Meta-analyzing the relationship between grades and job performance. *Journal of Applied Psychology,* 548–556.

Schmidt, F. L. (1996). Statistical significance testing and cumulative knowledge in psychology: Implications for training of researchers. *Psychological Methods, 1,* 115–129.

Schmidt, F. L., & Hunter, J. E. (1996). Measurement error in psychological research: Lessons from 26 research scenarios. *Psychological Methods, 1,* 199–223.

Schmidt, F. L., Law, K., Hunter, J. E., Rothstein, H. R., Pearlman, K., & McDaniel, M. (1993). Refinements in validity generalization methods: Implications for the situational specificity hypothesis. *Journal of Applied Psychology, 78,* 3–13.

Schwab, D. P. (1980). Construct validity in organizational behavior. In B. M. Staw and L. L. Cummings, (Eds.), *Research in organizational behavior* (Vol. 2, 3–43). Greenwich, CT: JAI Press.

Schwab, D. P., Olian-Gottlieb, J. D., & Heneman, H. G., III. (1979). Between subject expectancy theory research: A statistical review of studies predicting effort and performance. *Psychological Bulletin, 86,* 139–147.

Schwarz, N., & Sudman, S. (Eds.). (1994). *Autobiographical memory and the validity of retrospective reports.* New York: Springer.

Scott, K. D., & Taylor, G. S. (1985). An examination of conflicting findings on the relationship between job satisfaction and absenteeism: A meta-analysis. *Academy of Management Journal, 28,* 599–612.

Shavelson, R. J., Webb, N. M., & Rowley, G. L. (1989). Generalizability theory. *American Psychologist, 44,* 922–932.

Smith, P.C., Kendall, L. M., & Hulin, C. L. (1969). *The measurement of satisfaction in work and retirement.* Chicago: Rand McNally.

Steel, R. P., & Griffeth, R. W. (1989). The elusive relationship between perceived employment opportunity and turnover behavior: A methodological or conceptual artifact. *Journal of Applied Psychology, 74,* 846–854.

Stone, E. F., & Hollenbeck, J. R. (1989). Clarifying some controversial issues surrounding statistical procedures for detecting moderator variables: Empirical evidence and related matters. *Journal of Applied Psychology, 74,* 1, 3–10.

Sudman, S., & Bradburn, N. M. (1982). *Asking questions.* San Francisco: Jossey-Bass.

Van Eerde, W., & Thierry, H. (1996). Vroom's expectancy models and work-related criteria: A meta-analysis. *Journal of Applied Psychology, 81,* 575–586.

Weiss, D. J., Dawis, R. V., England, G. W., & Lofquist, L. H. *Manual for the Minnesota Satisfaction Questionnaire.* University of Minnesota. Minneapolic: Industrial Relations Center.

White, A. G. (1986). *Survey and questionnaire design: A bibliography.* Monticello, IL: Vance Bibliographies.

Author Index

A

Abelson, R. P., 287
Alwin, D. F., 391
Aquinis, H., 391

B

Bangert-Drowns, R. L., 300, 310
Baron, R. M., 391
Barrett, G. V., 66
Bernstein, I. H., 66
Bevier, C. A., 311
Blalock, H. M., Jr., 66
Bloom, M. C., 308
Bobko, P., 220
Bradburn, N. M., 66
Bretz, R. D., Jr., 311

C

Campbell, D. T., xxi, 66, 133
Campbell, J. P., 66, 357
Cardinal, L. B., 311
Cascio, W. F., 311
Cavender, J. W., 311
Cochran, W. G., 133
Cohen, J., 220, 287, 338, 342, 357, 391
Cohen, P., 220, 287, 338, 342, 357, 391
Cook, T., xxi, 133
Cook, T. D., 133
Cortina, J. M., 357
Craig, J. R., 73

Cronbach, L. J., 66, 357, 391
Cryer, J. D., 220

D

Daft, 321
Davis, 55*f*
Donner, A., 342

E

England, 55*f*
Erez, A., 308*n*

F

Fiske, D. W., 66
Frees, E. W., 220, 391

G

Ghiselli, E. E., 66, 357
Glass, G. V., 303*n*, 304*n*, 310
Gleser, G. C., 357
Griffeth, R. W., 311
Guion, R. M., 307*n*, 311

H

Haberfeld, Y., 311
Hackett, R. D., 307*n*, 311
Hagen, R. L., 287
Hauser, R. M., 391
Hays, W. L., 220
Hedges, L. V., 310

Subject Index